Story Listening and Experience in Early Childhood

"This fascinating title lays out the innumerable, tangible benefits to listening to oral stories, while empowering new storytellers with essential tools and encouragement to get started. Thoroughly supported with well-integrated research and insights drawn from these experts' first-hand experiences, this will be an invaluable resource for educators. It also offers illuminating and essential reading for parents, business executives, and anyone else seeking ways to better understand how we learn, communicate, encourage creativity, and develop a sense of shared community."

—Gillian Engberg, Consultant of Children's Books and Media and Former Editorial Director of Books for Youth, American Library Association Booklist, USA

"From cave paintings to the epic of Gilgamesh to modern movies, storytelling has been central to human culture and communication. Despite the earlier emphasis on oral storytelling in classrooms, limited current research and analysis is available. This wonderful book from two expert storytellers and educators fulfils this urgent need in the literature. Schatt and Ryan present a comprehensive and powerful view of oral storytelling from multiple perspectives—by describing their own experiences as storytellers, citing empirical literature on the topics as well as providing practical suggestions for aspiring storytellers. A must-read for not only educators and researchers, but anyone who is interested in children's language and literacy development."

—Ece Demir-Lira, Assistant Professor, Department of Psychological and Brain Sciences, Iowa Neuroscience Institute, University of Iowa, USA

"*Story Listening and Experience in Early Childhood* is an engaging and accessible exposition on the art of storytelling. Displaying an in-depth knowledge and expert grasp of their subject the authors unpack the theory, practice, and application of oral storytelling in a clear and highly readable book that fairly skips along. Of interest to teachers and librarians as well as scholars and researchers, the interweaving of anecdotal and theoretical perspectives serves to illustrate and illuminate what is actually a highly theoretical treatise on the art and science of storytelling. The authors challenge scholars in education, literacy, psychology, and neurology to initiate quantitative research on the topic. With extensive reading lists, web-based resources and very useful appendices introducing and equipping the novice storyteller with strategies for beginning their own storytelling, this book is a valuable, welcome and timely addition to the field."

—Jane O'Hanlon, Education Officer with Poetry Ireland

"With this book, Donna Schatt and Patrick Ryan have done us all a great service by bringing together a wealth of knowledge and experience from their careers as storytellers and educators, as well as thinking from across the disciplinary spectrum. However, this is not just a book for storytellers and educators, but for anyone interested in how we equip our children for the future."

—Michael Wilson, Head of Creative Arts and Director of the Storytelling Academy, Loughborough University, UK

"The great significance of this book cannot be overstated. This is a marvelous book, and Donna Schatt and Patrick Ryan are to be commended for combining personal experience, theory, and research to demonstrate how children learn through listening to oral stories and how educators learn by listening to children. In addition, Schatt and Ryan provide numerous examples and methods that will enable educators and parents to deepen the experience of children when they listen to diverse stories. Their insights call for more reform in how we educate our children today. It should be a standard book for storytellers and educators alike!"

—Jack Zipes, Professor Emeritus, University of Minnesota, USA, and author of *Creative Storytelling* (1995) and *Speaking Out* (2004)

"Every rare once in a while a book emerges that is required for our times. *Story Listening and Experience in Early Childhood* is such a book. The early childhood field has long understood the importance of storytelling as the perfect antidote to modern life and didactic education practices. Telling stories to young children improves vocabulary acquisition and promotes trust between the narrator and the child. Now the larger education community understands the importance of visualization as a vehicle for understanding complicated concepts. In a new world filled with technology, what could make more sense than implementing a personalized method to deliver fact and fiction. This book gives us the proof of its impact and provides a road map for implementation."

—Harriet Meyer, Former President, The Ounce of Prevention Fund, USA

Donna Schatt • Patrick Ryan

Story Listening and Experience in Early Childhood

palgrave
macmillan

Donna Schatt
Chicago, IL, USA

Patrick Ryan
Belfast, Antrim, UK

ISBN 978-3-030-65357-6   ISBN 978-3-030-65358-3   (eBook)
https://doi.org/10.1007/978-3-030-65358-3

This Palgrave Macmillan imprint is published by the registered company Springer Nature Switzerland AG.
The registered company address is: Gewerbestrasse 11, 6330 Cham, Switzerland

To the Schatt Boys and the Ryan Kids
who are central to every story we tell.

FOREWORD

STORY MATTERS

If you were asked to recall a significant memory in your primary school-ing, what would it be? The trip to the Smithsonian Museum when you saw dinosaur skeletons for the first time? Being a wise man with gold to give in the nativity play? Your class's poetry performance at the arts festival which your mom said was amazing? Reading by the campfire with marshmallows at that residential? Those occasions when your teacher told stories and transported you to worlds of wonder?

When you stop to consider why these events are so memorable, what can be distilled? It's tricky. It could be the allure of somehow being in a place beyond the classroom? It could be the people with whom you con-nected? It could be the sense of imaginative engagement in the activity? It's probably all of these. But I suspect there's something more—some-thing more about story. School trips and arts festivals are often shaped as stories; framed around a narrative arc they provide entertaining events to retell later. Dramatic performances, reading, and story times offer oppor-tunities to live vicariously, allowing spells of enchantment to enter minds and bodies.

Story matters. As humans we think in stories, make sense of life experi-ence through story, and imagine this and other worlds through story. In school, children experience story directly in various ways, mainly through listening to teachers reading aloud from books and through reading them-selves. Some will also participate in telling and re-enacting their own stories, watching or participating in created worlds though drama, and listening to traditional tales and literary stories.

Story Listening and Experience focuses on this last form—the oral telling of traditional or literary stories told from memory, without books, props, or a high degree of drama. Drawing on their work as tale tellers and educators over many decades, Donna Schatt and Patrick Ryan share their experience of oral storytelling and the benefits that accrue when children listen to such stories repeatedly. They offer us the voices of alumni from the University of Chicago Laboratory Schools, who frequently heard stories as young people, alongside those of other interviewees, and they share insights about the power of story listening from psychology, neurology, and education. The research reviewed is accessibly explained, and the argument is illuminated with personal narratives and anecdotes. This makes for fascinating reading, the kind that sucks you in and draws you onward, making this an unusually engaging academic book. But I digress, let's get back to the story, to narrative itself, and to its potency as a tool for learning and for life.

NARRATIVE: A TOOL FOR ADULTS AND CHILDREN

In the early years, as James Moffett (1968, p. 121) famously argued over half a century ago, "young children must, for a long time, make narrative do for all." In many cultures and countries across the world, children voice their own stories, reflect on the events of the day, and use narrative as a way of thinking, to construct explanations and to make sense (Smidt 2006). However, narrative is not merely used by children; rather, many argue, it is a sense-making tool deployed by humans throughout the life span. The sociocultural psychologist Bruner (1986) argued that narrative is a "fundamental mode of thought," a process of meaning-making, and that "our capacity to render experience in terms of narrative is not just child's play, but an instrument for making meaning that dominates much of life in culture—from soliloquies at bedtime to the weighing of testimony in our legal system" (Bruner 1990, p. 97). He later reasoned that we construct our understandings of the world "mainly in the form of narrative—stories, excuses, myths, reasons for doing and not doing, and so on" (Bruner 2003, p. 44).

The centrality of narrative as a crucial aspect of cognition is also widely recognized by scholars from other disciplines. The literary theorist Hardy (1977 p. 12) seminally declared that narrative is the "primary act of mind transferred to art from life," the linguist Langer (1953) claimed narrative is a major "organizing device," and Barthes (1977), another literary theorist, contended that narrative as a tool for making meaning is "international, transhistorical and transcultural." Within this universality, anthropologists such as Heath (1983) and Hymes (2003) have documented the cultural diversity in oral and literary storytelling traditions and practices. Educationalists too have affirmed the significance of narrative, with Rosen claiming that story "is nothing if not a supreme means of rendering otherwise chaotic, shapeless events into a coherent whole saturated with meaning" (Rosen 1988, p. 164), and Wells asserting that making sense, constructing stories, and sharing them with others is "an essential part of being human" (1986, p. 222). We are all storytellers.

This need for and use of narrative starts early; through participating in family conversations we learn from the age of two how to talk about and organize our mental representations of past events and activities (Nelson and Fivush 2004; Wang and Fivush 2005). As children we develop autobiographical memories as we listen to the stories our families tell about our shared past. We also contribute to these tellings and in the process are helped to make sense of our world. Some everyday family tales bear repetition, due perhaps to their highly affective nature, and serve to build the family's collective identity (Congleton and Rajaram 2014). In my own family, many of the same stories about us as children are retold each Christmas; it is almost as if by gathering together we remember who we were, consider who we are, and make new stories together. From an early age, we develop our sense of self in part by storying our lives and we continue to do so throughout our lives. Stories sketch out landscapes of possibility for us. For adults, as for children, narrative remains a potent force and a tool for thinking.

STORIES IN CHILDHOOD

As Hollingdale argues, stories play a particularly significant role for children:

> we need stories as we need food, and we need stories most of all in childhood, as we need food then in order to grow. (Hollingdale 1997, p. 70)

In relation to the practice of storytelling in early childhood, both the symbolic potential of language—"its power to create possible and imaginary worlds through words" (Bruner 1986, p. 156)—and the relationship between narrative and imaginary play are recognized as significant. Such play contributes to children's development as they come to think through story. Analyses of young children's storytelling reveal its generative nature, the fluid interplay between oral and written language, and the scope for play and enactment (Engel 2005; Fox 1993). In the words of Paley "play... [is] story in action, just as storytelling is play put into narrative form" (1990, p. 4). These vital forms of symbolic activity make a sustained impact upon children's social, emotional, and language development, and influence their identity formation (McCabe and Bliss 2003). For instance, the storytelling and story-acting approach of Paley (1990), which involves children dictating and dramatizing their own stories, has been shown to be valuable for cognitive, social, and emotional development (for an overview see Cremin et al. 2017). This story-based pedagogy creates pathways to literacy, enriching children's spoken language and vocabulary and fostering their involvement as young apprentice writers (Cremin 2020; Nicolopoulou et al. 2015).

Through the stories they tell, young children move easily between "what is" narratives (in which their play connects to everyday life) and "what if" narratives (in which they play in an imaginary world of fictive possibilities) (Engel 2005). They oscillate, Engel argues, between these two domains of experience with ease and explore the boundaries between them. My grandson, Gus, on a recent "Granny T story time" regaled me with the pleasures of his day: a trip to Greenwich, mixed up with meeting dinosaurs and having tea with a boy called Tom. Knowing I had read him Michael Foreman's (2004) *Dinosaur Time* regularly in our Zoom story times (the protagonist is called Tom) and that he had recently made dinosaur cookies, I could hear echoes of his life, literature, and current fascinations in this retelling. Gus's "what is" and "what if" worlds played out before me with an evident, almost-knowing delight in his four-year-old eyes. As Rosen (1984) asserts, "any story presupposes the existence of other stories...for both reader and listener (or teller and told) threads of connection exist, threads of many different kinds" (p. 33).

The foundational nature of narrative in later school-based learning has also been documented, linked to the concept of "possibility thinking" and the creativity with three-to-eleven-year-olds (Craft et al. 2012; Cremin et al. 2013). In playful outdoor contexts as well as focused science and mathematics lessons, reciprocal relationships between questioning, imagination, and narrative were identified. Narrative, particularly fantasy narratives told by their teachers, appeared to provide a possibility space for children's questioning and deep emotional and imaginative engagement. Conversely, leading questions created a space in which young people's imaginations contributed to the development of narratively framed sequences of possibility thinking (Cremin et al. 2013). Nonetheless, the ways in which children deployed narrative playfully in subject-specific lessons often went unnoticed by their teachers.

STORY IN POLICY AND PRACTICE

Despite the wealth of empirical evidence demonstrating the power of narrative, its role in learning and in child development, it remains under-recognized and under-developed in policy and practice internationally. In school, narrative as a tool for thinking and learning across the curriculum is relatively infrequently employed—at least in a planned and intentional manner. Stories are commonly read aloud to young children, but this tends to drop off in the later years, when reading aloud is often viewed an entertaining extra, included only if time permits. Additionally, despite its efficacy, Paley's (1990) approach is used in relatively few schools, and drama is often viewed as a performance art in which children perform others' words with scant chance to create their own narrative worlds. The oral telling of tales is particularly marginalized; relatively few teachers offer children such encounters, and when they do these tend to be confined to a narrow range with billy goats, little pigs, or gingerbread men taking center stage. Children may encounter professional writers in schools, but they are far less likely to encounter a professional oral storyteller. Thus, in formal schooling, listening to oral stories is very rarely given the attention it deserves. Bruner asks:

> Why are we so intellectually dismissive towards narrative? Why are we inclined to treat it as rather a trashy, if entertaining, way of thinking about and talking about what we do with our minds? Storytelling performs the dual cultural functions of making the strange familiar and ourselves private and distinctive. If pupils are encouraged to think about the different outcomes that could have resulted from a set of circumstances, they are demonstrating useability of knowledge about a subject. Rather than just retaining knowledge and facts, they go beyond them to use their imaginations to think about other outcomes, as they don't need the completion of a logical argument to understand a story. This helps them to think about facing the future, and it stimulates the teacher too. (Bruner 2007)

In many countries however teachers are not positioned as artistically engaged pedagogues, but as knowledge bearers and curriculum deliverers. In part this is due to the presence of structured curricula created to respond to the standards agenda and local and national assessment regimes. High stakes assessment has led to an instrumental approach to teaching and learning literacy which views literacy as a body of skills to be taught and tested, and fails to recognize it as highly complex, sociocultural practice. This constrains educators, triggering compliance and a downward pressure on the curriculum which restricts the ways children could be learning. As a result, the inherently social practices of storytelling and story listening are relegated backstage and English remains at the margins of debates about arts education. Furthermore, storytelling, like reading aloud, is too often viewed as an early years' practice, as if once children have reached their sixth birthday, narrative no longer holds sway. Even when opportunities are offered to experience the power of oral stories, these are often framed within functionalist drives toward raising attainment. It is clear, if tale telling is tethered too tightly to the standards agenda, this severely compromises its potential and *raison d'être*.

In sum, notwithstanding widespread recognition of the role of narrative in early learning, story-based activities and storytelling and listening are side-lined in favor of structured literacy routines and practices (Dyson and Dewayni 2013). As a consequence, the potential of listening to stories as an inspiring tool for learning and for life remains significantly under-developed.

TEACHERS AS LANGUAGE ARTISTS AND STORYTELLERS

Limited attention has been paid to teachers' creative use of language in school. Practitioners have not been supported to develop a sense of themselves as oral language artists—tale tellers, performance poets, or role players, for example; their imaginative engagement is rarely prioritized in pre-service education or later training, and as a result they are likely to lack the confidence to be storytellers. Modeling the inventive use of spoken language through tale telling involves taking risks and the adoption of a playful, improvisational, and artistic stance. Yet it is possible, and Schatt and Ryan offer invaluable support in this regard. The process of preparing to tell a tale to others is not a memory test, but an opportunity to share the soul of the story, lean on the narrative structure, and entice the listeners to imagine and respond.

As teachers quickly find, storytelling and listening is a two-way process. The experience helps build bonds between the teller and the told, and such stories are frequently shared without a marked sense of hierarchy. As language artists, teacher-storytellers are freed from the traditional patterns of classroom interaction and are arguably more personally and affectively involved. So, although the creative social process of telling tales can be challenging at first, storytelling offers educators real pleasure and satisfaction. Convinced of the myriad benefits of the story listening experience, so adeptly presented by Schatt and Ryan, teachers will want to give voice to narratives with intonation and imagination, and to do so repeatedly. As the authors argue, repeatedly listening to tales is critical in order to accrue the advantages on offer.

As their book unequivocally documents, listening to stories builds on children's narrative competence and in particular fosters their imaginative engagement. When children are exposed to oral stories regularly they learn to pay attention, to visualize, and to exercise their imaginations—they live in and through such stories, and, significantly, they are enabled to think through the stories too. These are core skills, linked to their development as readers, philosophers, and empathetic human beings. Alexander (2010) maintains that exciting the imagination should be a core aim of the primary curriculum: "we need to assert the intrinsic value of exciting children's imagination. To experience the delights—and the pains—of imagining, and of entering into the imaginative worlds of others, is to become a more rounded and capable person" (p. 199). Such an aim can be progressed through listening to stories.

In order to realize the latent cognitive, social, and moral benefits of story listening experience, teachers, librarians, and other educators need to be enabled to exercise professional agency and incorporate storytelling into their educational settings, documenting the impact as they travel. This book offers very rich support on the journey and significantly advances our understanding of the experience of listening to stories. As Schatt and Ryan recognize, more research is needed, but the wealth of scholarly inquiry shared here makes one thing crystal clear—story matters.

The Open University, Milton Keynes, UK   Teresa Cremin

REFERENCES

Alexander, R. 2010. *Children, Their World and Their Education*. London: Routledge.

Barthes, R. 1977. *Poètique du récit*. Paris: Éditions du Seuil.

Bruner, J. 1986. *Actual Minds, Possible Worlds*. Cambridge, MA: Harvard University Press.

Bruner, J. 1990. *Acts of Meaning*. Cambridge, MA: Harvard University Press.

Bruner, J. 2003. The Narrative Construction of Reality. In *Narrative Intelligence*, eds. M. Mateas and P. Sengers, 41–62. Amsterdam: John Benjamins.

Bruner, J. 2007. The Lesson of the Story. *The Guardian*. https://www.theguardian.com/education/2007/mar/27/academicexperts.highereducationprofile. Accessed August 31, 2020.

Congleton, A. R. and Rajaram, S. 2014. Collaboration Changes Both the Content and the Structure of Memory. *Journal of Experimental Psychology*, 143(4): 1570–1584. DOI: https://doi.org/10.1037/a0035974.

Craft, A., McConnon, L., and Matthews, A. 2012. Child-Initiated Play and Professional Creativity. *Thinking Skills and Creativity*, 7(1): 48–61. DOI: https://doi.org/10.1016/j.tsc.2011.11.005.

Cremin, T., Chappell, K., and Craft, A. 2013. Reciprocity between Narrative, Questioning and Imagination in the Early and Primary Years. *Thinking Skills and Creativity*, 9: 136–151. DOI: https://doi.org/10.1016/j.tsc.2012.11.003.

Cremin, T., Flewitt, R., Mardell, B., and Swann, J. (eds.). 2017. *Storytelling in Early Childhood: Language, Literacy, and Classroom Culture*. London and New York: Routledge.

Cremin, T. 2020. Apprenticing Authors: Nurturing Children's Identities as Writers. In *Developing Writers Across Primary and Secondary Years*, eds. H. Chen, D. Myhill, and H. Lewis, 113–130. London and Sydney: Routledge.

Dyson, A. H. and Dewayni, S. 2013. Writing in Childhood Cultures. In *International Handbook of Research on Children's Literacy, Learning, and Culture*, eds. K. Hall, T. Cremin, B. Comber, and L. Moll, 258–274. Oxford: Wiley Blackwell.

Engel, S. 2005. The Narrative Worlds of What-Is and What-If. *Cognitive Development*, 20: 514–525. DOI: https://doi.org/10.1016/j.cogdev.2005.08.005.

Foreman, M. 2004. *Dinosaur Time*. London: Anderson.

Fox, C. 1993. *At the Very Edge of the Forest: The Influence of Literature on Storytelling by Children*. London: Continuum.

Hardy, B. 1977. Towards a Poetics of Fiction: An Approach Through Narrative. In *The Cool Web*, eds. M. Meek, A. Warlow, and G. Barton. London: Bodley Head.

Heath, S. B. 1983. *Ways with Words: Language, Life and Work in Communities and Classrooms.* Cambridge: Cambridge University Press.

Hollingdale, P. 1997. *Signs of Childness in Children's Books.* Stroud: The Thimble Press.

Hymes, D. 2003. *Now I Only Know So Far: Essays in Ethnopoetics.* Lincoln: University of Nebraska Press.

Langer, S. K. 1953. *Feeling and Form.* London: Routledge and Kegan Paul.

McCabe, A., and Bliss, L. S. 2003. *Patterns of Narrative Discourse: A Multicultural, Life-Span Approach.* Boston, MA: Allyn and Bacon.

Moffett, J. 1968. *Teaching the Universe of Discourse.* Boston: Houghton Mifflin.

Nelson, K. and Fivush, R. 2004. The Emergence of Autobiographical Memory. *Psychological Review*, 111: 486–511. DOI: 10.1037/0033-295X.111.2.486.

Nicolopoulou, A., Cortina, K. S., Ilgaz, H., Cates, C. B., and de Sá, A. B. 2015. Using a Narrative- and Play-Based Activity to Promote Low-Income Preschoolers' Oral Language, Emergent Literacy and Social Competence. *Early Childhood Research Quarterly*, 31: 147–162. DOI: https://doi.org/10.1016/j.ecresq.2015.01.006.

Paley, V. G. 1990. *The Boy Who Would Be a Helicopter: The Uses of Storytelling in the Classroom.* Cambridge, MA: Harvard University Press.

Rosen, H. 1984. *Stories and Meanings.* Sheffield: National Association for the Teaching of English.

Rosen, H. 1988. The Irrepressible Genre. In *Oracy Matters*, eds. M. Maclure, T. Phillips, and A. Wilkinson. Milton Keynes: OUP.

Smidt, S. 2006. *The Developing Child in the 21st Century.* London: Routledge.

Wang, Q. and Fivush, R. 2005. Mother-Child Conversations of Emotionally Salient Events. *Social Development*, 14: 473–495. DOI: https://doi.org/10.1111/j.1467-9507.2005.00312.x.

Wells, G. 1986. *The Meaning Makers.* Portsmouth, NH: Heinemann.

PREFACE[1]

BELIEVE, BUT DON'T BELIEVE ME: AN INTRODUCTORY NOTE

Dear Reader of any age or background,

Allow me to pull you into a book that matters. Given a chance, it will change what you offer to the children in your life and scatter happiness over everyone who witnesses or listens. This is a book that can open doors—for you, for the kids who are lucky enough to join you in this adventure, and for others who may then want to learn how to try this, or simply to observe and absorb.

What are we talking about? The ancient and powerful art of storytelling. Face-to-face, without a book in hand. Heart to heart. Before I saw the librarians at the University of Chicago Laboratory Schools practicing this almost thirty years ago, I had no idea what a powerful tool this time-honored activity is. One story in and I was hooked, as were the hundreds of kids who came to listen once a week in the school library and still remember the experience of losing themselves inside a story told in this way. Don't believe me; this is something to be tried.

Wait! What? You don't have time to think about what this book offers? I understand, but hold on. I'm afraid you may miss something huge but accessible. It's not rocket science, but it's rarely seen or heard in schools in the United States. I almost missed it myself.

---

[1] The author, Blue Balliett, holds the copyright to the preface.

I'm quite sure that listening to Donna and the other librarians telling stories is part of the reason I went on to tell many of my own, in print, out in the classroom of the world. They taught me the power of *giving* a story to the listener, of looking at the story itself as an interactive experience.

I came to the University of Chicago Laboratory Schools as an inexperienced assistant teacher, in the early 1990s. I took my third- and fourth-grade students to the library "for their Story," one period a week. They could enter the library all week at other times to explore and check out books, but the weekly "Story" was a different activity. That was all I'd been told about this period. It sounded kind of silly. I still remember sitting on a small chair at the back of an open area in the library and listening for the first time to Donna tell one of her stories. I had never heard anyone do this, without a book in hand. I wasn't prepared.

She reached out but quietly, without theatrics or any dramatic razzmatazz. The props were clearly inside the children's heads, as their faces told you. Sitting on the rug in front of her, the kids were soon dead quiet, even the wiggliest ones, and the rapt expressions that go with active listening and imagining filled the room. It's a kind of a spell, this mode of storytelling. The first story I heard her tell was *The Billy Goats Gruff*, and I still remember how quickly the pictures of what was happening bubbled up in my head. Can you believe I remember that, decades later? I do, right down to the sounds of hooves on the bridge! That day, there was a tangible magic woven between the teller and the listeners, and I took note.

During my many years as a teacher at Lab, I heard hundreds of stories told in the Lower School library. I couldn't wait to come in for this special half hour. My class always became calm, immersed in the swirl of the story, leaving with plot and characters filling their heads. Every librarian working in that lower school library was a skilled storyteller, and this activity was a high point of every child's week. The stories went on for twenty to thirty minutes, but kids were rarely restless. Some had to be reminded to stand up and leave with their class.

While a classroom teacher, I went on to write the mystery *Chasing Vermeer* (2004), which I truly wrote as a read aloud to be shared at school or home. I created the book I wanted as a teacher and parent, packed with ideas I longed to share with all of the kids in my life. As Donna does with her storytelling, I put together what I hoped was an unusual tool that kids could pick up and keep, a story woven around dreams and skills that could lend power to their thinking, but painlessly. A story that encouraged active participation on the part of the reader, whatever age they might be of.

I have gone on to write six more mysteries for kids, and to my amaze-ment, my stories are now in thirty-five languages and a startling number of editions and formats. If I hadn't listened to, witnessed, and been thrilled by the storytelling in the Lab library so many years ago, would I have gone on to weave potent spells of my own?

Perhaps not. What Donna and Patrick share here about the art of the Told Story, as opposed to the Read Story, is riveting. It pulls at anyone who has focused on children, words, stories, and books. They learned first-hand that literacy and a fascination with narrative often begins, for kids, with "Now I'm going to tell you a story." Such listening fosters inde-pendent reading, as it creates a hunger for plot lines. It offers a path to the printed word. Perhaps that holds true for any of us, at any age and stage. This mode of telling empowers. It is a wake-up call, whispering that it's never too late to imagine and to use the art of storytelling to enrich and strengthen lives.

I believe that inspiring children inspires us all and that that is how the world best changes. We desperately need our stories, our tellers, and a book like this, one that will make many of us bold enough to sit on an imagined rug, absorb any or all of what this book offers, and then use any part of it in a way that fits.

Enjoy. Believe, but don't believe me—learning is doing, as John Dewey said.

Nantucket, MA   Blue Balliett
June 2020

Acknowledgments

There are many people and institutions we would like to thank for their help regarding our research and this book.

First, we'd like to gratefully thank and acknowledge the former students of UCLS for generously sharing their memories of the storytelling program. Without them we never would have written this book. Likewise, thanks to the UCLS librarians, especially Mary Ogilvie, Lee McLain, Irene Fahrenwald, and Cynthia Oakes: fine teachers, storytellers, and friends who provided encouragement as well as access to the storytelling program records. We'd also like to thank Dr. Catie Bell for her patience and kind help. She was as generous a teacher with us as she is with all the students who have ever been lucky enough to work with her.

Many thanks to Liz Weir and Arti Prashar, fellow storytellers, and good friends who shared their observations and anecdotes.

Special thanks to Gillian Enberg and the late Vivian Paley, who both offered good advice in the early stages of the book, and to Professor Jack Zipes and Professor Michael Wilson, each of whom offered valuable guidance as the book progressed. We'd also like to thank Dr. Ece Demir-Lira and Maria Carriel for collaborating with us on other projects and providing important resources and data.

A special mention to the faculty at International School of Brussels, especially Jeffrey Brewster and Heidi Dechief (ISB's fantastic librarians), and Gordon Eldridge who arranged for us to teach at ISB Summer Institutes. We're grateful for all the ideas and opportunities they provided.

A number of friends and colleagues offered advice, help, and/or support at different times during the research and writing. These include

Dr. Daniella Karidi, Dr. Susan Goldin-Meadow, Dr. Susan Levine, Dr. Janice Del Negro, Roscoe Nicholson, Dr. Barnaby Reidel, Dr. Monica Vela, Emily Spangler, Dr. Jacqueline Harrett, Peter Rhoades-Brown, Arturo Regal-Mendez, Dovie Thomason, Shifra Werch, Jim Sells and Samir Singh. Thank you all.

Patrick would like to extend his gratitude to colleagues at the George Ewart Evans Centre for Storytelling (GEECS) and University of South Wales, particularly Professor Hamish Fyfe and Dr. Emily Underwood-Lee. Also, Patrick thanks Professor Warren Cariou and the Centre for Creative Writing and Oral Culture (CCWOC) at University of Manitoba. Much of Patrick's research for this study happened while he was Research Fellow at GEECS and Writer/Storyteller-in-Residence at CCWOC. Both institutions also provided the time and space to write. The support and advice of the people at both institutions, and that of other colleagues in Cardiff and Winnipeg, is much appreciated.

Donna would like to thank her family and all of her friends for their encouragement, patience, and kindness. And for allowing her to share their stories.

And Patrick, too, thanks family and friends for their support and happily listening to updates on how the research was going.

Finally, Patrick also gratefully acknowledges the support of the National Lottery through the Arts Council of Northern Ireland.

LOTTERY FUNDED

About the Book

Storytellers and educators Patrick Ryan and Donna Schatt show connections between oral story listening and unique, enduring educational effects. Using scientific studies and interviews, as well as personal observations from more than thirty years in schools and libraries, the authors examine learning outcomes from frequent story listening. Experiencing stories told entirely from memory transforms individuals and builds community, affecting areas such as reading comprehension, visualization, focus, flow states, empathy, attachment, and theory of mind.

Contents

ABOUT THE AUTHORS

Patrick Ryan, PhD FEA is a storyteller, teacher, researcher, and writer. Based in Belfast, he works throughout Ireland and the UK, much of Europe, and in North America. He is the author of *Shakespeare's Storybook* and several articles on storytelling.

Donna Schatt, MLS MA is a storyteller, researcher, librarian, and writer. She resides in Chicago, Michigan, and New York. She is researching the effects of oral story listening on visualization abilities and writing a novel.

"I knew where I was the whole time." *What storytelling is and isn't: an introduction*

Donna's son was in kindergarten when he decided to walk home with his friend. When he didn't show up in the library where she was waiting for him, she went down to his classroom. No one had any idea where he was. She frantically ran outside and asked everyone lined up for dismissal if they had seen Daniel. Finally one teacher said she saw him walking down the street with his best friend Joe (so much for security). When she called Joe's house, his older brother answered and said that Joe and Daniel had just walked in. Daniel came to the phone and Donna explained to him that no one knew where he was, that he was not allowed to leave school with anyone but his parents and that he had frightened her because she thought he was lost. Daniel was completely unconcerned and responded, "I wasn't lost! I knew where I was the whole time."

We love this family story of Donna's. It's very much who Daniel was and who he has remained—the adventurer, calming others down with common sense. It is also a story with a lesson, not unlike folklore. Sometimes we know where we are but no one else does. It is up to us to communicate our "location" to others.

We are two educators and storytellers who recognized that there was a unique and specific type of learning going on when our students listened to stories in and outside of our classrooms—but few other people could see it. Through our observations and the scientific work of others we will attempt to illuminate our "location" to you, the reader. We are hoping

D. Schatt, P. Ryan, *Story Listening and Experience in Early Childhood*, https://doi.org/10.1007/978-3-030-65358-3_1

that after reading this book, educators will be able to locate the benefits that we have observed—cognitive, social, and practical—which occur from the use of oral storytelling in the classroom.

A BIT ABOUT OURSELVES AND STORYTELLING

We are both tellers of tales. Between us we have more than eighty years of professional storytelling and hundreds of stories in our repertoires. Patrick is an educator and academic raised in an extended Irish American family that found great pleasure in telling stories to maintain their identity, history, and culture. As a teacher, folklorist, and storyteller Patrick has served as a storytelling consultant to education systems throughout the world. Donna is a children's librarian, a teacher, and a researcher who grew up in a Jewish immigrant family that loved to pass along their traditions and superstitions through stories. For seventeen years, Donna was involved as librarian-storyteller in the storytelling program at University of Chicago Laboratory Schools (UCLS), founded by educational philosopher John Dewey. As a student-teacher training at UCLS, Patrick became familiar with that storytelling program and met Donna, and they began sharing thoughts on different storytelling experiences. The results they both observed from the weekly storytelling program, and the children who participated in that program, play a prominent role in the motivation for writing this book.

Years of telling stories in schools and libraries afforded us the opportunity to observe beneficial outcomes to students and teachers when listening to stories. Story listening transforms individuals, in the sense of Phillip Jackson's definition of transformative education. A leader in education and curriculum studies and Dewey scholar (Abowd 2015), Jackson had a close relationship with UCLS. He believed by hearing stories students are "changed in ways that are both beneficial and enduring" (Jackson 1995, p. 4). We agreed, feeling more people should be mindful of the place of story listening in the classroom, playground, and home.

We believed it would be simple to persuade educational administrators, teachers, and parents that storytelling should have a greater presence in their interactions with children. At conferences, when visiting schools, or in informal gatherings we found ourselves waxing poetic about the benefits of oral stories told in classrooms both as a curricular tool and to manage classroom behavior. While often indulged, we were not in a position to make lasting changes in education. It didn't seem to matter that we were speaking from years of personal observation. Although people frequently nodded in agreement at how much everyone loved stories, few felt capable of bringing storytelling into their schools or homes. Some even believed it was a dying art, readily replaced by new technology. Others declared oral storytelling no more than entertainment, certainly not an appropriate pedagogical tool. Many thought teachers were incapable of telling stories, even some teachers themselves. And typical of these times, we were asked to show data on the outcomes of oral story listening.

It took a while for us to recognize that most people were unclear as to what we meant when speaking about storytelling. Many thought we were talking about shared picture books or chapter books read aloud, which we all agreed should be present in early childhood classrooms. But their concept of storytelling was muddy. Patrick tells how when visiting schools to tell stories, even with paperwork sent in advance explaining what he would be doing, he still was introduced as a writer. The idea of storytelling and stories being solely associated with books and reading aloud predominated.

Some teachers did tell us they used storytelling in their instruction. We watched as these teachers narrated, with children reciting along, making choreographed gestures to identify parts of a sentence. The teachers were using storytelling as a *vehicle* to attain easily measurable targets. This use of story codifies or prescribes content and strategies, with the teacher modeling a personal process that children repeat and rehearse (DCSF 2008, p. 8). Carole Bignell identified this as a method "that assumes that the child should internalize the teacher's thinking and learn by heart the teacher's stories to participate in the curriculum" (Bignell 2012, p. 51). In essence, a type of rote learning. This, too, is not the type of storytelling we want to talk about.

We met educators who were aware of the works of Vivian Paley, Susan Engel, Donald Graves, and others. They thought we were speaking about stories children tell and make up, and what happens in classrooms when adults attend to children's storytelling and story writing. To a small extent our observations are connected with those practices; Paley taught at UCLS and the child storytellers Paley reported upon went to the weekly storytelling program that Donna ran. Some are among those we relied on for our research. But we were not talking about oral and written stories *created by children*. We always spoke of the effects of listening to traditional and literary stories told to children orally.

There were people we spoke with who had heard oral stories told by adults, but most often they were thinking of listening to programs like "The Moth" on NPR, where people tell personal stories. Or they had seen a theatrical performance teller at a live event and were intimidated at the thought of recreating the slick voice and exaggerated choreographed gestures (by the way so are we!). That seemed like a lot of work for a classroom teacher to take on. We agree that it would be, if that were the type of storytelling we were talking about. Fortunately it is not.

After years of lectures, conversations, and discussions we decided a book was needed to persuade educators that they should seriously examine the effects of story listening on early childhood learning. This was a bigger challenge than we envisioned. There was little hard data to support our arguments. We had our observations and the observations of others, but few empirical studies. Lacking significant data about something as transient and subtle as the effects of story listening made convincing doubters a Sisyphean task. Over the last fifty years there has been a body of convincing data on benefits of shared reading. However, quantitative research on the outcomes of storytelling started appearing only recently.

Sharing picture books with your children at bedtime, or any time, reaps great benefits and is a wonderful experience for everyone. But as education professor Elaine Reese says, "we should supplement shared book-reading with a rich range of other types of conversations and language interactions" (Reese 2012, p. 65). She reports that shared reading doesn't always work for middle- and low-income families due to a variety of valid reasons (Reese 2012, p. 60). For many, telling traditional and family stories might prove easier and equally effective. Oral storytelling is the missing link between spoken language and the printed word. We knew it, we had observed it. But how could we demonstrate this knowledge and convince others?

You could say all this set the stage for a heroic journey. To alert "magic helpers" to gather, analyze, and explain the data, we needed to define clearly what we meant, about something we knew to be practically invisible to the scholars who could design quantitative research examining why and how oral story affects the listener.

WHAT DO WE MEAN WHEN WE TALK ABOUT STORYTELLING?

If you have three people in a conversation about storytelling you may have three or more definitions and expectations. So, from the start we would like to be sure that, like Daniel, we all know exactly where we are.

In this book when we speak about storytelling, we are speaking about simple oral telling of traditional tales or literary stories, told from memory in a conversational manner without books, flannel boards, or other props and with no grand choreographed gestures or overly dramatic or exaggerated body movements or voices. This is the type of storytelling we are speaking about when we describe our research into the unique outcomes that develop when children listen repeatedly to stories. This is the definition we are using when we discuss the application of storytelling in education. This is the definition we are using when we make the connection between story listening and current cognitive and neurological research. This is the type of storytelling we would like you to bring into your classroom, library, and home.

A BRIEF HISTORY OF EDUCATIONAL STORYTELLING IN AMERICA

Now that we've defined storytelling as we are using the term, it is important to explore its history in American education. We already knew it was part of the UCLS historical pedagogy, but had it been widespread in the US? If so, why did it disappear from most classrooms? And historically, were teachers trained to tell stories? Here's what we discovered.

Learning how to tell a story had been an integral part of teacher training programs during the Progressive Era. Teachers and librarians were expected to be comfortable telling stories (Parker 1883, 1894; Gregor 2010). According to published studies and primary source materials, the use of storytelling was widespread in both public and private schools from the 1890s through the 1920s (Alvey 1974; Bryant 1905; Dewey, E. 1919a, 1922, 1919b; Dewey, J. and Dewey, E 1915; Gregor 2010). We found articles written by teachers as far back as the 1880s who used storytelling in their classrooms and found that it made classroom management easier. Storytelling helped those teachers manage the same challenges teachers face in classrooms today: diverse multi-lingual communities, disaffected or challenging students, and a rapidly changing society. We also found evidence that during this time many educational philosophers and teachers believed that listening to stories developed students' critical thinking, love of literature, and fluency in reading (Chubb 1902, 1929; Coe and Christie-Dillon 1913; Thorne-Thomsen 1901, 1903; Wiggin, 1892; Wiggin and Smith 1895).

Now it is the rare teacher who uses storytelling as part of the curriculum. Why? The decline of educational storytelling in America can be attributed to historical causes that will sound familiar. In the 1930s political and economic trends brought new education policies that emphasized standardization, new technologies, easily measured outcomes, and testing. Storytelling outcomes did not (and still don't) lend themselves to easy measurement and storytelling was incorrectly believed to duplicate what could be taught using basal readers and the newly popular genre of picture books (Dewey, J. 1933, pp. 261–262; Jackson 1986, pp. 121–122; Warren 1997, p. 66). Teachers were encouraged to read aloud from picture books. Storytelling became used less frequently. Where oral story was still being used, it was seen as the provenance of the library, viewed simply as a tool to promote interest in books to be read for pleasure.

From the 1930s until recent times, classroom storytelling throughout the country was receding, However, storytelling has remained central to the curriculum and pedagogical philosophy at UCLS to this day. The University of Chicago Laboratory Schools (UCLS), known colloquially as The Lab School, is where Donna taught and Patrick trained as a teacher.

STORYTELLING AT THE UNIVERSITY OF CHICAGO LABORATORY SCHOOLS

When John Dewey founded UCLS in 1896 he did so to test out his child-centered experiential pedagogy. He espoused the idea that a child's experience as a member of a social community should be the starting point for learning. Dewey envisioned that teachers and students would develop educational experiences collaboratively. He argued that a child's mind was not like blotting paper absorbing knowledge or an empty vessel to be filled. It's an active, living organism that accepts and rejects according to its conditions and needs (Dewey 1933, pp. 261–262). He believed learning comes not solely from experience, but from reflecting on and applying that experience (Dewey 1933, 1938).

Not long after setting up UCLS Dewey brought a renowned educator, Colonel Francis Parker, to the school. They both advocated the use of oral storytelling in the classroom. In a series of influential lectures over the 1880s, Parker stated, "Every teacher should be an excellent storyteller, so as to make the half hour each day given to storytelling, a delightful one to the children" (Parker 1883, p. 143). To promote the use of storytelling in the classroom, Dewey and Parker employed Gudrun Thorne-Thomsen, an educator and folklorist, to teach third grade, work with other Lab School Staff, and teach storytelling to trainee teachers in the University's School of Education.

From the start Dewey, Parker, and Thorne-Thomsen articulated a convincing message, demonstrating connections between storytelling, literacy, literature, and what today is called cognition. Thorne-Thomsen (Thorne-Thomsen 1901, p. 229; Greene and Del Negro 2010, pp. 18, 23) asserted that the thought process that occurred when listening to a story was similar to or the same as the thought process of a fluent reader when reading. Other specialists at the time commonly shared this belief.

Catie Bell, a Dewey expert as well as a colleague and current Lab School teacher, reminded us

> that the power of storytelling for any listener lies in the quality of the experience. Dewey would point to the enjoyment the child undergoes hearing the story for the first time, what she comes to reflect on later and the extent to which the experience sets her up for congruous future experience. (Bell 2019)

The storytelling we advocate leads to the type of experience that Dewey promoted for optimum learning.

Storytelling, over time, achieves a great deal through this type of experience. When Dewey spoke of reflecting on and applying experience, he saw collateral learning as a result of this process. Story listening could be considered a working definition of that term.

> Perhaps the greatest of all pedagogical fallacies is the notion that a person learns only the particular thing he is studying at the time. Collateral learning in the way of formation of enduring attitudes, of likes and dislikes, may be and often is much more important than the spelling lesson or lesson in geography or history that is learned. For these attitudes are fundamentally what count in the future. The most important attitude that can be formed is that of desire to go on learning. (Dewey, J. 1933, p. 48)

Dewey's ideas have informed our own work in classrooms and libraries. Dewey's focus on experiential learning is why we named our book *Story Listening and Experience in Early Childhood*. Collateral learning and experience are recurring themes throughout this book.

THE UCLS STORYTELLING PROGRAM

Extensive teacher work reports, minutes of faculty meetings, and articles by UCLS staff from the first years of the school's existence indicate that many teachers practiced oral storytelling to initiate classroom activities during this time. Drama, creative writing, visual arts, spelling, grammar, and history lessons were all derived from storytelling (DePencier 1960; Rice and Thorne-Thomsen 1901; Thorne-Thomsen 1901, 1903).

However, The Lab School was not totally immune to the new educational philosophies and practices. Somewhere in the 1930s teachers began to tell stories with less frequency. The Lab School librarians gradually took over the telling of stories, where storytelling was treated as a means to promote book circulation and reading. The difference was that at The Lab School the oral story program continued to be highly regarded by the school and the University community. Records show that in 1949 a formal storytelling program was instituted in the lower school library. This program has remained much the same for seventy years. Children in grades K–2, in addition to their regular weekly library time, are brought to the library to hear thirty minutes of formal stories once a week. The stories are primarily traditional folk and fairy tales, or literary stories of a similar style to these genres, from cultures all around the world. The librarians tell these stories entirely from memory, tales are never read aloud. These stories are unrelated to classroom curricula or practices. Children enrolled in the school since kindergarten will have exposure to approximately two hundred told stories by the end of second grade (eight years of age).

THE STUDY

We found the continuing storytelling program at the Lab School an ideal site for beginning our study on the impact of storytelling in an educational setting. As a starting point we chose to examine what meaning alumni made of the program. As far as we knew, no one had ever asked the students why *they* thought they were being brought to the library to listen to stories that were totally unrelated to the work they were doing anywhere else in the school.

We initiated a series of interviews with former students, one current second grader, and two former librarians. The alumni ranged between nineteen and forty-four years of age, and all had experienced at least two full years of the storytelling program. An equal number of men and women were interviewed, as were people with and without learning disabilities. Although we attempted to represent the ethnic demographics of the school in our sample, we were not fully successful. The interviews were semi-structured and open ended. Snowball sampling was used to recruit our interviewees. All interviews were held either in person or over Skype.

As we transcribed and analyzed these interviews certain themes emerged:

- The pleasure of the experience and wanting to repeat it
- A feeling of warmth and closeness with the person telling the story
- Understanding how narratives are structured
- An ability to construct images from the story that were from their own experiences
- Recognizing that not everyone "saw" stories the same way
- Losing sight of time and place while listening to a story

These themes and the questions they raised guided our research and provided the structure for this book. Quotations from these interviews gave us the titles for each chapter.

To our surprise, many teachers and librarians of the past espoused similar findings and outcomes when telling stories to their students. We started speaking about these similarities in conference papers, on consulting projects and with our colleagues. It became clear that this was not just coincidence. We found insight by looking at studies in the fields of cognitive psychology, emergent literacy, visualization, neurology, and executive function. We uncovered quantitative data on shared reading, reading comprehension, vocabulary growth, narrative understanding, attachment—basically every area our informants spoke about and connected directly to oral story listening. While the data found in these studies cannot be used to claim oral storytelling causes similar achievements, it does start to explain phenomena related to our observations and point out the need for research to find correlations and causality.

Had scientists working in the above fields started gathering data before oral story began fading from classrooms, and before shared picture book reading began to dominate, there is a good chance that more educational research would have focused on oral story. It's an interesting "What if" thought experiment. Because educational storytelling took the historical course outlined above, oral story listening went off everyone's radar. Therefore, most of today's students have yet to benefit from regular story listening.

With our experiences and observations of telling stories in schools and libraries, knowledge of the history of storytelling, and review of the literature, we felt uniquely placed to start this particular ball rolling. By extrapolating a lot of our data from tangentially related studies, we are connecting dots that many do not see. We will compare our results with recent quantitative studies on story listening. We'll also discuss research in the fields of literacy studies, developmental psychology, cognitive and neurological sciences, linguistics, folklore, and anthropology. We are not claiming causality. We are pointing out what, in our opinion, needs to be noticed and addressed. In the following chapters we will attempt to give you a map to our "location" showing the importance of oral story in the educational process and help you to make it part of your class, your home, your life.

You may wonder why, at a time when teachers are already being asked to work harder than ever before with fewer resources, we are suggesting that educators integrate storytelling into their classrooms. Especially given that the storytelling we describe will most likely be a new tool that most teachers haven't used or tried before. The reason is that we truly believe storytelling is worth the effort. It will make a teacher's job easier and affect students' learning in unique and important ways. It will make the classroom more cohesive and the students more understanding of others.

Ironically educators such as Dewey and Parker believed this was true at the turn of the twentieth century, but the educational landscape changed and what they knew was forgotten. We are suggesting a return to what was lost.

Story Listening and Experience in Early Childhood, and the Reader

We know first-hand how difficult it is to teach, administrate, have a family, and still find time to read professional materials. We designed this book with that in mind. The chapters are, for the most part, independent of each other and cover different outcomes of story listening. These are summarized here to help you navigate your way to the various points we make.

Chapter 2 looks at *increasing engagement and focus.* Here we examine how narrative causes the listener to focus, and how this focus supports emergent literacy skills.

Chapter 3 goes on to discuss *how reader comprehension is enhanced through visualization.* We show that listening is not a sedentary experience. We demonstrate how oral story fosters visualization as opposed to picture book reading, and also discuss how visualization factors into both oral and reading comprehension.

Chapter 4 delineates *the benefits of repeated story listening.* This chapter describes how oral story listening can put the listener in a state of flow, fostering a desire to recreate the learning experience. It explains how frequent listening can cause a trance-like state, relaxing the listener and supporting the development of metacognition and theory of mind.

Chapter 5 examines *the social effects of the listening experience.* We discuss how oral story listening affects empathy, attachment, and community cohesion, and also look at oral story as a classroom management tool.

Chapter 6 gives *reasons for investing time in storytelling and how to get started.* Here we give directions for how to become a storyteller, and why it is worth the challenges you may face. We advise how to choose stories to tell, how to learn them, and what to expect from your audience.

And we provide three appendices with additional support for learning to tell stories and establishing an educational storytelling practice. Appendix A has four easy-to-learn, tellable stories. Appendix B lists further resources supporting any storytelling practice. And Appendix C consists of case studies describing three different types of successful storyteller training.

If your main interest is learning to tell stories, start by reading Chap. 6 and the Appendices. To know how story listening is different from picture book reading, start with Chap. 3. Should you wish to know about story listening effects in relation to emergent literacy, look at Chaps. 2, 3, and 4. You get the picture.

While we do hope you eventually read the entire book, what would really be the best outcome for us is to see you bring storytelling into your classroom and your home. Many teachers and librarians have been able to do just that.

One of our interviewees summed up the effects of her story listening experience this way:

> I'm intending to teach elementary school and I think that the stories and all of this… you know the stories, listening to those stories, may be why. You know when I got older, I always wanted to go back to the lower school (where the stories were told), because everything was paradise. There was no "you're bad at that." It was beautiful. Whatever grade I was in, story time was the BEST. I just loved listening. I want to bring that to the kids I teach.

References

Abowd, M. 2015. Philip W. Jackson, Education Scholar Committed to Children' Flourishing, 1928–2015. *UChicago News*, July 31. https://news.uchicago.edu/story/philip-w-jackson-education-scholar-committed-childrens-flourishing-1928-2015. Accessed May 14, 2020.

Alvey, R. G. 1974. *The Historical Development of Organized Storytelling to Children*. Dissertation, University of Pennsylvania. Ann Arbor, MI: University Microfilms International.

Bell, C. 2019. Email correspondence. November 2019.

Bignell, C. 2012. Talk in the Primary Curriculum: Seeking Pupil Empowerment in Current Curriculum Approaches. *Literacy* 46(1): 48–55. https://doi.org/10.1111/j.1741-4369.2011.00602.x.

Bryant, S. C. 1905. *How to Tell Stories to Children*. Boston and New York: Houghton Mifflin Co.

Chubb, P. 1902. *The Teaching of English in the Elementary and the Secondary School*. New York: The Macmillan Company.

Chubb, P. 1929. *The Teaching of English in the Elementary and the Secondary School, Revised and Largely Rewritten*. New York: The Macmillan Company.

Coe, I. and Christie-Dillon, A. J. 1913. *The Story Hour Readers Manual*. New York: American Book Company.

DCSF. 2008. *Talk for Writing*. DCSF Publications. http://www.education.gov.uk/publications/eOrdeeringDownload/Talk-for-writing.pdf. Accessed June 2020.

DePencier, Ida. 1960. *The History of the Laboratory Schools: The University of Chicago, 1896–1957*. Chicago: University of Chicago Press.

Dewey, E. 1919a, 1922. *The Dalton Laboratory Plan*. New York: E. P. Dutton and Co.

Dewey, E. 1919b. *New Schools for Old*. New York: E. P. Dutton and Co.

Dewey, J. 1933. *How We Think*. Lexington: D. C. Heath and Co.

Dewey, J. 1938. *Experience and Education*. New York: Collier Books.

Dewey, J. and Dewey, E. 1915. *Schools of To-morrow*. New York: E. P. Dutton and Co.

Greene, E. and Del Negro, J. M. 2010. *Storytelling: Art and Technique*. Santa Barbara, CA; Denver, CO; Oxford, UK: Libraries Unlimited.

Gregor, M. E. 2010. *Storytelling in Home, School and Library, 1890–1920*. MA Thesis. Portland, OR: University of Oregon. https://scholarsbank.uoregon.edu/xmlui/bitstream/handle/1794/10639/Gregor_Martha_E_ma2010sp.pdf?sequence=1. Accessed March 10, 2012.

Jackson, P. W. 1986. *The Practice of Teaching*. New York: Teachers' College Press.

Jackson, P. W. 1995. On the Place of Narrative in Teaching. In *Narrative in Teaching, Learning and Research*, 3–23, eds. Hunter McEwan and Kieran Egan. New York and London: Teachers College Press.

Parker, F. W. (Reported by L. E. Partridge). 1883. *Notes of Talks on Teaching Given by Francis Parker at the Martha's Vineyard Summer Institute, 1882*. New York: E. L. Kellog and Co.

Parker, F. W. 1894. *Talks on Pedagogics: An Outline on the Theory of Concentration*. New York and Chicago: E. L. Kellogg and Co.

Reese, E. 2012, The Tyranny of Shared Book-Reading. In *Contemporary Debates in Childhood Education and Development*, eds. Sebastian Suggate and Elaine Reese, 59–68. Abingdon: Taylor and Francis Group.

Rice, Emily J., and Gudrun Thorne-Thomsen. 1901. History and Literature. *Elementary School Teacher and Course of Study*, 2(1): 40–48.

Thorne-Thomsen, G. 1901. Reading in the Third Grade. *Elementary School Teacher and Course of Study*, 2(3): 227–235.

Thorne-Thomsen, G. 1903. The Educational Value of Fairy-Stories and Myths. *Elementary School Teacher*, 4(3): 161–167.

Warren, H. 1997. Character, Public Schooling, and Religious Education, 1920–1934. *Religion and American Culture: A Journal of Interpretation*, 7(1): 61–80. https://doi.org/10.1525/rac.1997.7.1.03a0003.

Wiggin, K. D. 1892. *Children's Rights: A Book of Nursery Logic*. Boston: Houghton, Mifflin and Company.

Wiggin, K. D. and Smith, N. A. 1895. *The Story Hour: A Book for Home and Kindergarten*. New York: Gay and Bird.

CHAPTER 2

"I am able to really listen. It's because of the stories." *Increasing engagement and focus*

Donna's family was attending a Christmas Party where at least seventy-five children were running throughout the house. A good many of the children attended the Laboratory Schools. After a while the hostess wanted to gather the children for Santa's arrival. Donna suggested that having the children listen to a story would be an easy way to get them settled. The hostess was thrilled. Sitting down in the middle of a wide wooden staircase Donna announced that she would tell a story while they waited for Santa.

The children who attended the Laboratory Schools sat down quietly. The other children continued playing. The children from the Laboratory Schools kept looking around, clearly agog that anyone would ignore the fact that a story was about to be told. Finally, one little boy starting shouting, "Come on, we're going to hear a story! Come on, sit down, let's hear the story." Other seated children took up the cry. After a while everyone sat down…

For the children who attended the Laboratory Schools listening to a story was an experience so pleasurable they gave it preference over playing or even Santa's arrival.

WHAT WE OBSERVED

We've lost count of the times teachers have expressed surprise at how children they were certain couldn't sit still long enough to listen to a story, would sit attentively to long, complex tales. Donna had it happen again while we were writing this book. She asked if she could tell stories in her

D. Schatt, P. Ryan, *Story Listening and Experience in Early Childhood*, https://doi.org/10.1007/978-3-030-65358-3_2

four-year-old grandson's preschool class. The teachers assumed she was asking to read to the children, but she explained she was going to just use her voice. The teachers reminded her the children, being so young, wouldn't sit still. Donna said she could handle it. There was a little wiggling when she began telling the two stories her grandson had requested. But everyone soon focused. When Donna returned that afternoon at dismissal time, one teacher came up and asked if Donna could come back the next day. "I've never seen these children so focused. They talked about the stories all day and kept telling them to each other." Donna was not surprised.

Early in our careers, we dismissed teachers' claims of unusually intense focus as an aberration, but it happened time and again. Over the years we recognized that most children who could not sit still or focus during class, even those with ADHD or facing stressful situations in their home life, would be quiet and calm during a story. At the Laboratory Schools this fact was acknowledged to the point where counselors evaluating children would come to observe them during story time. Those who couldn't attend to a story were thought to be in extreme distress.

Over time it also became evident that even the youngest children, when told stories weekly, exhibited a rapid increase in the length of time they could sit still, focus, and listen. Within weeks of the start of school, kindergarten children were capable of listening for as long as thirty minutes to unfamiliar, multi-themed stories and then could retell those stories in detail to their friends and family.

This has been independently confirmed in recent quantitative studies. A team of psychologists and educators, one of the few doing such work on oral storytelling in classrooms, established that "during oral storytelling children were less restless...and paid more attention to the stories...than during read-aloud" (Lenhart et al. 2020, p. 345). And qualitative studies looking at storytelling for students with special needs have also reported unanticipated intense focus while pupils listen. One researcher had difficulty keeping storytelling sessions for her study within the allotted time, because the class didn't want her to stop. The participating teacher was quite impressed because her pupils were known to have very short attention spans (Mello 1997, 2001, p. 6).

Not only were the children at the Lab School intensely focused during story times, the children put pressure on others to pay attention too. While a tale was told, children would ignore outside distractions, like a bee getting in on a hot spring day, or a snow plow throwing snow up against the windows. Even an errant squirrel running around behind them did not stop the children from focusing on the story being told. One woman we interviewed recalled:

> I do remember sometimes when I would get uncomfortable when some kids wouldn't be paying attention and I just could never understand that. I was always thinking how could you possibly not be paying attention? It was rare, you only would see a few of them, but I could NEVER understand. I was always, like, "HOW could you not be listening?" And not because I was a kiss ass, but I was genuinely interested in just being there.

This phenomenon wasn't particular to The Lab School situation. Even in extreme instances, when children lost focus in the middle of a story, that focus quickly returned.

A good friend and colleague, Liz Weir was head of Children's Services in Belfast Public Libraries during the worst of "The Troubles" in Northern Ireland. She pioneered a summer storytelling program, in which librarian-tellers visited parks and community centers where children could play safely during school vacations. Violent outbreaks had made it too danger-ous for children to visit libraries, so librarians came to the children. One morning Liz heard that a community center she was to tell stories at had burned down in a riot the previous evening. The play leaders assured her their summer camp would go on anyway, but it would be held in the lot beside the rubble. She related *The Three Billy Goats Gruff* to a large group of three-to-sixteen-year-olds gathered among piles of broken glass and bricks. In the middle of the story, a British army vehicle full of soldiers drove by. The children ran after the truck, throwing stones and bottles at the soldiers. Liz was horrified—would the soldiers react, would the kids in her charge start a new riot? But the soldiers, used to this reaction from the local children, just continued on. When the soldiers were out of range, her audience ran back to where they'd been sitting and demanded to hear the end of the tale. As Liz said, that's the power of storytelling. Children can focus on a story among the most extreme disturbances.

Every storyteller we know has tales of deep focus. We've all seen chil-dren so focused on the story that they shouted at the protagonist to stay away from the witch, or the listener who glazed over and had to be reminded that they were in a room with other people when it was time to leave. Yet no one we knew could explain the underlying causes. Why was it listening to a story put you in a state that one of our interviewees said, "was similar to taking a sedative?" Why do people attend to narrative with such intense focus? How is listening to a story different than hearing other forms of speech such as common conversation or classroom instruction?

WHY HUMANS FOCUS ON NARRATIVE

Auditory comprehension, "the human ability to listen and comprehend orally presented stimuli" (Horowitz-Kraus and Hutton 2015, p. 650), is innate, a primary act, much like seeing or speaking (Turner 1996, p. 13; Moffett 1968, p. 121). No one needs to show you how to do it, you are born attending to language, as suggested by fetal preference for human voice and sound (Dehaene 2009). The ability to comprehend orally presented narrative, in normally developing children, evolves over time with exposure to conversation and stories.

Storytelling and story listening are thought to be primary acts of the mind, actual ways of thinking. In his study of the origins of thought and language, Mark Turner claims, "Narrative imagining—story—is the fundamental instrument of thought. Rational capacities depend upon it. It is our chief means of looking into the future, of predicting, of planning, and of explaining. It is a literary capacity indispensable to human cognition generally" (Turner 1996, pp. 4–5). Stories are how we make sense of our world. For years, authors like Isaac Bashevis Singer (1976), Robert Leeson (1985), and Umberto Eco (1994), educators like Francis Parker (Parker 1883) and John Dewey (Dewey and Dewey 1915, pp. 29, 35), mathematicians and scientists such as Charles Hermite (Shedlock 1915, pp. 116–117; Winick 2013) and Albert Einstein (Winick 2013) have stated that stories, and storytelling, are essential to our make-up as humans. In her introduction to *The Cool Web: the pattern of children's reading*, Margaret Meek observed that "Storying is the most significant way we explain how we came to be where we are at, and a universal language habit that transcends all cultural barriers" (Meek et al. 1977, p. 8). Nobel Prize winner Isaac Bashevis Singer ends his well-known tale of *Naftali the Storyteller and his Horse, Sus* with a similar sentiment:

> When a day passes, it is no longer there. What remains of it? Nothing more than a story. If stories weren't told or books weren't written, man would live like the beasts, only for the day. The whole world, all human life is one long story. (Bashevis Singer 1976, pp. 20–21)

Barbara Hardy, a British literary scholar, asserted that narrative "is not to be regarded as an aesthetic invention used by artists to control, manipulate, and order experience, but as a primary act of the mind transferred to art from life" (Hardy 1977, p. 12). Yet few front-line educators and policy makers currently acknowledge storytelling and story listening as a *way of thinking* that's integral to children's development. This is both unfortunate and misinformed. As we stated in our introduction, it wasn't always so. Educators during the Progressive Era, such as Francis Parker and John Dewey, understood, based on intuition and observation, that storytelling was a powerful tool for teachers to use in early childhood education. Educator A.S. Artley argued that a child's ability to interpret any narrative she reads grows out of an appreciation of stories she hears spoken, and the "teacher sets the stage for this type of growth with much storytelling" (Artley 1953, p. 326).

Researchers are now exploring what educators intuited over a century ago. The ability to hear "our world of sound" is believed to begin in utero. "A newborn human shows preference for his/her mother's voice and to musical pieces to which he/she was previously exposed, indicating a capacity to learn while in utero" (Gerhardt and Abrams 2000, p. S1). When one of Donna's sons was a week old, she was convinced he was deaf because he did not wake up when their dog barked. When she contacted her pediatrician, the doctor laughed saying, "He's been hearing that dog bark for months. No wonder he's not reacting."

The innate ability to tune into and start making sense of human voices and sounds heard in utero starts at birth. Infants are born with billions of neurons, but most brain cells are not yet connected in networks. By interacting with their surroundings via all the infant's senses, including hearing, connections called synapses are created at an amazing speed (Greene and Del Negro 2010, p. 131). In her studies, Patricia Kuhl details amazingly complex brain activity in infants engaging in language they hear spoken to and around them (Kuhl 2004, 2010; Meltzoff and Kuhl 2016). Marianne Wolf states in her work *Proust and The Squid* that early childhood is one of the richest times for language growth due to the intertwining of oral language and cognition (Wolf 2008, p. 84).

We also know that narrative production and understanding appears early in life. There is a dramatic development of narrative production and understanding in children aged three to five years due to increasing linguistic sophistication (Friend and Bates 2014, p. 1; Fernyhough 2008, pp. 93, 165, 167). Psychologists have gone so far as to suggest that almost "every brain structure is involved in the process of narrative construction, and thus, we may say that the human brain is, indeed, a *narrative brain*" (Gonçalves et al. 2004, p. 103). Even so, narrative abilities must be developed, encouraged, and supported. Horowitz-Kraus and others stress that while listening is innate, "the development of higher-level abilities for comprehension depends on environmental factors such as verbal exposure" (Horowitz-Kraus and Hutton 2015, p. 650).

To recap—humans attend to sound in utero. We begin organizing and attending to language we are exposed to at birth and attain language skills over time. Listening to and producing story is part of this innate process. Between three and five years of age there is a developmental leap in language skills, and we begin producing and understanding the structure of narrative. Innate language and narrative development need exposure to different types of discourse to blossom. That's the biology of narrative listening. But chemistry is involved, too.

Neuroeconomist Paul Zak and his associates conducted experiments examining why certain stories are more persuasive than others. In their experiments, they found that if a story follows a "classic narrative arc" the listener becomes attentive to the story and emotionally attaches to the protagonist. This happens because two hormones, cortisol and oxytocin, are released during the narrative. Cortisol makes us alert and focuses our attention. This causes listeners to engage with the characters and their situation (Zak 2015, p. 4). Oxytocin, a chemical associated with care, gives the listener a sense of connection and empathy (Zak 2015, 2016a; Barraza et al. 2015). In some ways, the listener really has no choice but to attend to "a good story." Your brain is telling you, "*This is important. Pay attention,*" and while you're at it, "*Relax, empathize with the protagonist and feel good about the whole experience.*"

Other scientists have started studying physiological reactions prompted by stories. Mary Helen Immordino-Yang and her associates conducted qualitative analyses of listeners' reactions to emotional stories, using brain scans to identify physiological responses (Science Daily 2011; Immordino-Yang 2011, p. 314). Recent BBC and NPR documentaries on narrative and the brain (Kanthal 2019; Renken 2020a, b) both presented various findings on neurological and physiological effects of story listening. When immersed in a story, certain narratives can make your palms sweat, eyes blink, or heart skip a beat. Facial expressions change and eyebrows shift, further indications of intense focus (Green and Sestir 2017). We see this with children, whose eyes widen, jaws drop, and mouths gape open when engaged in story times. And fMRI scans reveal that listening to narratives engages parts of the brain associated with immersive states, so that "regions not traditionally thought to be part of a 'language network' in the brain become consistently activated when people listen to narratives" (Martinez-Conde et al. 2019, p. 8286).

Vivid, emotional stories make a subject appear important or more real, hence affecting focus and physiology. Zak's team found that in order for all this to happen the story had to follow a classic dramatic arc, as described by Aristotle and Gustav Freytag, what the latter delineated as exposition, rising action, climax, and denouement (Zak 2015, p. 7, 2016a, b; Freytag 1863, 1968). This is a description of most classic literature and of all folklore, fairy tales, and mythology.

It is interesting to note that since its inception, the material used for storytelling in the Lab School program consisted mainly of folk and fairy tales, or literary stories that mimic traditional narratives in terms of language, content, and structure. Such narratives all follow the classic dramatic arc. And the original teacher-storytellers at the Lab School weren't alone in preferencing folklore. Over a century ago teacher-storyteller Sara Cone Bryant identified listening to folk tales "as a simple and effective means of forming the habit of concentration, of fixed attention" (Bryant 1905, p. 9). When training teachers, she claimed storytelling was a practical aid, "fundamental and indispensable" for classes with children that policy makers would today identify as having challenging backgrounds or special needs.

Zak and his colleagues conducted their experiments on adults and have no findings concerning cortisol or oxytocin release in children listening to narrative. However, based on more than forty years of observation while telling stories to groups of children, we have seen behavior in young listeners that indicates outward signs of both attention and relaxation. We have repeatedly seen the dramatic arc "hook" listeners in a powerful and compelling way. We will be discussing this in greater detail later in the book. We do believe more investigation into the brain chemistry of young listeners experiencing these narratives would be beneficial for a better understanding of this phenomenon.

We should also mention that one early indication we had of chemical processes involved in listening came from our interviews with adults, who participated as children in the Lab School storytelling program. Almost all our informants talked of being excited about the weekly story times, looking forward to the *experience of listening*. It was the way that listening to a story made them *feel* that they wanted to experience as often as possible. Many of the people we interviewed said they were able to recreate the experience themselves once they could read well enough to get lost in books. We think some of that enjoyment came from the intense focus and empathy stimulated by the play between cortisol and oxytocin in their bloodstreams and brains.

Of what importance, in terms of human development, would the intense listening and engagement with an emotional story have? Current research suggests both contribute to reading comprehension and reading achievement. Listening to stories is one variable that is foundational to school success.

READING NEEDS TO BE TAUGHT, FOCUS IS A NECESSARY PART OF THE PROCESS

We were never born to read. Human beings invented reading only a few thousand years ago. And with this invention, we rearranged the very organization of our brain, which in turn expanded the ways we were able to think, which altered the intellectual evolution of our species. (Wolf 2008, p. 3)

Reading is not a 'natural' act; if it was we would all be able to do it effortlessly. (Tennent 2015, p. 2)

Reading and writing are unnatural acts, more unnatural, say, than speaking and listening. No one can master them in a short time. (Sanders 1994, p. 88)

Reading with comprehension is necessary for school and life success. Unfortunately, it does not always occur without intervention. The National Center for Education Statistic's 2019 "nation's report card" indicates that in the United States only 35% of fourth graders are at or above National Assessment of Educational Progress (NAEP) Proficiency in Reading, with only 34% of eighth graders and 37% of twelfth graders at or above NAEP Reading Proficiency (2019). In a 2010 report by the Annie E. Casey Foundation, "83% of children from low-income families...failed to reach the 'proficient' level in reading" (2010). Kate Walsh, of the National Council of Teacher Quality, attributes this to teaching methods, and expresses frustration regarding the fact that too many teachers are not adequately prepared, with most teachers-in-training receiving just one course in how to teach reading (Gonser 2018). We are certain little of this training covers storytelling—either the how to or the why. Oral story listening promotes the ability to focus, as we've shown above, and we believe can be an effective intervention to support foundational reading skills. We're backed by studies showing story listening experience utilizes social interaction and collaboration, enhancing word acquisition, recall, and fluency (Miller and Pennycuff 2008, pp. 37, 38; Myers 1990).

The process of reading has no genetic program allowing it to be passed between generations (Wolf 2008, pp. 12–13). Reading is a relatively new *phylogenetical* skill. It is believed to have come about a few thousand years ago due to evolutionary development and adaptation in the parts of our brain that are used for reading. "Underlying the brain's ability to learn reading lies its protean capacity to make new connections among structures and circuits originally devoted to other more basic brain processes such as vision and spoken language" (Wolf 2008, p. 5). Vision and language, including listening, are known to be innate and have genetic structures that are passed from one generation to the next. Neuroscientists believe that brain regions originally devoted to these innate cognitive functions and others are utilized to comprehend written symbols and other processes supporting decoding written words and reading comprehension (Horowitz-Kraus et al. 2014, p. 2).

Since reading is not natural to our genetic make-up, how do we prepare our elastic brains to adapt so that we can acquire the skills that allow us to learn to read? With the natural development of our language skills, supported by repeated exposure to language and language experience, we build the neural pathways we will need to learn to read (Horowitz-Kraus and Hutton 2015). "These accrue during specific age ranges, beginning with nonverbal communication in infancy and culminating in reading fluency" (Hutton et al. 2019, p. 2). Through this exposure we acquire a developmental continuum of "skills, knowledge, and attitudes that are precursors to reading and writing" (Whitehurst et al. 1988, p. 848). This continuum is referred to as emergent literacy (EL).

Emergent literacy is a concept introduced fifty years ago by Marie Clay. It describes young children's behavior when interacting with books and writing materials before they are able to read or write in any meaningful way (Clay 2013). Since the 1960s reading specialists have identified various behaviors that define EL and which contribute to or predict later reading success. EL skills pertinent to story listening experience that also pertain to reading development are:

- Understanding narrative hierarchy (or story structure/story grammar)
- Vocabulary
- The ability to visualize
- Semantic recognition

Active, focused listening to narrative supports development of these four areas of EL which help lay the foundation for our brain adapting in ways that allow us to learn to read. Shared reading has similar outcomes. But increasingly, studies suggest that oral storytelling results in a "collaboration between storyteller and listener that [doesn't] manifest itself as readily between reader and listener" (Myers 1990, p. 829), and that such collaboration makes a greater impact on story comprehension and building vocabulary, requisites for reading success.

The point we are making is that one of the long-term benefits of our natural focus on oral narrative is setting the groundwork for our subsequent reading abilities. By intense focus on story the listener is attending to the language and its meaning, building vocabulary, and learning to visualize (Nicolopoulou 2017, p. 50; Hutton 2015, pp. ii, 8, 12). For young children, decontextualized oral discourse makes greater demands than conversation when it comes to semantic clarity. Oral stories—one type of decontextualized language—requires them to create a world picture using only words, and "unlike many other forms...narrative is an important, engaging, and enjoyable activity for children from an early age" (Nicolopoulou 2017, p. 50). All these skills are needed for later reading. "Language networks provide critical support for emergent literacy, and a critical factor fueling literacy is a level of verbal simulation" (Horowitz-Kraus et al. 2017, p. 541).

John S. Hutton and Tipzi Horowitz-Kraus found that the development of neural circuits supporting verbal decoding and narrative comprehension at pre-reading stages are necessary for later reading and narrative comprehension (Horowitz-Kraus and Hutton 2015, p. 651). Hutton and his team have shown that the quality of cognitive stimulation in the home through oral narrative and shared reading provides "more grammatically correct vocabulary and range of subject matter than everyday conversation, especially in low-socioeconomic status (SES) households" (Hutton 2015, p. 2). They state that the more exposure children have to oral language and oral narrative from a young age, the more likely it is that they've built the mental "hardware" that is needed for emergent literacy and early literacy in primary school.

Hutton elaborates. Using fMRIs and narrative with young children he has shown that the quality of cognitive simulations and nurturing in early childhood has a long-term impact on brain development. His studies have shown that exposure to narrative (in his experiments, oral story reading with three-to-five-year-olds) contributes significantly to future reading success. His team has found that children who have a stimulating home reading environment which includes listening to stories show a "more robustly engaged neural circuitry supporting narrative comprehension, a foundational component of emergent literacy" (Hutton et al. 2015, pp. 469–470). In her overview of neuroscience in education, Delores Liston asserted that theories in this field

> demonstrate the significance of storytelling and narrative to education by relating brain function to learning. Storytelling and narratives are a good way to encourage new connections and the recognition of new patterns and relationships among objects and ideas. (Liston 1994, p. 1)

INTERNALIZING VOCABULARY, STORY STRUCTURE, AND FOCUS

Unfortunately, many children arrive at school with a gap in their vocabulary when compared to their peers. This establishes a significant disadvantage in their reading readiness (Hart and Risley 1995; Hutton et al. 2015, p. 469; Stanovich 1986). Disadvantaged students may never manage to close the vocabulary gap between themselves and their more advantaged peers in later reading ability. As Wolf eloquently summarizes:

> Children who begin kindergarten having heard and used thousands of words, whose meanings are already understood, classified, and stored away in their young brains, have the advantage on the playing field of education. Children who have never had a story read to them, who never hear words rhyme, who never imagine fighting dragons or marrying a prince, have the odds overwhelmingly against them. (Wolf 2008, p. 20)

Keith Stanovich termed what Maryanne Wolf is talking about above as "The Matthew's Effect" in relation to reading. In a seminal article he used the concept of the Matthew's Effect as a possible explanation of individual reading differences (Stanovich 1986; Walberg and Tsai 1983). The term is based on the Gospel according to Matthew: "For unto everyone that hath shall be given, and he shall have abundance: but from him that hath not shall be taken away even that which he hath" (XXV–29). As Stanovich relates, the Matthew's Effect, with regard to reading, refers to those children who enter school lacking in vocabulary compared to their peers. Children with inadequate vocabularies may find decoding of words and comprehension more difficult than their peers, and because it is difficult and unenjoyable, they will practice less and read more slowly. As a result, they will have less practice reading and that will inhibit further growth in their reading ability. Meanwhile those with adequate vocabulary will find learning to read enjoyable, and therefore will practice more, their vocabulary will grow quickly, and their reading abilities progress at a rapid rate. Thus, "The Matthew's Effect in reading arises from the fact that it is the better readers who have the more developed vocabularies" (Stanovich 1986, p. 381; Cunningham and Stanovich 1997, 1998).

Oral story listening may address some concerns regarding attainment of vocabulary (Artley 1953, p. 325; Elley 1989; Beck and McKeown 2001; Weisleder and Fernald 2013). For decades now educators, literacy experts, and psychologists have investigated the role narrative experience plays in building children's vocabulary. Particular attention has been devoted to students who are struggling to succeed in school, including those from lower socio-economic groups. But most of these studies looked at shared reading experiences using picture book narratives and not oral story as we define it. Sometimes the story is simply read out loud, while other studies use dialogic approaches with conversations between adult and child regarding text and/or illustrations as the story is read aloud. All of these studies found significant gains in vocabulary: shared reading as story listening does have impact (Dickinson and Smith 1994; Whitehurst et al. 1988; Trostle and Hicks 1998; Bus 2002; Whitehurst and Lonigan 2002; Mol et al. 2008; Murulis and Neuman 2010, 2013).

It has also been acknowledged that other forms of spoken discourse builds vocabulary. And in numerous publications storytellers, teachers, and librarians report on the efficacy of oral storytelling for word acquisition (MacDonald et al. 2013; Mello 2001; Tooze 1959). Both quantitative and qualitative studies have demonstrated that listening to oral stories, overheard conversational narratives, and hearing and participating in nursery rhymes and songs influence linguistic development. These speech forms, experienced *apart* from books, seem to offer rich and interactive opportunities for implicit and explicit language learning to occur because they represent highly ritualized dialogue, in which the narrator guides the attention, asks questions, provides explanations, and gives feedback. (Lenhart et al. 2020)

Shared reading can also enhance this enriched language, but anecdotes and qualitative reports of oral story practitioners, as well as recent quantitative studies, indicate oral story listening does so more effectively. Jan Lenhart, Enni Vaahtoranta, and Sebastian Suggate and their colleagues have run experiments with different methods of story delivery: oral storytelling versus read-aloud. They found oral storytelling resulted in the largest gains in vocabulary and best story comprehension. The listeners were also less restless and more attentive during oral storytelling (Lenhart et al. 2020; Vaahtoranta et al. 2017, 2019; Suggate et al. 2013).

This may be due to oral storytelling being more enjoyable than shared picture book reading for a large percentage of listeners. Those who spend time with young children—parents, child-care workers, and teachers—will remember situations where playful, enjoyable expressions of language led to kids spontaneously and creatively using new words. A recent anecdote demonstrating this comes, again, from Donna's family. Her grandson Victor asked if she would come to his kindergarten class and tell *The Woman Who Flummoxed the Fairies* for his birthday. Victor's younger brother, Noam, had never heard the story (or the word "flummox") but was there listening when Donna told it to Victor's class. Two weeks later, Noam tricked his mother in the kitchen: he then turned and informed her, "Ha! I flummoxed you!"

And it's not only words that Noam and other children pick up from story listening, but elements and actions within narratives that they can contemplate and emulate. Many of the studies referenced above not only examined the role of shared reading and oral narratives in vocabulary development, but also the part played in comprehension. Understanding what you read depends on decoding the text to get the content of a story, but also requires knowing and understanding how stories work. Gaining a knowledge of story structure is vital and comes from regular story listening experience. The process of acquiring it is enjoyable and once embedded helps when encountering new stories.

As Hutton et al. (2015, 2019) have shown, regular, frequent experience with oral narrative has a cumulative effect on neural development that benefits later reading. Conversely, a lack may inhibit reading development and comprehension. We suggest that such a lack of story listening experience for young children adds to the deficit that Stanovich identified as the Matthew's Effect. The lack of vocabulary and a deficient knowledge of and experience with story grammars and hierarchies in comparison to their peers puts children at a serious disadvantage. On the other hand, exposure to frequent, regular oral narrative listening develops regions of the brain that help adapt it to reading (Hutton et al. 2015; Horowitz-Kraus et al. 2017). And just as importantly, we would argue, it provides a child with a knowledge of what stories are and how they work, what experts call narrative hierarchies and narrative structure or story grammar (Nezworski et al. 1982; Stein 1982; Stadler and Ward 2005).

It may seem to be a stretch to assert regular story listening experience embeds a practical understanding of story structure. But one of our informants, many years after taking part in the UCLS storytelling program, passionately expressed that it does, telling us:

> I hate the way my husband tells stories, you know, like at a dinner party. You know we have these stories that we tell and I'm always correcting the story he's telling—at least in my head. You know there's a way that a story needs to be told, that certain things need to come before other things and he will miss out on some key character development elements, or he'll leave out the setting before he delves into the funny part of the story. I think that comes from the fact that I spent so much time listening to stories. But the way my husband tells a story drives me crazy. He doesn't know what makes up a good story and I do! And the funny thing is, you know, he's a writer.

In summary, story listening supports emergent literacy, establishing precursors needed for being able to learn to read.

The second identified area of skills that need to develop in order to learn to read are called executive functions (EF). Commonly thought of as "the CEO of the brain" (Gooch et al. 2016; Anderson 2002), it is a collective term that identifies a set of processes necessary in controlling cognitive, emotional, and physical behaviors (Diamond and Lee 2011; Miyake et al. 2000). EF is needed when creating, telling, or comprehending a narrative (Friend and Bates). The executive function skills cognitive scientists recognize as underpinning reading include:

- Attention (the ability to focus on a particular object, activity or person),
- Inhibition (self-control, self-regulation),
- Metacognition (also known as theory of mind).
  (Diamond and Lee 2011, p. 959; Horowitz-Kraus et al. 2014)

Those familiar with the term "executive functions" may see similarities between EF and the behavior we describe when children are focused on an oral story. Teachers who have observed their students listening to stories say there is a dramatic effect on listening and concentration; both aspects of Executive Function development (Gardner 1973, p. 203; Greene and Del Negro 2010, p. 45 and 112; MacDonald et al. 2013, p. 59). Remembering the story times, one of our Lab School informants saw an outcome of story listening rather didactically:

We learned to sit and listen and focus on the speaker. You listen to the story and got an appreciation of the story arc, the importance of a theme, coming back to motifs over and over again. You're hearing patterns over and over. It registered.

Seeing potential connections, researchers have experimented to see if and how EL and EF are related to or via narrative. Friend and Bates recognized that narrative and EF are different but complementary, finding "that narrative and executive functions are comprised of a set of skills that appear to develop asynchronously during the preschool period and that support subsequent development across skill sets" (Friend and Bates 2014, p. 10). And the findings of Gooch and her associates "suggest that executive function and language skills have separate but correlated origins" (Gooch et al. 2016, p. 185). Various studies have also found correlations between EF and EL, but nothing causal.

Recent findings on how babies and young children think, and what they're thinking about, suggest a line for future inquiries about story listening and how it might support EF qualities such as attention and inhibition. Alison Gopnik, with students and colleagues, has revealed a better understanding of babies' and young children's consciousness. In Gopnik's opinion, babies are more conscious than adults (Gopnik 2012). She describes young and mature brains as exhibiting different ways of focusing. Adults have a highly focused, purpose-driven kind of attention, while

> babies and young children seem to have more of a lantern of consciousness than a spotlight of consciousness. So babies and young children are very bad at narrowing down to just one thing. But they're very good at taking in lots of information from lots of different sources at once. And if you actually look in their brains, you see that they're flooded with these neurotransmitters that are really good at inducing learning and plasticity, and the inhibitory parts haven't come on yet. So when we say that babies and young children are bad at paying attention, what we really mean is that they're bad at not paying attention. So they're bad at getting rid of all the interesting things that could tell them something and just looking at the thing that's important. (Gopnik 2011)

Assuming this is so, then regular, frequent oral story listening could be one way adults guide children's brain development toward a "spotlight" kind of consciousness. Considering how oral narrative is natural, captures our attention, and what it does to us, requires creating a consciousness where a listener is so focused on the story content and elements of its performance that everything else disappears. Experienced repeatedly, children become able to "really focus."

One final point to consider regarding focus in relation to EF: a number of teachers and parents we've encountered have asked what's the difference between experiencing recorded stories and those told live. Many adults see the advantages of talking books and animated picture books, readily available via electronic devices. They're great babysitters, and certainly keep children quiet and "focused." In education, policy makers look to digital resources to supply narrative and other language experiences, seeing it as both enrichment and a money- and labor-saving device. This isn't really new—toward the end of the Progressive Era in the 1930s, educational storytellers were replaced in the name of efficiency with storytelling on phonographs and the radio, and then by movies, filmstrips, and television in subsequent decades (Alvey 1974, pp. 89–90).

But some of the studies we've referenced earlier compared not only shared reading and oral storytelling, but also live versus recorded narration. Patricia Kuhl's research into linguistic development found that "babies are listening intently to us, and they're taking statistics as they listen to us talk" (Kuhl 2010). Wondering what role adult humans played in live experiments on language acquisition, her team repeated the study with different eight-month-old children. One group was provided "language experiences" via television, the other from audio recordings. Using magnetoencephalography, they found no learning whatsoever going on in either the video or audio results (Kuhl 2010; Meltzoff and Kuhl 2016). In another fMRI study by Hutton and his team, twenty-seven children between four and five years of age were scanned listening to three short stories: one read aloud, one read with illustrations, and one in animated form. They found substantial differences in functional brain network activity between the animated and more traditional story formats, suggesting the latter were more efficient in scaffolding language development (Hutton et al. 2018). And in their most recent experiment, Lenhart's team also included audiotaped versions alongside live presentations of read-aloud and oral storytelling (Lenhart et al. 2020). As previously mentioned, live presentations showed the largest gains in all areas. Involvement of a live adult narrator appears to be the most beneficial form of storytelling to contribute to foundational literacy or executive functions.

THE FOCUS EXPERIENCE

We are innately programmed to listen to sounds and language, to create patterns that make meaning. As a primary act of the mind, it's natural and enjoyable for us to think in stories. From a very early age voice catches our attention, especially unusual sounds, rhyming, and patterns. Early focus that comes while listening to stories is partly inherent due to aspects within ourselves and our environment from the start of life.

The structure of narratives, especially classic story arcs like those found in folk and fairy tales, produces a physiological response. Listening becomes pleasurable and so we want more of it. Neurologists, cognitive scientists, developmental psychologists, and reading specialists have measured how frequent, regular exposure to stories read aloud re-structures parts of the young brain to make it a reading brain, and this contributes to later reading success. We believe listening to stories told aloud also contributes in a foundational way to creating the reading brain.

Whether they do so equally, but in different ways, may be significant. The testimony of our informants, accounts from educators over the last century, and our own anecdotes and those of fellow teacher- and librarian-storytellers, as well as the limited quantitative data we have, all makes a case for more research in this area. We would like to see educators encouraged to tell stories as part of their curriculum, and more specialists gathering quantitative observations and data on such practices.

Story listening, as a way of thinking, deserves consideration as a natural way to teach, something Sara Cone Bryant understood over one hundred years ago. She believed that when children listened happily to stories on a regular, frequent basis, then

> the habit of listening and deducing has been formed, and the expectation of pleasantness is connected to the opening of the teacher's lips. These two benefits are well worth the trouble they cost... [Any teacher who tells stories will observe] the quick gaining of a confidential relation with the children, and the gradual development of concentration and interested attention in them. (Bryant 1905, p. 12)

References

Alvey, R. G. 1974. *The Historical Development of Organized Storytelling to Children*. Doctoral dissertation, Graduate School of the Arts and Sciences, University of Pennsylvania, 1974. Ann Arbor, MI: University Microfilms International. Microfilm.

Anderson, P. 2002. Assessment and development of executive function (EF) during childhood. *Child Neuropsychology* 8(2): 71–82. DOI: https://doi.org/10.1076/chin.8.2.71.8724.

Annie E. Casey Foundation. 2010. *Early Warning! Why reading by the end of third grade matters. A kids count report on the importance of reading by third grade*. https://www.aecf.org/resources/early-warning-why-reading-by-the-end-of-third-grade-matters/. Accessed 1 November 2019.

Artley, A.S. 1953. Oral-language growth and reading ability. *The Elementary School Journal* 53(6): 321–328. doi. 0.1086/458497.

Barraza, J.A., Alexander, V., Beavin, L.E., Terris, E.T., Zak, P.J. 2015. The heart of the story: peripheral physiology during narrative exposure predicts charitable giving. *Biological Psychology* 105: 138–143. DOI: https://doi.org/10.1016/j.biopsycho.2015.01.008.

Bashevis Singer, I. 1976. *Naftali the storyteller and his horse, Sus, and other stories*. Oxford and New York: Oxford University Press.

Beck, I. and McKeown, M.G. 2001. Text talk: capturing benefits of read-aloud experiences for young children authors. *The Reading Teacher* 55(1): 10–20.

Bus, A. G. 2002. Joint care-giver—child storybook reading; A route to literacy development. In *Handbook of Early Literacy Research, Vol. 1*, eds. Susan B. Neumand and David K. Dickinson. New York, London: The Guildford Press.

Bryant, S. C. 1905. *How to Tell Stories to Children*. Boston: Houghton, Mifflin and Co.

Clay, M.M. 2013. *An Observation Survey of Early Literacy Achievement*. New Zealand: The Marie Clay Literacy Trust.

Cunningham, A.E. and Stanovich, K.E. 1997. Early reading acquisition and its relation to reading experience and ability 10 years later. *Developmental Psychology.* 33(6): 934–945. DOI: https://doi.org/10.1037/0012-1649.33.6.934.

Cunningham, A.E. and Stanovich, K.E. 1998. What reading does for the mind. *American Educator* 22: 8–17.

Dehaene, S. 2009. *Reading in the Brain. The new science of how we read*. New York: Viking Penguin, Penguin Group (USA).

Dewey, J. and Dewey, E. 1915. *Schools of To-Morrow*. New York: E. P. Dutton and Company.

Diamond, A. and Lee, K. 2011. Interventions shown to aid executive function development in children 4 to 12 years old. *Science,* 333(6045): 959–964. DOI: https://doi.org/10.1126/science.1204529.

Dickinson, K. and Smith, M.W. 1994. Long-term effects of preschool teachers' book readings on low-income children's vocabulary and story comprehension. *Reading Research Quarterly,* 29(2); 104–122. DOI: https://doi.org/10.2307/747807.

Eco, U. 1994. *Six Walks in Fictional Woods*. Cambridge, Mass.: Harvard University Press.

Elley, W.B. 1989. Vocabulary acquisition from listening to stories. *Reading Research Quarterly,* 24(2): 274–287. DOI: https://doi.org/10.2307/747863.

Fernyhough, C. 2008. *The Baby in the Mirror, a child's world from birth to three*. London: Granta Books.

Freytag, G. 1863, 1968. *Die Technik des Dramas / Technique of the drama; an exposition of dramatic composition and art. An authorized translation from the 6th German*. Ed., Trans. E.J. MacEwan. New York: B. Blom.

Friend, M. and Bates, R. P. 2014. The union of narrative and executive function: different but complimentary. *Frontiers in Psychology,* 5(465): 1–12. DOI: https://doi.org/10.3389/fpsyg.2014.00469.

Gardner, H. 1973. *The Arts and Human Development*. New York and London: Wiley.

Gerhardt, K.J. and Abrams, R.M. 2000. Fetal exposures to sounds and vibro-acoustic stimulation. *Journal of Perinatology,* 20(S200S29). DOI: https://doi.org/10.1038/sj.jp.7200446.

Gonçalves, Ó. F., Henriques, M.R., Machado, P.P.P. 2004. Nurturing nature, cognitive narrative strategies. In *The Handbook of Narrative and Psychotherapy. Practice, Theory and Research*, eds. L.E. Angus, L.E. and J McLeod, 103–117. Thousand Oaks, London, New Delhi: Sage Publications.

Gonser, S. 2018. How to help struggling readers. *Early Education, The Hechinger Report.* https://hechingerreport.org/how-to-help-struggling-young-readers/ Accessed 1 November 2019.

Gooch, D., Thompson, P. Nash, H.M., Snowling, M.J., Hulme, C. 2016. The development of executive function and language skills in early school years. *Journal of Child Psychology and Psychiatry,* 57(2):180–187. https://doi.org/10.1111/jcpp.12458.

Gopnik, A. 2011. What do babies think? TedTalk. https://www.ted.com/talks/alison_gopnik_what_do_babies_think/footnotes?language=en. Accessed August 1, 2020.

Gopnik, A. 2012. Scientific thinking in young children: Theoretical advances, empirical research, and policy implications. *Science* 337, 1623–1627. DOI: https://doi.org/10.1126/science.1223416.

Green, M. C. and Sestir, M. 2017. Transportation Theory. *International Encyclopedia of Media Effects*. Hoboken, New Jersey: John Wiley and Sons, Inc. doi:https://doi.org/10.1002/9781118783764.wbieme0083.

Greene, E. and Del Negro, J.M. 2010. *Storytelling: Art and Technique.* Santa Barbara, California, Denver, Colorado, Oxford, England: Libraries Unlimited.

Hardy, B. 1977. Narrative as a primary act of mind, towards a poetics of fiction: an approach through narrative. In *The Cool Web*, eds. M. Meek, A. Warlow and G. Barton, G., 12–23. London: The Bodley Head.

Hart, B. and Risley, T. 1995. *Meaningful Differences in Everyday Experience of Young American Children.* Baltimore, MD: Brookes.

Horowitz-Kraus, T., Vannest, J.J., Gozdas, E., Holland, S.K. 2014. Greater utilization of neural-circuits related to executive functions is associated with better reading: a longitudinal fMRI study using the verb generation task. *Frontiers in Human Neuroscience.* 8(447): 1–13. DOI: 0.3389/fnhum.2014.00447.

Horowitz-Kraus, T., and Hutton, John S. 2015. From emergent literacy to reading: how learning to read changes a child's brain. *Acta Paediatrica,* 104(7): 648–686. DOI: https://doi.org/10.1111/apa.13018.

Horowitz-Kraus, T., Schmitz, R., Hutton, J.S., Schumacher, J. 2017. "How to create a successful reader? Milestones in reading development from birth to adolescence" *Acta Paediatrica,* 104(7); 648–9. DOI: https://doi.org/10.1111/apa.13738.

Hutton, J. S. 2015. Home Reading Environment and Brain Activation in Preschool Children Listening to Stories. M.Sc. Thesis. Cincinnati: University of Cincinnati.

Hutton, J. S., Horowitz-Kraus, T. Mendelsohn, A.L., DeWitt, T., Holland, S.K., and the C-MIND Authorship Consortium 2015. "Home reading environment and brain activation in preschool children listening to stories" *Pediatrics*, 136(3): 466–478. DOI: https://doi.org/10.1542/peds.2015-0359.

Hutton, J. S., Dudley, J., Horowitz-Kraus, T., DeWitt, T., Holland, S. K. 2018. Differences in functional brain network connectivity during stories presented in audio, illustrated, and animated format in preschool-age children. *Brain Imaging and Behavior.* 14: 130–141. DOI:https://doi.org/10.1007/s11682-018-9985-y.

Hutton, J.S., Justice, L., Huang, G., Kerr, A., DeWitt, T., Ittenbach, R.F. 2019. The reading house: A children's book for emergent literacy screening during well-child visits. *Pediatrics*, 143(6): 1–11. DOI: https://doi.org/10.1542/peds.2018-3843.

Immordino-Yang, M. H. 2011. Me, my "self" and you: Neuropsychological relations between social emotion, self-awareness, and morality. *Emotion Review*, 3(3): 313–315, DOI: https://doi.org/10.1177/1754073911402391.

Kanthal, S. 2019. Why do stories matter? *The Why Factor*. BBC World Services. https://www.bbc.co.uk/sounds/play/w3csytz8. Accessed April 30, 2019.

Kuhl, P.K. 2004. Early language acquisition: cracking the speech code. *Nature Reviews Neuroscience*, 5, 831–843. DOI: https://doi.org/10.1038/nrn1533.

Kuhl, P. K. 2010. The linguistic genius of babies. TedTalk. https://www.ted. com/talks/patricia_kuhl_the_linguistic_genius_of_babies/transcript?language=en#t-598636. Accessed August 1, 2020.

Leeson, R. 1985. *Reading and Righting, the past, present and future of fiction for the young*. London, Glasgow, Sydney, Auckland, Toronto, Johannesburg: William Collins Sons and Co. Ltd.

Lenhart, J., Lenhard, W., Vaahtoranta, E., Suggate, S. 2020. More than words: Narrator engagement during storytelling increases children's word learning, story comprehension, and on-task behavior. *Early Childhood Research Quarterly*, 51: 338–351. DOI: https://doi.org/10.1016/j.ecresq.2019.12.009.

Liston, D.D. 1994. Storytelling and narrative: a neurophilosophical perspective. Conference paper/non-journal. https://files.eric.ed.gov/fulltext/ED372092.pdf. Accessed July 10, 2018.

MacDonald, M. R., MacDonald-Whitman, J. and Forrest-Whitman, N. 2013. *Teaching with Story, classroom connections to storytelling*. Atlanta, GA: August House.

Martinez-Conde, S. Alexander, R. G., Blum, D., Britton, N., Lipska, B. K., Quirk, G. J., Swiss, J. I., Willems, R. M., Macknik, S. L. 2019. "The storytelling brain: How neuroscience stories help bridge the gap between research and society". *The Journal of Neuroscience.* 39(2): 8295–8290. DOI: https://doi.org/10.1523/JNEUROSCI.1180-19.2019.

Meek, M., Warlow, A. and Barton, G. (Eds.). 1977. *The Cool Web*. London: The Bodley Head.

Mello, R. 1997. "Creating pictures in my mind": A qualitative study of children's responses to *storytelling in the classroom*. *Primer: The Journal of the Massachusetts Reading Association*. 26(1): 4–11.

Mello, R. 2001. Building bridges: How storytelling influences teacher/student relationships. *Conference Paper: Storytelling in the Americas Conference, St. Catherine's Ontario, Canada, Aug. 2001*. ERIC Number: ED457088.

Meltzoff, A. N. and Kuhl, P. K. 2016. Exploring the Infant Social Brain: What's Going on in There? *Zero to Three Journal*. 36(3): 2–9.

Miller, S. and Pennycuff, L. 2008. The power of story: Using storytelling to improve literacy learning. *Journal of Cross-Disciplinary Perspectives in Education*. 1(1): 36–43.

Miyake, A. Friedman, N.P., Emerson, M.J., Witzky, A.H., Howerter, A., Wager, T.D. 2000. The unity and diversity of executive functions and their contributions to complex 'Frontal Lobe' task: A latent variable analysis. *Cognitive Psychology*, 41(1): 49–100. DOI: https://doi.org/10.1006/cogp.1999.0734.

Moffett, J. 1968. *Teaching the Universe of Discourse*. Boston: Houghton Mifflan.

Mol, S. E., Bus, A. G., de Jong, M. T., Smets, D. J. H. 2008. Added value of dialogic parent-child book readings: A meta-analysis. *Early Education and Development*. 19(1): 7–26. DOI: 10.1080/10409280701838603.

Murulis, L. M. and Neuman, S. B. 2010. The effects of vocabulary intervention on young children's word learning: A metanalysis. *Review of Educational Research*, 80(3): 300–335. DOI: https://doi.org/10.3102/003465431 0377087.

Murulis, L. M. and Neuman, S. B. 2013. How vocabulary interventions affect young children at risk: A meta-analytic review. *Journal of Research on Educational Effectiveness*. 6(3): 223–262. DOI: https://doi.org/10.108 0/19345747.2012.755591.

Myers, P. 1990. Stories from print. *Language Arts*. 67(8): 824–831. Jstor.org/stable/41961806.

NAEP Report Card: 2019 NAEP Reading Assessment. 2019. *National Assessment of Educational Progress*. National Center for Education Statistics. https://www.nationsreportcard.gov/highlights/reading/2019/. Accessed 1 November 2019.

Nezworski, T., Stein, N. and Trabasso, T. 1982. Story structure versus content in children's recall. *Journal of Verbal Learning and Verbal Behavior*. 21(2): 196–206. DOI: https://doi.org/10.1016/S0022-5371(82)90561-8.

Nicolopoulou, A. 2017. Promoting oral narrative skills in low-income preschoolers through storytelling and story acting. In *Storytelling in Early Childhood, Enriching language, literacy and classroom culture.*, eds. Teresa Cremin, Rosie Flewitt, Ben Mardell, and Joan Swann, 49–66. London and New York: Routledge.

Parker, F. W. (Reported by L. E. Partridge). 1883. *Notes of Talks on Teaching Given by Francis Parker at the Martha's Vineyard Summer Institute, 1882.* New York: E. L. Kellog and Co.

Renken, E. 2020a. How stories connect and persuade us: Unleashing the brain power of narrative. *Short Wave.* NPR: April 22. https://www.npr.org/sections/health-shots/2020/04/11/815573198/how-stories-connect-and-persuade-us-unleashing-the-brain-power-of-narrative?t=1597173557106. Accessed May 10, 2020.

Renken, E. 2020b. Your brain wave on storytelling. *Short Wave.* NPR: January 14. https://www.npr.org/2020/01/13/795977814/your-brain-on-storytelling. Accessed May 10, 2020.

Sanders, B. 1994. *A is for Ox, the collapse of literacy and rise of violence in an electronic age.* New York: Vintage Books.

Science Daily. 2011. Brain co-opts the body to promote moral behavior, study finds. https://www.sciencedaily.com/releases/2011/07/110707092443.htm. Accessed May 21, 2020.

Shedlock, M 1915, 1951 (3rd ed.). *The Art of the Storyteller.* New York: D. Appleton and Company; Dover Publications Inc.

Stadler, M. A. and Ward, G.C. 2005. Supporting the narrative development of young children. *Early Childhood Education Journal,* 33(2):73–80. DOI:https://doi.org/10.1007/s10643-005-0024-4.

Stanovich, K. E. 1986. Matthew effects in reading: some consequences of individual differences in the acquisition of literacy. *Reading Research Quarterly,* 21(4): 360–407. DOI: https://doi.org/10.1177/0022057409189001-204.

Stein, N. 1982. The definition of a story. *Journal of Pragmatics,* 6: 487–507. DOI: https://doi.org/10.1016/0378-2166(82)90022-4.

Suggate, S. P., Wolfgang, L., Neudecker, E., Wolfgang, S. 2013. Incidental vocabulary acquisition from stories: Second and fourth graders learn more from listening than reading. *First Language.* 33(6): 551–571. DOI: https://doi.org/10.1177/0142723713503144.

Tennent, W. 2015. *Understanding Reading Comprehension, processes and practices.* Los Angeles, London, New Delhi, Singapore, Washington DC: SAGE.

Tooze, R. 1959. *Storytelling, how to develop skills in the art of telling stories to children.* Englewood Cliffs NJ: Prentice-Hall, Inc.

Trostle, S., Hicks, S. J. 1998. The effects of storytelling versus story reading on comprehension and vocabulary knowledge of British primary school children. *Reading Improvement* 35(3): 127–135.

Turner, M. 1996. *The Literary Mind.* Oxford, New York: Oxford University Press.

Vaahtoranta, E. and Suggate, S., Jackman C., Lenhart, J., Lenhard, W. 2017. Can explaining less be more? Enhancing vocabulary through explicit versus elaborative storytelling. *First Language* 0(0): 1–20. DOI: https://doi.org/10.1177/0142723717737452.

Vaahtoranta, E., Lenhart, J., Suggate, W., Lenhard, W. 2019. Interactive elaborative storytelling: engaging children as storytellers to foster vocabulary. *Frontiers in Psychology.* 10(1534):1–13. DOI: https://doi.org/10.3389/fpsyg.2019.01534.

Walberg, H. J., and Tsai, S. 1983. Matthew effects in education. *American Educational Research Journal,* 20: 359–373.

Weisleder, A. and Fernald, A. 2013. Talking to children matters: early language experience strengthens processing and builds vocabulary. *Psychological Science,* XX(X): 1–10. doi: https://doi.org/10.1177/0956797613488145.

Whitehurst, G. J., Falco, F. L., Lonigan, C. J., Fischel, J.E., DeBaryshe, B. D., Valez-Menchaca, M. C., and Caulfield, M. 1988. Accelerating language development through picture book reading. *Developmental Psychology* 24(4): 552–559. DOI: https://doi.org/10.1037/0012-1649.24.4.552.

Whitehurst, G. J. and Lonigan, C. J. 2002. Emergent literacy: Development from prereaders to readers. In *Handbook of Early Literacy Research, Vol. 1.* eds. Susan B. Neumand and David K. Dickinson. New York, London: The Guildford Press.

Winick, S. 2013. Einstein's folklore. *Folklife Today* [blog] Washington D.C.: Library of Congress. https://blogs.loc.gov/folklife/2013/12/einsteins-folklore/. Accessed March 17, 85.

Wolf, M. 2008. *Proust and the Squid, the story and science of the reading brain.* New York and London: HarperCollins.

Zak, P. J. 2015. Why Inspiring stories make us react: the neuroscience of narrative. *Cerebrum,* 2: 1–13.

Zak, P.J. 2016a. Empathy, neurochemistry and the dramatic arc. *The Future of Storytelling.* https://futureofstorytelling.org/video/paul-zak-empathy-neurochemistry-and-the-dramatic-arc. Accessed July 1, 2019.

Zak, P.J. 2016b. Why the story arc is important. *The Future of Storytelling.* https://www.youtube.com/watch?v=2K3WIsVi850 Accessed July 1, 2019.

CHAPTER 3

"So, it was like, in my mind an activity."
Enhancing reader comprehension through visualization

One of our informants spoke descriptively about an image he still remembers from a very long and complicated British tale about a young girl who skips rope with the fairies while she sleeps:

> I have an image of a Tim Burton kind of character, and I think it was in *Elsie Piddock*. I can see a big hill, and it's really dark and scary, and there's this little girl jumping rope. Am I seeing that because they made a movie of it or something?

We told him there was no movie version of that story. Only in recent years, long after he'd heard it, was there a picture book version in pastel watercolors (Farjeon 2000), making it nothing like a Burton film. The image was entirely of his own making.

AN ACTIVITY OF THE MIND

Storytelling in school settings is often considered entertainment, a frivolous activity, a waste of time in a packed school day. As already discussed, most people who observe children listening to stories are impressed with how focused and still the children are, and often that their bodies are relaxed, and their breathing is shallow. But instead of seeing this focus as having educational or developmental relevance, many assume from these observations that the listeners are passive recipients of the narrative and

D. Schatt, P. Ryan, *Story Listening and Experience in Early Childhood*, https://doi.org/10.1007/978-3-030-65358-3_3

not enactors of it—the children are being "entertained," as if there is no activity or learning going on.

What remains unnoticed is the activity going on in the minds of the children. Professor Craig R. Roney asserted story listening is active because listeners create images, causing reactions delivered back to the teller, affecting the telling, and increasing comprehension (Roney 1996, p. 7). Our students convinced us early on that their listening was not passive. As Roney claimed, they were co-creating the stories they were hearing, by creating visualizations and bringing their life experiences to their understanding of the stories.

Here's an example: in the middle of listening to *Kate Crackernuts* (a Scottish folk tale about two sisters defying fairy enchantments, including replacing one sister's head with that of a sheep), a second grade boy stood up shaking and proclaimed, "I don't believe a word of this! I'm leaving!" Donna calmly replied, "It's just a story." "Oh" he said, looking around and realizing he was in a library with forty other children. He smiled and sat back down and listened to the rest of the story. Later when Donna asked him why he had wanted to leave, he said the pictures were too scary.

Donna was telling the story without the use of a book or visual props. The student's response of "the pictures were too scary," certainly seems to be evidence that he was actively visualizing the story as it was told. According to Keith Oatley, when we read, we create our own version of the story, running simulations in our minds. "As partners with the writer, we create a version based on our own experience of how the world appears …and of how we might understand its deeper properties" (Oatley 2011, p. 18). This co-creation of story between the narrator and the reader (or listener) is called "reader response" (Oatley 2011; Davis 2013; Gold 2002). Although Oatley is speaking about adult readers, we believe that what he describes is also true for story listeners no matter their age.

Our listener is not an isolated example of this. Author Jane Yolen recalled a similar experience when listening to the myth of *Perseus* as a child at summer camp. She wrote that

> when the storyteller came to the part where the hero held up the head of the gorgon Medusa, she held her own hand aloft. I could have sworn then—and I can swear now—that I saw snakes from the gorgon's head curling and uncurling around the storyteller's arm.

Yolen goes on to try and rationalize this but finally admits it was "simply the power of the teller and the tale" (Yolen 1981, pp. 41–42).

Yolen and the child in our example became engrossed by the images of the story each had created in their minds. Both found themselves inside the story, which is also referred to as being embedded or transported (Gerrig 1993; Green 2004, pp. 247, 248; Kuyvenhoven 2005, 2007). To comprehend the narrative, our student drew on memories of other stories he had heard and from his life experience (Roney 1996; Woolley 2011, pp. 18, 84, 87). He created images that were either too frightening or stretched his ability to believe what he was hearing. He was so absorbed in the story that he lost sight of where he was. The story became reality and he wanted to be somewhere else. When he was brought out of the story that *he visualized*, he was able to sit back down and listen to the end of the story. The mental activity of listening to and co-creating a story is enough to cause both physical and emotional responses in the listener, enhancing story recall and comprehension (Roney 1996; Sturm 2000; Martín-Loeches, et al. 2008; Martinez-Conde et al. 2019).

Awareness that a listener co-creates the story by creating images in their mind is not a recent discovery. Ellin Greene and Janice Del Negro in *Storytelling: Art and Technique* observed that for years many teachers had used storytelling and what we now call guided imagery or visualization techniques to teach reading (Greene and Del Negro 2010, p. 23). What those teachers intuitively thought to be useful has now been shown to be correct—*the ability to visualize plays an important role in reading comprehension* (Joffe et al. 2007; Woolley 2011; Horowitz-Kraus et al. 2013; Agosto 2016; Hutton et al. 2018) and story listening promotes the ability to visualize. Jeffrey D. Wilhelm, in his observational work, *You Gotta BE the Book*, relates working with eighth grade children who wouldn't read until he realized he had to get them to visualize the story. He goes on to say, "Much of what these students revealed to me made me begin to believe that these students did not see anything when they read, and therefore they could not experience and think about what they had read. They had no ownership over the process and no sense that it would work for them in personally meaningful ways" (Wilhelm 2008, pp. 157–158).

In their meta-study De Koning and Van Der Schoot cite numerous works showing that "reading comprehension depends on the construction of a coherent meaning-based mental representation (visualization) of the situation described in a text." They observe that situation model representations are gradually constructed "by continuously updating information from different text dimensionss (e.g., space, time, protagonist, causation, and intentionality) and integrating this information with the readers' [or listeners'] background knowledge, as text unfolds" (De Koning and Van Der Schoot 2013, p. 287). Visualization (making a mental representation) is a fundamental literacy skill, and children develop comprehension by visualizing stories (Agosto 2016, pp. 23, 24; Hassett 2008, p. 314). Children who visualize while reading comprehend what they read better than children who don't visualize as they read (Hassett 2008; Woolley 2011, pp. 81–97). De Koning and Van der Schoot go on to explain that this is because

> comprehension depends on the construction of a coherent meaning-based mental representation of the situation described in a text.… The result is a coherent and richly connected visuospatial representation of the situations and events that are described in a text, which enables readers to draw inferences. (De Koning and Van Der Schoot 2013, p. 287)

Although most of us will think of visualization as strictly referring to a mental image, visualization while reading has been found to refer to a wider range of senses. While some of us do "see" an image when we visualize, recent studies recognize all ways of "visualizing" or using one's imagination to comprehend narrative (Carey 2005; Davis 2013; Oatley 2011). The mental representations created by listening to a story "often include memories of sights, sounds, tastes, touch, smells, feelings, events and stories that may be replayed in the mind" (De Koning and Van der Schoot 2013, p. 265).

The obvious question to ask at this point is whether the promotion of mental visualization skills is also being reenforced when a picture book is read to children. There are many cross-over benefits between reading a picture book and telling a story. Both promote vocabulary development, complex syntax usage, the understanding of narrative structure, and desire to read. Previously referenced studies indicated listening to oral stories was more effective when compared with shared reading (Lenhart et al. 2020; Vaahtoranta et al. 2017, 2019). Perhaps this is because of the situation modeling and mental simulations required by oral listening. Listening to oral stories has some unique benefits, and developing the ability to create and use mental representations is a big one.

To become a real reader the child must go from what is concrete and present to developing the capability to conceptualize what is abstract and distant (Daniel 2012, pp. 36–37). Oral story listening allows children "to use a sophisticated form of communication—decontextualized talk—that is not bound by immediate context.... [This] is important because it promotes higher-order thinking like reminiscing and planning" (Curenton 2006, p. 81). Picture books provide set representations with little or no chance to go off on mental tangents and visualize alternatives to what listeners see in the book (Reese 2012; Spaulding 2011, pp. 56, 137). Regular listening to oral story requires listeners in a "here and now" situation to access what is distant (their personal knowledge and experiential memories) to create something abstract: the mental images of a narrative which in turn takes them to another "distant" context, into a story world of imagined characters, settings, and actions. These become as "real" as *Kate Crackernuts* (Jacobs 1968; Minard 1975) did to our second grader.

Not all stories work equally well in promoting mental simulation. The structure of certain folk tales, and stories that have folkloric formats, is particularly good at promoting creative visualization in the listener.

Folk and Fairy Tale Formats: Why They Promote Visualization

For the most part folk and fairy tales are thought of as the provenance of children's literature. But originally folk tales were told to entertain adults and included violence, sexual passages, and lots of talk of bodily functions. In early versions of *Rapunzel*, the Witch finds out that Rapunzel has been seeing someone other than her when she notices that Rapunzel is pregnant. Over time these tales evolved to be thought of as children's stories. The Hollywood versions of these stories helped to move that evolution forward.

However, folklorists and storytellers have long recognized the appeal and importance of traditional folk and fairy tales for all audiences (Lüthi 1984; Warner 1994; Zipes 2004, pp. 58–59, 2006, 2012; Pullman 2017, pp. 305–313). Critical studies identify how regular exposure to such stories rehearses the importance of metaphorical language in listener/reader response (Applebee 1978, p. 133; Lüthi 1984, p. 44; Oatley 2011, pp. 28–35; Parkinson 2011, p. 18). Exposure also encourages visualizing and imagination to aid comprehension and the appreciation of good literature (Thorne-Thomsen 1903; Cooper and Collins 1992, pp. 11–12, 19–20; Collins and Cooper 1997, pp. 11, 15–16; Spaulding 2004, pp. 51–58). And in addition, exposure also encourages critical thinking due to subversive elements in the narratives (Agosto 2016, p. 24; Fisher 1998, 2001;

Zipes 2004, p. 53). Other scholars in both the humanities and sciences (Zipes 2006; Tartar 2009, 2010; Greenfield 2011a, b; Nijhof and Willems 2015) have examined folk and fairy tales, recognizing this narrative format contains elements supporting acts of imagining and remembering that help listeners to visualize, comprehend, and retain knowledge.

Neurologists and cognitive scientists came gradually to an awareness of this genre's importance when examining reading and listening comprehension. Manuel Martín-Loeches observed that scientists focused mainly on discourse features such as irony, metaphors, and figurative language when really they needed to look at long and contrasting texts as "a sound way to deal with the question of the brain areas and presences of a truly global comprehension" (Martín-Loeches et al. 2008). Ten years since this observation, Martinez-Conde et al. admit that the

> neuroscience of language has traditionally focused on understanding how the comprehension and production of words and single sentences is implemented in our brains. Despite the importance of stories in our everyday lives, the neuroscience of narrative has only recently begun to be an area of active research. (Martinez-Conde et al. 2019, p. 8286)

Around the same time, Wendy Suzuki, Uri Hasson, and their colleagues concurred. Storytelling is clearly the focus of a growing body of cognitive neuroscientific exploration (Suzuki et al. 2018, p. 9468).

Even though today's neurologists give an impression of suddenly "discovering" storytelling, there were scientists and mathematicians in previous centuries who recognized its importance. There's an urban myth that's gone around for decades claiming that Albert Einstein believed intelligence arose from listening to fairy tales. Everyone from Marie Shedlock, who popularized storytelling in schools and libraries a century ago, to Jack Zipes, today's world expert on fairy tales, and even the librarians at the Library of Congress have told versions of this contemporary legend:

> There was once a professor of children's literature and drama. One day he told his students that, back in his college days, he got caught in a near-riot in Manhattan. A crowd stampeded past him, knocking over an old man. He went and helped the older guy, who was unhurt. Turned out it was none other than Albert Einstein. Unrecognized, Einstein had nearly been trampled by a bunch of crazy New York tourists who had spied Marilyn Monroe and chased after her instead.

Seeing the scientist was okay, and being a father of a little girl, the younger man took this chance encounter to ask Einstein for parenting advice. How could he bring up his young daughter to be a great scientist. What should he tell her? What books should he get? What could he do to make her really smart?

"Fairy tales!" Einstein proclaimed.

The younger man thought he had misheard the genius. "Pardon?" he asked again.

"Tell her fairy tales," the scientist repeated, without hesitating.

"Right. Well, what do I do after that?" the young father asked.

"Tell more fairy tales," Einstein suggested with a shrug.

"Ok, sure," he said, "but what then?"

"Even more fairy tales!" smiled the great genius, "Just tell the kids fairy tales, that's the way to do it!"

And Einstein puffed on his pipe and walked away in a cloud of smoke.

We want to believe this is a true story.

Given the recent research from all these different fields what do we now know about the format of folk and fairy tales and its connection to visualization and co-creation of the story by the listener?

First of all, we know that folk and fairy tales provide a minimal amount of detail to describe characters, settings, objects, and actions. Characters and scenes are practically anonymous (the king, the witch, the youngest son, the castle, the hill, the bridge) with little if any character development occurring. For the most part, objects are generic, too. The magic ball can be interchanged with the magic animal (Parkinson 2011, pp. 142–143). It is exactly this flexibility and lack of detail that encourages listener co-creation and visualization of the story. As Oxford professor John Carey repeatedly emphasizes, simple texts require creativity on the part of the reader or listener, and precisely because texts are simple the listener or reader may be "unaware of what he or she is having to supply" (Carey 2005, p. 233).

Co-creating the story leads to better comprehension, story recall, and a sense of the story belonging to the listener. It becomes part of the listener's thinking (Meek 1982, pp. 37–38; Roney 1996; Woolley 2011, pp. 87, 88–89). The listener or reader (or teller remembering or writer creating the story) will draw on personal memories so that a story makes sense. Even more, these mental representations become so visceral that the listener experiences the story physically. When Elfrida Vipont's *The Elephant and the Bad Baby* (Vipont 1969), a tale about a baby riding a runaway elephant and being treated to all kinds of goodies, is related orally the children smack their lips and shout "yummy" and "yuk" over all the cookies, cakes, sausages, vegetables, fruits, and ice cream mentioned, often proclaiming afterward that the story has really made them hungry.

Occasionally the listener is aware of what he or she is creating when hearing a story. We asked an adult we know what he remembered about listening to stories as a child at the Laboratory Schools. He recalled how enthralled he was by the creation of images in his mind:

> I think that's what always fascinated me about visualization: you guys weren't telling us every little detail, but my brain was able to put together the absent details and populate the image.

He went on to call it "an activity in my mind". John Carey would agree with him. Stories that provide few descriptive details encourage the listeners to become mentally active. Folkloric structure does this beautifully.

Also common in folkloric narratives are tropes that wander from one tale to another but in their brevity conjure images and connections to other stories in listeners' minds. Many maidens besides Snow White possess "Lips red as blood, hair black as ebony, and skin white as snow." Just a protagonist's name in a lesser-known tale like a persecuted heroine called *The Maiden without Hands*, or a dauntless dim-witted youngest son referred to as *The Lad Who Went Forth to Learn Fear* can respectively send shivers down a listener's spine or make you hold your breath in anticipation of frights to come. These tropes act as triggers stimulating a series of images from past experiences or stories previously heard.

Literary short stories for children can imitate the folk and fairy tale format by incorporating the same motifs of traditional tales and utilizing similar structures such as few descriptive details, common tropes, repetition of events, or rhythmic and figurative language. They promote visualization in the same way that folklore does. It's the structure of the tale that is important. Joan Aiken's *A Necklace of Raindrops* (Aiken 1968), popular with many storytellers and elementary school children, includes the North Wind giving a girl a magic necklace, issuing strict warnings about the necklace, talking animals, childhood jealousy, and reversals of fortune to create a story that has the structure and format of a traditional tale. Rudyard Kipling's *Just so Stories* (Kipling 1902), although written like folklore, did not come from "the folk" but from Kipling's pen, so too the stories of Hans Christian Andersen. But listeners get the same benefits from these stories as from *The Three Little Pigs.*

Aside from format and structure these stories, both folkloric and literary, help the listener visualize and co-create the narrative by incorporating popular subjects and activities familiar to listeners.

> Fairy tales are more realistic than they may appear to be at first sight; while the magic in them almost heightens the realism. The magic sets us wondering how we ourselves would react in similar circumstances. It encourages speculation. It gives a child license to wonder. (Opie and Opie 1974, p. 16)

Think of all the tales you know where the young protagonist is left to outwit the enemy or where the youngest foolish child turns out to be the bravest, the wisest, the best loved: for examples, *Jack and Beanstalk*, or John Burningham's *Avocado Baby* (Burningham 1986), in which an infant who only eats avocadoes fights off the bullies and saves his family. Or recall the seemingly impossible tasks "big people" (parents and teachers in life, giants and monsters and witches in stories) order "little people" to do. Or temptations like trying something new to eat or resisting opening a door or box you were told not to. It is easy for many children to identify with these motifs. By relating to these elements, listeners can picture themselves in the stories. They easily draw upon their life experience to understand and comprehend what is happening in the story they are hearing.

Stories that follow this format can also broaden listeners' understanding and experience, moving them to think of previous encounters and present everyday objects and situations in novel ways. To explain this process, Sadoski, Paivio, and Goetz proposed Dual Coding System (DCS) theory. In cognitive terms, they envisioned DCS as "two separate but interconnected mental systems, a verbal system and an imagery system" (Sadoski et al. 1991, p. 472). DCS theory supports mental situation modeling, as discussed in De Koning and Van Der Schoot's meta-study. The way DCS theory works, according to Woolley, is that "a concrete object or event may invoke a visual representation, or be associated with a verbal label, or vice versa" (Woolley 2011, pp. 81–82). Woolley goes on to explain that by constructing mental images from words (read or heard) by remembering concrete objects and experiences, personal meanings and emotional content also become involved for there to be comprehension (Woolley 2011, p. 87).

Patrick was once telling seven-year-olds a ghost story. While working through the night spinning flax into thread, an old woman got lonely and wished for company. Company (a ghost) came in bit by bit—feet, legs, body, etc.—and between each entrance there was a refrain: "And still she spun and still she spun and still she wished for company." Although Patrick had explained about spinning wool and weaving cloth, just before the story's climax one boy exclaimed, "Gosh! She must have been really dizzy, with all that spinning!" This typifies what Sadoski, Paivio, and the rest are talking about. Adult knowledge associates "spinning wheel" and "spinning" (whether heard or read) with manufacturing textiles, conjuring images of someone making thread; young children are more likely to relate the same words to roundabouts and flinging around with arms spread wide on playgrounds. In both situations, it's nice to have company.

In their experiments. and critiques of various methods for teaching literacy and literature, Sadoski and Paivio expressed concerns about mimetic approaches to rehearse better visualization for comprehension. "Images and feelings are deeply personal, and instruction in *what* to imagine and feel is surely less appropriate *than* to imagine and feel" (Sadoski and Paivio 2004, p. 50). In other words, it's better for the engaged listener doing her own work to picture and fully comprehend the story, and oral story listening requires that she does. In this way it is as if the child's own experiences have been broadened.

The language used to relate these stories also facilitates the process of co-constructing the story through images and nonverbal expressions. The rhythm created by repetition of words, phrases, and narrative episodes, and the use of simple but striking formulaic language describing characters, objects, and settings support listener comprehension (Myers 1990; Del Negro 2014, pp. 10–11; Meek 1982, pp. 45, 53). The refrain of "Trip-trap, Trip-trap, Trip-trap! Who's that walking across my bridge?" in the Norwegian folk tale of *The Billy Goats Gruff* and the skipping rhyme "Andy Spandy Sugardy and Candy" from literary fairy tale *Elsie Piddock Skips in Her Sleep* by Eleanor Farjeon provoke anticipation of what comes next in the plot and provide choruses for listeners to join in on and so become more engaged in the story.

This type of deep listener involvement is more commonly seen with orally told stories, whether folk tales or literary constructs using a traditional story format, than when a picture book of the same story is presented (Malo and Bullard 2000; Curenton 2006; Reese 2012). When you are telling a story there is an intimacy that cannot be achieved when holding a picture book or looking at words in the story. With picture book reading, the child is focused on the illustrations, the reader is focused on the words, the teller's hands are holding the book and cannot use gesture for emphasis or to enhance understanding. With the oral telling the eye contact and mirroring of facial expressions and gestures between teller and listeners provides nuance to the words, aiding meaning (Myers 1990; Roney 1996; Parkinson 2011, pp. 171–174). As Margaret Read MacDonald observes, "Storytelling delivers emotions, information, culture and language in a package that nothing else can approach" (MacDonald et al. 2013, p. 11).

As happened to our young listener who stood up in the middle of *Kate Crackernuts* to declare his disbelief in the story, the ability to produce images by listening to narratives causes a way of thinking that evokes physical and emotional responses. The confidence and ability to question and criticize, gained by multiple experiences of visualizing by being engaged with both stories and the storyteller, is empowering. As Jeffrey Wilhelm observed, when students are "given the support to create a concrete visualization of a story, then they often become excited about reading that particular piece, and become capable of empathizing, connecting, and reflecting on the literary experience" (Wilhelm 2008, p. 88). Story listening gives pre- and emergent readers this support.

By challenging the fantastic, or explaining it, children create mental representations additional to those described in the story. Regular story listening experience is like a mental workout to develop imagination and the skill to visualize in a way that can lead to formulating questions or alternate versions of a story that criticize and challenge the original. Merely by listening to stories regularly a child absorbs information naturally. They discover new ideas and gain knowledge both from hearing and experiencing the words and sounds, and through any natural playful language among participants that occurs in or around a story. Through listening experiences children evaluate information and ideas, decide what to believe, what to accept in a way we expect an accomplished independent reader to do (Thorne-Thomsen 1901; Haven 2007, pp. 90–95; Reese 2012).

In summary we are saying that folkloric-type stories told out loud promote visualization and comprehension because of:

- Format and structure
  - Few descriptors
  - Generic characters and objects
  - Spare settings
  - Common tropes
- Use of recognizable situations in novel ways
- Rhythmic, repetitive language
- Intimacy with teller

Denise Agosto found, in her study of children's post-listening thank-you cards, that a single storytelling session enables children to practice a variety of important literacy skills, including cognitive engagement, critical thinking, story sequencing, and most importantly for our purposes, visualization (Agosto 2016, pp. 21–25).

BUT DON'T MOST READERS LEARN TO VISUALIZE ON THEIR OWN ANYWAY?

In our experience many adults, even teachers working in early years, assume children automatically visualize as they learn to read. One teacher said, "They sound out a word, decoding it and picturing it at the same time." It is true that for some early readers visualization develops as they learn to read but for a portion of the population this doesn't happen. Emergent literacy scholars and cognitive scientists have experimented with interventions to promote the ability to visualize, or visualize better, to improve reading comprehension (Pressley 1976; Harris and Pressley 1991; Maguire et al. 1999, Horowitz-Kraus et al. 2013, p. 2659; Hutton 2015, p. 12). Currently Ece Demir-Lira, at the University of Iowa, and Donna are doing research to see whether repeated story listening can be used as an intervention to promote visualization skills (Demir-Lira and Schatt 2017). This will be the first controlled study looking into the use of storytelling as an intervention tool for visualization and comprehension.

Patrick has anecdotal evidence which points toward positive findings in this area. For years he participated in a sport and education literacy project, training professional soccer players, coaches, and high school students to tell stories to young children. Comments and observations regarding visualization and storytelling came up repeatedly in this work. As one pupil informed us:

> Well, when I read now, I can actually, like, visualize things. And before I couldn't see anything, I just read it and it meant nothing. Now it gives me a bit...I can, like, go over stories again and again and never get bored, because I can find new things just by visualizing. (Ryan 2012, p. 9)

Accompanying this use of visualization to tell stories and read better this young man also found new confidence and enjoyment in being able to hold other listeners' attention.

One of the teachers we recently worked with comes from a background of traditional storytelling in the French Caribbean. From an early age he saw the importance of listening to stories and being able to create your own images. He is passionate about the importance of passing this along to his students. As he relayed to us:

> It's like, we give an image [*i.e., a printed illustration*] to the kid, and, I mean, at that moment we just limit his way of seeing the world.... [So the kid thinks,] "You take away my imagination. It's like this is what the character looks like, and even if I want to see something different, my brain is conditioned to be based on that model that you gave me." ...I [tell stories to] make it very easy for them to create the story.

WHAT THE LISTENERS TELL US

Our Lab School study provided first-hand information on how aware story listeners were of visualizing while listening to stories, and what they thought about it. Our contacts enthusiastically discussed their remembrances of what happened when they listened to stories in order to help us understand an experience that they may not have consciously reflected upon or considered for a long time. Almost everyone described story listening as active not passive. They spoke of what was "going on in my head." When asked to elaborate, they mentioned being "in" the story, and of it "belonging" to them.

Having control of the images was frequently mentioned. Here are quotes from two alumni:

> When you read you get one image and what you hear provides another kind of image, based on the way it's said, and the way the person actually speaks

that particular scenario. When the storyteller would say, "This is the story, this is the character, this is the house they're in, or the path they're taking," it [the image] was always instant. I never had to think about it. It was my way, the way I wanted to see it. Whereas, when I was reading a [picture] book it was dictated to me.

So my seeing pictures in a book, despite having someone read it to me, that's the image in my head, and that's the image that stays. There isn't another option. And when you tell a story to me, I'm instantly given an image, but I've given it to myself, I was in control of those images.

This sense of ownership of the story, which alumni mentioned to us during their interviews, mirrors what De Koning and Van der Schoot found in their meta-analysis on reading comprehension and visualization. They note that nonverbal representations prompt "private sensory experiences and images [making] the story personal to the reader" (De Koning and Van der Schoot 2013, p. 265). It seems clear to us that similar processes take place during the listening experience. Or as Oxford Professor John Carey puts it, a story exists only in our mind. "The fact that it has never existed beyond that makes it more wholly ours. We create and possess it, rescuing it from nothingness" (Carey 2005, p. 237).

Our informants also mentioned "working harder" and spoke of being "struck with the vividness of the images" of the story. They claimed that they were "more involved in the story," and had "become part of the story." Some even said that they felt like they were "standing inside the story" when it was being told. Over numerous interviews it became clear that creating vivid images and the feeling of being part of or inside the story were connected. Creating images—using their imagination—was the "hard work," because it put you in the story and gave you possession of it.

The alumni we spoke with described the experience as pleasurable, something to seek out and look forward to. Statements such as "It was the best" and "It was paradise" predominated. They considered listening to stories to be significantly better than listening to a picture book or prose story read aloud. Picture books limited their imagination. While a told story made them "work harder," books read aloud provided images too easily. Many felt picture books offered "no other option" in how one sees the images. However, a told story was "totally unlike" being read to or being shown the book's illustrations. One young woman said that the story listening experience was "unmediated, nothing between you and the story. No pictures or words to focus on, only a voice and the images in my head" (Schatt 2010).

In our sample, every person talked about creating images. And importantly, their comments raised the prospect that unique, significant differences exist between listening to stories told and sharing picture books read aloud. There is much scientific literature confirming the multiple benefits of reading aloud to children (Isbell et al. 2004; Hutton et al. 2018; Lenhart et al. 2020). But we should all be aware that listening to a story told from memory provides powerful and profoundly different experiences related to the processes entailed in visualizing, imagining, and comprehending narrative. The construction of images connected to the narrative frequently happens when fluent readers read because they have developed this skill over time. However, it may be that for preliterate or struggling readers who have not yet developed this ability, the interactive nature of storytelling and story listening provides a scaffold (in the sense proposed by Bruner and Vygotsky) promoting the ability to visualize and create situational models and thus comprehend (Bruner 1986, pp. 73–74). Successful oral storytelling relies on a social context structured by interactions between teller and listeners that allow the child to concentrate on acquiring new and difficult skills without the encumbrance of decoding words or looking at pictures at the same time.

The power of stories to create images

When discussing how children capable of generating images find it easier to read and remember, Kieran Egan stated that educators "would be foolish to ignore this power of language in planning how to teach" (Egan 2005, p. 27). And Wayne Tennent points out in *Reading Comprehension, Processes and Practices* that "children enter schools with a spoken language comprehension in advance of their ability to decode. From the perspective of teaching, it might seem odd to avoid supporting this development until the decoding component has been mastered" (Tennent 2015, p. 15). These are just the points we are making. It is true that picture book reading can provide pleasure and help to develop vocabulary, syntax usage, and narrative understanding. And a myriad of cognitive studies confirm benefits in terms of acquiring lifelong reading habits. However, the inability to visualize has been identified as a factor that contributes to children's inability to comprehend when they read. To Tennent's point, the storytelling we describe can support and extend language comprehension from the moment the child enters formal education in a way that is uniquely different from shared picture book reading. It does so because oral stories do not limit the imagination of the listener by providing an image. Instead, oral stories provide a scaffold to support the ability to visualize, a foundational skill in reading comprehension.

Story listening is an activity of the mind. Storytelling is not passive entertainment: it requires the construction of meaning-based mental representations, such as visualization, to be comprehended. The social aspects of storytelling, and the narrative structures of stories most commonly found in storytelling, prompt ways of thinking important for reader development, for school success, and for life.

REFERENCES

Agosto, D. E. 2016. Why Storytelling Matters, Unveiling the Literacy Benefits of Storytelling. *Children and Libraries.* 14(2): 21–26. DOI: https://doi.org/10.5860/cal.14n2.21.

Aiken, J. 1968. *A Necklace of Raindrops: And Other Stories.* London: Cape.

Applebee, A. N. 1978. *The Child's Concept of Story.* Chicago and London: University of Chicago Press.

Bruner, J. 1986. *Actual Minds, Possible Worlds.* Cambridge, MA and London: Harvard University Press.

Burningham, J. 1986. *Avocado Baby.* London: PictureLions.

Carey, J. 2005. *What Good Are the Arts?* London: Faber and Faber.

Collins, R. and Cooper, P.J. 1997. *The Power of Story: Teaching Through Storytelling.* Needham Heights, MA: Allyn and Bacon.

Cooper, P. J. and Collins, R. 1992. *Look What Happened to Frog, Storytelling in Education.* Scottsdale, AR: Gorsuch Scarisbrick, Publishers.

Curenton, S. M. 2006. Oral Storytelling: A Cultural Art That Promotes School Readiness. *Young Children*, 61(5): 78–89.

Daniel, A. K. 2012. *Storytelling Across the Primary Curriculum.* London and New York: Routledge.

Davis, P. 2013. *Reading and the Reader.* Oxford: Oxford University Press.

De Koning, B.B. and Van der Schoot, M. 2013. Becoming Part of the Story! Refueling the Interest in Visualization Strategies for Reading Comprehension. *Educational Psychology Review*, 25: 261–287. DOI: https://doi.org/10.1007/s10648-013-9222-6.

Del Negro, J. M. 2014. *Folktales Aloud, Practical Advice for Playful Storytelling.* Chicago: ALA Editions.

Demir-Lira, E. O. and Schatt, D. 2017. *Storytelling as an Intervention for Visualization Skill: A Pilot Study.* A paper presented to the Psychology Department, University of Chicago, Chicago, IL. March 1, 2017.

Egan, K. 2005. *An Imaginative Approach to Teaching.* San Francisco: Jossey-Bass, A Wiley Company.

Farjeon, E. 2000. *Elsie Piddock Skips in her Sleep.* London: Walker Books.
Fisher, R. 1998. Stories for Thinking: Developing Critical Literacy Through Use of Narrative. *Analytic Teaching* 18(1): 16–27.
Fisher, R. 2001. Philosophy in Primary Schools: Fostering Thinking Skills and Literacy. *Literacy*, 35(2): 67–73. DOI: https://doi. org/10.1111/1467-9345.00164.
Gerrig, R. J. 1993. *Experiencing Narrative Worlds: On the Psychological Activities of Reading*, New Haven, CT: Yale University Press.
Gold, J. 2002. *The Story Species: Our Life-Literature Connection.* Markham, Ontario and Allston, MA: Fitzhenry and Whiteside Limited.
Green, M. C. 2004. Transportation Into Narrative Worlds: The Role of Prior Knowledge and Perceived Realism. *Discourse Processes*, 38(2): 247–296. DOI: https://doi.org/10.1207/s15326950dp3802_5.
Greene, E. and Del Negro, J. M. 2010. *Storytelling: Art and Technique.* 4th Edition. Santa Barbara, CA and Oxford: Libraries Unlimited.
Greenfield, S. 2011a. Susan Greenfield on Storytelling. *Sunday Sermons* [video]. London: The School of Life. https://vimeo.com/33716283. Accessed December 2011.
Greenfield, S. 2011b. *You and Me: The Neuroscience of Identity.* London: Notting Hill Editions.
Harris, K. R. and Pressley, M. 1991. The Nature of Cognitive Strategy Instruction: Interactive Strategy Instruction. *Exceptional Children*, 57: 392–404. DOI: https://doi.org/10.1177/001440299105700503.
Hassett, D. 2008. Teacher Flexibility and Judgment: A Multidynamic Literacy Theory. *Early Childhood Literacy*, 8(3): 295–327. DOI: https://doi. org/10.1177/1468798408096479.
Haven, K. 2007. *Story Proof: The Science Behind the Startling Power of Story.* Wesport, CT and London: Libraries Unlimited.
Horowitz-Kraus, Vannest, J. J., and Holland, S. K. 2013. Overlapping Neural Circuitry for Narrative Comprehension and Proficient Reading in Children and Adolescents. *Neuropsychologia*, 51(13): 2651–2662. DOI: https://doi. org/10.1016/j.neuropsychologia.2013.09.002.
Hutton, J. S. 2015. *Home Reading Environment and Brain Activation in Preschool Children Listening to Stories.* M.Sc. Thesis. Cincinnati: University of Cincinnati.
Hutton, J., et al. 2018. Difference in Functional Brain Network Connectivity During Stories Presented in Audio, Illustrated, and Animated Format in Preschool-Age Children. *Brain Imagining and Behaviour*, 14: 1–12. DOI: https://doi.org/10.1007/s11682-018-9985-y.
Isbell, R., Sobol, J, and Lowrance, L. A. 2004. The Effects of Storytelling and Story Reading on the Oral Language Complexity and Story Comprehension of Young Children. *Early Childhood Education Journal*, 32(3): 157–163. DOI: https://doi.org/10.1023/B:ECEJ.0000048967.94189.a3.

Jacobs, J. 1968. Kate Crackernuts. In *English Fairy Tales (English Fairy Tales and More English Fairy Tales)*, 124–126. London; Sydney; and Toronto: The Bodley Head.

Joffe, V.L., Cain, K., and Maric, N. 2007. Comprehension Problems in Children with Specific Language Impairment: Does Mental Imagery Training Help? *International Journal of Language and Communication Disorders*, 42: 648–664. DOI: https://doi.org/10.1080/13682820601084402.

Kipling, R. 1902. *Just So Stories*. London: Macmillan and Co.

Kuyvenhoven, J. 2005. *In the Presence of Each Other: A Pedagogy of Storytelling*. Doctoral Dissertation, University of British Columbia. https://open.library. ubc.ca/cIRcle/collections/ubctheses/831/items/1.0055624. Accessed July 10, 2020.

Kuyvenhoven, J. 2007. "What Happens Inside Your Head When You Are Listening to a Story?" Children Talk About Their Experience During a Storytelling. *Storytelling, Self and Society: An Interdisciplinary Journal of Storytelling Studies*, 3(2): 95–114. DOI: https://doi.org/10.1080/15505340701282755.

Lenhart, J., Lenhard, W., Vaahtoranta, E., and Suggate, S. 2020. More Than Words: Narrator Engagement During Storytelling Increases Children's Word Learning, Story Comprehension, and On-task Behavior. *Early Childhood Research Quarterly*, 51: 338–351. DOI: https://doi.org/10.1016/j. ecresq.2019.12.009.

Lüthi, M. 1984. *The Fairytale as Art Form and Portrait of Man*. Trans. John Erikson. Bloomington, IN: Indiana State University.

MacDonald, M. R., Macdonald-Whitman, J., and Whitman, N. F. 2013. *Teaching with Storytelling; Classroom Connections to Storytelling*. Atlanta, GA: August House.

Maguire, E.A., Frith, C.D., and Morris, R.G.M. 1999. The Functional Neuroanatomy of Comprehension and Memory: The Importance of Prior Knowledge. *Brain*, 122: 1839–1850. DOI: https://doi.org/10.1093/ brain/122.10.1839

Malo, E. and Bullard, J. 2000. *Storytelling and the Emergent Reader*. Paper presented at the International Reading Association World Congress on Reading. Auckland, New Zealand, July 11–14, 2000. https://files.eric.ed.gov/fulltext/ ED448464.pdf. Accessed November 11, 2014.

Martín-Loeches, M., Cassado, P., Hernández-Tamames, J., and Álvarez-Linera, J. 2008. Brain Activation in Discourse Comprehension: A 3t fMRI Study: NeuroImage, 41(2): 614–622. DOI: https://doi.org/10.1016/j. neuroimage.2008.02.047.

Martinez-Conde, S., Alexander, R. G., Blum, D., Britton, N., Lipska, B. K., Quirk, G. J., Swiss, J. Ian, Willems, R. M., and Macknik, S. L. 2019. The Storytelling Brain: How Neuroscience Stories Help Bridge the Gap between Research and Society. *The Journal of Neuroscience*, 39(42): 8285–8290. DOI: https://doi.org/10.1523/JNEUROSCI.1180-19.2019.

Meek, M. 1982. *Learning to Read*. London: The Bodley Head.
Minard, R. 1975. Kate Crackernuts. In *Womenfolk and Fairy Tales*, 65–70. Boston: Houghton Mifflin Company.
Myers, P. 1990. Stories from Print. *Language Arts*, 67(8): 824–831. http://jstor.com/stable/41961806.
Nijhof, A. D. and Willems, R. M. 2015. Simulating Fiction: Individual Differences in Literature Comprehension Revealed with fMRI. *PloS ONE*, 10(2): 1–17. DOI: https://doi.org/10.1371/journal.pone.0116492.
Oatley, K. 2011. *Such Stuff as Dreams, the Psychology of Fiction*. Malden, MA; Oxford; Chichester; and West Sussex: Wiley-Blackwell.
Opie, I. and Opie, P. 1974. *The Classic Fairy Tales*. London; New York; and Toronto: Oxford University Press.
Parkinson, R. 2011. *Storytelling and Imagination. Beyond Basic Literacy*. London and New York: Routledge.
Pressley, G. M. 1976. Mental Imagery Helps Eight-Year-Olds Remember What They Read. *Journal of Educational Psychology*, 66(3): 355–359. DOI: https://doi.org/10.1037/0022-0663.68.3.355.
Pullman, P. 2017. *The Daemon Voices, Essays on storytelling*. Oxford: David Fickling Books.
Reese, E. 2012, The Tyranny of Shared Book-Reading. In *Contemporary Debates in Childhood Education and Development*, eds. Sebastian Suggate and Elaine Reese, 59–68. Abingdon: Taylor and Francis Group.
Roney, R. C. 1996. Storytelling in the Classroom: Some Theoretical Thoughts. *Storytelling World*, 9: 7–9
Ryan, P. 2012. Junior Reading Champions: Storytellers as Role Models for Reading. *English 4-11*, 44, 7–11.
Sadoski, M., and Paivio, A. 2004. A Dual Coding Theoretical Model of Reading. In *Theoretical Models and Processes of Reading* (5th ed.), eds. R. B. Ruddell and N. J. Unrau, 1329–1362. Newark, DE: International Reading Association.
Sadoski, M., Paivio, A., and Goetz, E. T. 1991. Commentary: A Critique of Schema Theory in Reading and a Dual Coding Alternative. *Reading Research Quarterly*, 26: 463–484. DOI: https://doi.org/10.2307/747898.
Schatt, D. 2010. *Why Quantify a Dream?* Unpublished presentation, Department of Social Sciences, University of Chicago.
Spaulding, A. 2004. *The Wisdom of Storytelling in an Information Age*. Lanham; Toronto; and Plymouth, UK: The Scarecrow Press, Inc.
Spaulding, A. 2011. *The Art of Storytelling. Telling Truths Through Telling Stories*. Lanham; Toronto; and Plymouth, UK: The Scarecrow Press, Inc.
Sturm, B. W. 2000. The "Storylistening" Trance Experience. *The Journal of American Folklore*, 113(449): 287–304. DOI: https://doi.org/10.2307/542104

Suzuki, W. A., Feliú, M. I., Uri, H., Yehuda, R., and Zarate J. M. 2018. The Science and Power of Storytelling. *The Journal of Neuroscience*, 38(44): 9468–9470. DOI: https://doi.org/10.1523/JNEUROSCI.1942-18.2018.

Tartar, M. 2009. *Enchanted Hunters: The Power of Stories in Childhood*. New York: W.W. Norton and Co.

Tartar, M. 2010. Why Fairy Tales Matter: The Performative and Transformative. *Western Folklore*, 69(1): 55–64.

Tennent, W. 2015. *Understanding Reading Comprehension, Processes and Practices*. Los Angeles; London; New Delhi; Singapore; and Washington, DC: SAGE.

Thorne-Thomsen, G. 1901. Reading in the Third Grade. *Elementary School Teacher and Course of Study*, 2(3): 227–35.

Thorne-Thomsen, G. 1903. The Educational Value of Fairy-Stories and Myths. *The Elementary School Teacher*, 4(3): 161–167.

Vaahtoranta, E., Suggate, S., Jackman C., Lenhart, J., and Lenhard, W. 2017. Can Explaining Less be More? Enhancing Vocabulary Through Explicit Versus Elaborative Storytelling. *First Language*, 28: 1–20. DOI: https://doi.org/10.1177/0142723717737452.

Vaahtoranta, E., Lenhart, J., Suggate, W., and Lenhard, W. 2019. Interactive Elaborative Storytelling: Engaging Children as Storytellers to Foster Vocabulary. *Frontiers in Psychology*, 10(1534): 1–13. DOI: https://doi.org/10.3389/fpsyg.2019.01534.

Vipont, E. 1969. *The Elephant and the Bad Baby*. London: Hamilton.

Warner, M. 1994. *From the Beast to the Blonde: On Fairytales and Their Tellers*. London: Chatto and Windus.

Wilhelm, J. D. 2008. *You Gotta BE the Book, Teaching Engaged and Reflective Reading with Adolescents*. New York and London: Teachers College Press.

Woolley, G. 2011. *Reading Comprehension, Assisting Children with Learning Difficulties*. Heidelberg; London; and New York: Springer Dordrocht.

Yolen, J. 1981. *Touch Magic, Fantasy, Faerie and Folklore in the Literature of Childhood*. New York: Philomel Books.

Zipes, J. 2004. *Speaking Out, Storytelling and Creative Drama for Children*. New York and London: Routledge.

Zipes, J. 2006. *Why Fairy Tales Stick, The Evolution and Relevance of a Genre*. New York and London: Routledge.

Zipes, J. 2012. *The Irresistible Fairy Tale, The Cultural and Social History of a Genre*. New York and London: Routledge.

"Sometimes I get so hypnotized I forget where I am…" *The benefits of repeated story listening*

An Experience Like No Other

Former UCLS students remember having a unique reaction to oral story listening. Some went so far as to describe it as mind altering. Many reported that listening to stories brought them to "another world," causing them to lose sight of time or place, making other listeners disappear as though they were "no more alive than the rug." One of the alumni recalled:

> It was a really warm feeling…it was really relaxing. A time of no pressure. You were sitting with all your friends and everybody. It was a really nice thing to have a story wash over you. It was a really nice thing to have.

Others had similar recollections:

> Like klonipin. (laughing). That's exactly what it would feel like. No really, it was just, it absolutely, it was the best.

> It was definitely a WHOA experience. The description would be one that I would liken to meditating or taking hallucinogens.

More than a few of the alumni were interested in learning how to recreate the experience for their own children.

D. Schatt, P. Ryan, *Story Listening and Experience in Early Childhood*, https://doi.org/10.1007/978-3-030-65358-3_4

They told us that story listening provided a calm and neutral time, a complete escape from pressures in their lives. Even in early grades academic demands and social life caused frustrations and anxiety. Story listening allowed for a time when their imagination could take over without having to tell anyone what they saw or answer any questions. It felt like a solitary time for many, as if the story was being told just for them, only to them. The recollection of the storytelling program was that it was absolutely "the best," providing a treasured and valued experience. These students experienced a psychological and physical state, so intense and pleasurable that even years after they smiled when recalling it.

This reaction to story listening was not unique to our students. Across cultures, others have observed story listeners experiencing a similar kind of reverie and pleasure. In his travelogue, Paul Zweig related accounts of storytelling in Moroccan marketplaces. Among the hustle and bustle, the spot where a market storyteller performed became a quiet oasis, with listeners transfixed around him. The audience "seemed to have turned their backs on the world, creating a circle of vacancy so elusive and sudden that a man could search for that road everywhere over the earth and still not find it" (Zweig 1974, pp. 84–85).

Pleasure, absorption, and curiosity felt when listening to a story were often mentioned by students exposed to frequent oral story listening. The feeling was so pleasurable that they wanted the experience repeated. Many said it was the time they most looked forward to. A time they now recall with longing and happiness. The notion that storytelling motivates and engages students was well supported by teachers during the Progressive Era and then that notion was forgotten. Gudrun Thorne-Thomsen and Percival Chubb were among many who described how regular storytelling prompted reluctant or disaffected pupils to develop their imaginations, habits of thinking, reading for pleasure, and independent pursuit of many academic subjects (Thorne-Thomsen 1901; Chubb 1902, 1929). Motivating students is something teachers still strive to do, not always successfully.

Motivation and learning

In recent years, much effort has gone into attempting to discover how schools can better engage pupils. Educators acknowledge that young children have an enormous capacity to learn and take great joy in doing so, but that over time, many become incurious and fail to find any pleasure in formal education (Engel 2015, pp. 86, 89; Donaldson 1978, p. 127). In her study of the origins of curiosity in childhood, Susan Engel said:

Once children get to school, they exhibit a lot less curiosity. They ask fewer questions, examining objects less frequently... and in general seem less inclined to persevere in sating their appetite for information. Even if we expected children to get less curious as they got older (and there is no basis for such a simplistic or general expectation), the drop shouldn't be nearly as precipitous as the school data suggest. Something about schools is decreasing the expression of curiosity, above and beyond the inevitable, or intrinsic, developmental influences. (Engel 2015, pp. 104–105)

Mihaly Csikszentmihalyi speculated that this decrease in the pleasure of learning was a phenomenon of natural consequence "because 'learning' becomes an external imposition when schooling starts, and the excitement of mastering new skills gradually wears out" (Csikszentmihalyi 1990, p. 47).

While examining teacher's views on classroom motivation, David Shernoff and Deborah Vandell, associates of Csikszentmihalyi, noted that most teachers would like to provide lessons where student involvement consists of the "simultaneous experience of concentration, interest, and enjoyment" (Shernoff and Vandell 2007, p. 891). Concentration, interest, and enjoyment are apt descriptions of what we see in listeners during a story. We find it matches what informants told us when recalling their mental state during story listening.

Perhaps because oral storytelling has all but disappeared as an integral part of most classrooms, those doing research in educational motivation and engagement seem unaware of the excitement, pleasure, and motivation that the story listening experience can impart in educational situations. As a result, any analysis of this psychological state caused by story listening is missing from studies of what galvanizes learners.

STORY-LISTENING TRANCE, TRANSPORTATION, AND STORY LISTENING EXPERIENCE

But what exactly is the mental phenomenon story listeners experienced? Our youngest informant characterized the unique response to story listening this way:

Sometimes I get so hypnotized I forget where I am, and then I look around and I realize where I am. Sometimes I close my eyes when I listen to stories and one time the class almost left without me.

Another former student echoed our youngest informant by saying, "It was really easy to get lost inside those stories." Looking for definitions and explanations of altered mental states when encountering narrative led us to uncover three concepts, each from different fields of study, that spoke of states similar to those described by our alumni. The first two, story-listening trance and transportation, we examine here, and the third, flow, in the next section.

The first state, known as a "story-listening trance" was popularized in studies of contemporary storytelling (Sturm 2000; Stallings 1988, 1993; Parkinson 2011, pp. 11–12) and as "story trance" by educator-neuropsychologist Victor Nell (Nell 1988). As teacher and storyteller Rob Parkinson summarized, "Actual studies of the telling of stories and how it relates to 'hypnotic trance' and so on are less common than studies of reading absorption" (Parkinson 2011, p. 11). Nell's book relates how ludic reading (reading for pleasure) involves psychological mechanisms that, in skilled readers, produce hypnotic trance and pleasure. The enormously complex cognitive acts he describes focus entirely on reading physiology and skills. His descriptions of the trance state and pleasures derived from ludic reading are similar to our listener's memories of what they experienced, but Nell's study looked solely at reading.

Academic librarian Brian Sturm and Fran Stallings, a professional storyteller, focus entirely on story listening. They describe story-listening trance as:

- A lack of awareness of surroundings
- Intense engagement of receptive channels (particularly visual, auditory, kinesthetic, and emotional)
- Experiencing the story as something real (e.g., when a child listener shouts out a warning about an evil character or dangerous situation)
- A sense of distortion regarding time and place. (Sturm 2000; Stallings 1988, 1993)

Parkinson summarizes similar traits: diminished physical activity, fixed gaze with enlarged pupils, slower breathing, and a "marked response to emotionally loaded story events and other suggestions" (Parkinson 2011, p. 25). Stallings went on to describe how one can easily tell when listeners are in a story-listening trance.

You may have seen such listeners, child or adult, going so far into a story that you wonder if they are still present in the same room with you. They sit so still that they hardly seem to breathe. Their faces fall slack, their eyes grow large and luminous, seemingly focused not on the teller but deep within. (Stallings 1993, p. 1)

Sturm's and Stallings's breakdown of elements in story-listening trance mirrors our informants' recollections of "WHOA" experiences when listening to stories, including those who reported a sense of dislocation:

I remember the beginning and the end of the stories, but in the middle I don't know where I was. I could have been further out. Not in the story, just gone within my own head. The other people became part of the rug or something. They weren't any more alive to me than the rug.

While another observed:

When you come back to reality, you're not sure if the other place you were in was the reality, or this is.

Others spoke about a distorted sense of time:

I can remember the rug and then the voice and then coming to twenty minutes later with rug marks on my hands, my hands hurt and my feet were stiff. I remember thinking, "Wait, was I asleep?"

The elements of story-listening trance delineated by Stallings and Sturm seem to fit pretty closely with our informants' experiences.

The second term connecting to the state our listeners spoke about is "transportation," as coined by Richard J Gerrig, to describe intense mental states that occur in adults during silent reading (Gerrig 1993). He described it as:

- A distortion of time
- A sense of being in "another place"
- A sense of the story being more real than real life

Both Gerrig and Oatley have reported independently that avid readers frequently evoked a travel metaphor when describing the state they entered into when absorbed in a novel. "In the vehicle of narrative, we travel some distance from our ordinary world, and leave behind some of its aspects. When we return, we may find we have been changed by our journey" (Oatley 2011, p. 199). A journey with the characters who seem like friends, being carried into the actions and setting of a story, these are succinct explanations for the feelings readers have when forgetting everything around them and about themselves while "lost in a book."

In their meta-analysis of transportation, Tom Van Laer and colleagues expressed the view that transportation is an engrossing *temporary* experience that "specifically entails empathy and mental imagery" (Van Laer et al. 2014, p. 800). Transportation (and story-listening trance) is specific to experiencing narrative, relying on plot and characters. It appears that story-listening trance and transportation (S-LT/T) describe similar, if not exactly the same, phenomena, one prompted by oral story listening, the other by silent reading. Both are experiential responses to narrative, psychological states that encompass immersion in deep thought.

We have dozens of anecdotes where listeners—not only children but adults too—experienced an oral story as something more real than their immediate surroundings. With two of our most popular spooky tales, listeners jump at scary parts, or shout warnings when the rat is about to leap out in *Tailypo* (Galdone and Galdone 1979; Postgate 1998), or the child goes to open a window she shouldn't in *The Ruby Red Lips and Long Bony Fingers* (Weir 1995). One of our favorite personal recollections of an S-LT/T incident involves Donna's grandson Victor.

One night Victor's father was telling him *The Garden of Abdul Gasazi* by Chris Van Allsburg (1979), a mysterious picture book story about a young boy who has to rescue a runaway dog. Dogs are NOT welcomed in Mr. Gasazi's topiary garden. Victor was sitting on his father's lap listening intensely. When they came to the part where Mr. Gasazi asked if the boy wanted to know what happens to dogs who wander into his garden, Victor, immersed in the narrative, jumped up and slapped his father right across the face! Victor so shocked himself, he repeatedly assured his dad, "I'm so sorry, Daddy! I'm so sorry! I didn't mean to hit YOU." Victor wasn't seeing his father; he was seeing Mr. Gasazi in the room with him. (By the way, Victor had never been hit in his young life, nor had he ever hit anyone.)

We take this anecdote as evidence that story-listening trance and/or transportation (the terms seem interchangeable to us) do occur when listening to a story or fluently reading one, even when you're a four-year-old. Intuitively we know that there are important educational outcomes from this experience that have yet to be identified. There is a body of research into the educational outcomes of reading fluently and of shared reading done with young children (Whitehurst and Lonigan 1998, 2002; Bus et al. 1995; Bus 2002; Mol et al. 2008; Roberts and Burchinal 2002). And there are studies on reader response which suggest ways that experiencing transport affects readers' well-being and sense of self (Nell 1988; Davis 2013, pp. 43–43, 53, 90; Oatley 2011; Gold 2002). In a similar way we need to connect these psychological states tied to story listening experience to educational outcomes.

FLOW AND STORY LISTENING EXPERIENCE

The third term we've found that connects with our listeners' experience is flow, as defined by Mihaly Csikszentmihalyi. Csikszentmihalyi describes flow as a state of concentration or complete absorption with an activity or situation, coming about by sufficient challenge to engage attention while simultaneously having enough skills to meet the challenge (Csikszentmihalyi 1990, pp. 6, 53; Shernoff and Vandell 2007, p. 891). In describing what being in a flow state feels like, Csikszentmihalyi listed these elements:

- Completely involved—focused, concentrated
- Being outside of everyday reality—ecstasy
- Inner clarity
- Knowing that our skills are up to the task
- Sense of serenity
- Timelessness
- Intrinsic motivation—whatever produces flow becomes its own reward.
(Csikszentmihalyi 2004)

Most of these components are mentioned by our informants describing their experience when listening to a story.

Csikszentmihalyi recognizes that a flow state begins with *attention*, which we view as similar to the intense focus we see in story listeners as discussed at the start of our book. Csikszentmihalyi defines attention as psychic energy.

> Because attention determines what will or will not appear in consciousness, and because it is also required to make any other mental events—such as remembering, thinking, feeling, and making decisions—happen there, it is

useful to think of it as *psychic energy*. [....] We create ourselves by how we invest this energy. Memories, thoughts, and feelings are all shaped by how we use it. And it is an energy under our control, to do as we please, hence attention is our most important tool in the task of improving the quality of experience. (Csikszentmihalyi 1990, p. 33)

Csikszentmihalyi's objective is to establish that this optimal psychological state, flow, has an important role in developing a sense of self and creating a better life. With deep concentration consciousness is normally well-ordered: thoughts, feelings, and senses are focused on one goal. When we leave the flow state, we feel more "together" than before it started, within ourselves and also with respect to others and the world generally. "The self becomes more complex as a result of experiencing flow" (Csikszentmihalyi 1990, pp. 41, 42).

Csikszentmihalyi also states that "Any activity that transforms the way we perceive reality is enjoyable" (Csikszentmihalyi 1990, p. 73). Even though he doesn't identify story listening experience as an activity generating flow, he briefly discusses flow in relation to reading a book silently (Csikszentmihalyi 1990, pp. 49–50, 112, 120). We all have experienced being lost in a narrative as we listen to a story, or read one silently, and the calm and pleasure that produces. Csikszentmihalyi's observation provides another explanation for listeners' testimony regarding the pleasure story times provoke, providing a link between flow and story-listening trance. Csikszentmihalyi equates flow states with true happiness.

A main goal of educators is to generate activities and experiences that grab students' attention, so that teachers can guide and concentrate their students' mental energy in intellectual, creative, and social ways. Storytelling certainly gets attention, but as Philip Jackson pointed out, getting that attention is only an instrument to initiate experiences that improve a learner's well-being (Jackson 1968, p. 103). Attention and focus, in the way we use the latter term, are not the same. Attention is just the first step. The intense focus we identified and discussed in Chap. 2, which teachers wish to see in their students and which we believe can be supported by regular story listening, is something more. When something attracts attention to the point we fixate upon that object or activity, we display the deep focus discussed earlier. However, with that deep focus we're still aware of ourselves, our environment and the context we're operating in, and what we are doing and focusing upon. When we become so engrossed that we are unaware of our surroundings, and often ourselves as well, and the object, activity, or experience becomes more real than anything else, then we are in a state of absorption. And the kinds of absorption we're looking at here are story-listening trance, transportation, and flow.

We have observed and know that story listening can engage listeners in a story-listening trance or absorb them to the point that they are in a state of transportation. But if those mental states do no more than just hold a listener's attention, then it's difficult to see whether the mental energy required develops a child's intellect, creativity, or social skills.

When interviewing the alumni it became clear that story listening was doing more than grabbing attention; it was creating the desire to seek out and repeat or recreate the psychological state that story listening put the listener into. Listening became its own reward. It's this which suggests that the wonderful dream-like condition observed by storytellers and recalled by listeners is best explained by Csikszentmihalyi's definition of flow. Csikszentmihalyi views flow as necessary to develop a more complex self, with well-ordered thoughts and feelings. Perhaps experiencing a flow state through story listening contributes to this development. Listening to stories allowed our alumni to enter trance states that produced happiness, an experience they wanted to recreate for themselves and their children. To us it's pretty clear that of the three terms, flow best describes the state listeners enter into when deeply absorbed in an oral story. For educational purposes we need to understand how to reproduce this state, and to identify replicable outcomes for young listeners when flow is attained.

The mechanics of creating flow

Although it is noteworthy to identify the state that listeners experience, it is much more important to identify the factors that go into the creation of that state. Parkinson pointed out, "No one should expect all story activity to automatically produce [story-listening] trance. Conditions vary; pupils vary; we [storytellers] vary" (Parkinson 2011, p. 25). Both Sturm and Stallings individually and at different times attempted to identify factors contributing to story-listening trance, so that it might be reliably re-created with each story told, and easily identified whenever it happened (Sturm 2000, p. 301; Stallings 1988, 1993). They looked to the content and structure of the stories and specific elements of the telling (skills, styles, personalities and techniques of different tellers, and the nature of the audiences).

Sturm attended American Midwest storytelling festivals and events where he interviewed adult listeners immediately after they heard a story. Most, but not all, reported that the story's style (use of simple descriptions) and the storyteller's vocal style (low key supported by simple gestures) contributed to story-listening trance. Some listeners also indicated it was necessary for the teller or the story to generate a sense of comfort, or that the teller give the appearance of inhabiting or believing the story. The story's rhythm was also significant (Sturm 2000).

Stalling's "The Web of Silence" (Stallings 1988) and "Journey into Darkness" (Stallings 1993) both relied on a review of literature, as well as interviews and conversations with psychologists and professional storytellers to seek explanations for the occurrence of story-listening trance. Her summation similarly found story form or schema was key to putting listeners in a trance state. She also surmised that when listeners imagine and/or put effort into understanding a story, that effort could cause a trance, particularly because the brain seems wired for narrative. And she considered the speaker's or the teller's skills, and whether trance depends on the listener's ability to trust the teller and/or the whole storytelling process.

Stallings's and Sturm's findings were inconclusive. They didn't discover any specific aspects of storytelling that had a consistent *causal* effect tied to the occurrence of story-listening trance. However, they were able to identify one consistent factor that was present when S-LT did occur, which was that the stories being presented were folkloric in structure. Interestingly, the same has been found in other fields. M. Elizabeth Stevens-Guille and Frederci J. Boersma also recognized this in a review of therapeutic uses of fairy tales:

> Trance has been described along the dimension of absorption, with greater absorption being associated with the fading awareness of surroundings and alterations in perception and cognition. These are conditions that exist for children when fairy tales are told. Children are usually so absorbed in the story that they concentrate on the action and think of themselves as being involved to the extent that they shiver and hide their heads when the story reaches a scary part. (Stevens-Guille and Boersma 1992, p. 248)

We are in agreement. Traditional folk and fairy tales, as mentioned previously, require listeners to use their own memories and imaginations to mentally simulate narratives. This necessitates a deep degree of absorption. Minimal descriptions prompt mental simulations by using all the senses. Earlier discussions by us of story listening and visualization established listeners are active: there is effort in comprehending an oral story. In *You're Not Listening*, Kate Murphy points out: "To really listen is to be moved physically, chemically, emotionally, and intellectually to another person's narration." She reminds us that:

> it's important to emphasize that hearing is not the same as listening, but rather it's forerunner. Hearing is passive, listening is active. The best listeners focus their attention and recruit the other senses to the effort. Their brains work hard to process all that incoming information and find meaning, which opens the door to creativity, empathy, insight and knowledge. Understanding is the goal of listening, and it takes effort. (Murphy 2020, pp. 8, 30)

This is especially true in the case of young children listening to stories, since, for most children, formal storytelling is one new activity among many novel experiences in nursery or kindergarten. There's a challenge both in sitting still and concentrating on the words of one specific person while creating the images and understanding for yourself. Sitting still and really listening when you are young is challenging but you soon learn, with repeated story times, that it is a pleasurable and rewarding creative act.

One factor that made story listening pleasurable and rewarding for our informants was that they perceived the story as being told directly to them and them alone. We have both had individuals express this feeling to us after hearing a story. We think this impression might be explained by the absorption (whether it be intense focus, S-LT/T, or flow) the listeners enter into when listening. Transportation into the story makes the images of the story become more real than the physical space the listener is in. They feel the story is "happening" just for them.

But what listeners are usually unaware of is that they are *not* alone. They are co-creating the story with the teller. And they are also reacting to their fellow listeners' responses. The responses of others, whether laughter or shouts, impact each individual listener's comprehension and pleasure. Besides story content and structure, a storyteller's skill and understanding of their young listeners affect the experience. In addition, formulaic elements and figurative language in stories, prosody—the language of the text and the patterns of stress and intonation in the teller's voice—as well as the teller's gestures and eye contact all support listening. This leads to situational modeling which enhances both comprehension and the sense of being transported into the story. Taken together, all of these factors—story structure, formulaic elements, prosody, the socio-cultural aspects of story time—may "initiate certain mental states by triggering attitudes, listening poses, associative memories and recall of emotion" (Ryan 2007, p. 37), all of which support focused listening. But is it enough to create flow?

To achieve flow, Csikszentmihalyi emphasized the need for desirable difficulty and pleasure within the experience (Csikszentmihalyi 1990, pp. 6, 53). As we have shown, story listening, for most, is pleasurable. We also believe that sitting still and focusing, along with the new images and story created, the emotions processed, and the anticipated solutions to problems each time a story is heard, provide the degree of desirable difficulty and intense interest necessary to create a state of flow.

Not just the first encounter with a story but subsequent encounters with the same story can do this, as no two tellings are exactly the same. Listeners often notice things missed on the first hearing or slight differences the storyteller makes in a second rendition. The listener still must co-create the story with the teller and those around her, a challenging task. Repetition also provides comfort and relaxation at knowing what is going to happen, which adds to the enjoyment: another component needed for flow to be achieved. It becomes so pleasurable that you want to repeat the experience for, as Csikszentmihalyi said, "the sheer joy of doing it" (Csikszentmihalyi 1990, p. 51).

While reporting tremendous enjoyment, those interviewed about story listening confirmed they had to "work" more with the oral stories, in comparison with shared picture book reading. One recalled:

> You know, if you're provided with the picture there's only so much you can do to individualize it, but if you're just provided with descriptions you have to come up with the picture yourself. There's so many details in the stories.

Thinking about it some more, he acknowledged what kind of work was involved:

> Hearing a story without the pictures, it teaches you that words are only a portion of what you have to follow. If you only listen to the words, you get a pretty plain story, there's no imagination being put into the settings or the characters. I mean, you get vanilla characters, that's not really a good story. There's some imagination that has to be put into it, it's drawn out from the storyteller.

These impressions are supported in a study by Jo Kuyvenhoven. She spent one year observing a public school fourth/fifth grade class listening to stories told weekly by their teacher. Kuyvenhoven interviewed these pupils, asking what was going on in their heads when they listened to stories. The students talked about "getting into imagination," "entering the story" by making pictures or images. "The desired imaginative engagement, the sort that 'erased' the classroom, happened after 'making pictures'" (Kuyvenhoven 2007, p. 101).

Kuyvenhoven's subjects also described the importance of setting or, more precisely, space. Taking the teacher-teller's words they would build an environment. Kuyvenhoven didn't feel this alone facilitated the child listener's "entry into the story-world." She suspected, "engagement was created by complementarity and interesting complexity. The place had to become fully sense-able and defined. But it also had to hook the listener's interest or sympathy" (Kuyvenhoven 2007, p. 105). Kuyvenhoven's students said this state occurred unless there were distractions, which they found upsetting.

One of our alumni described the mental effort required to not only make the story real but what he saw as the listener's responsibility for entering one aspect of altered mental states:

> With storytelling it's more like you are passively listening and it's how you accept it. That's one side of it, but the other side is that you are pulled into a space, wherever the narrator is telling you are. It's not a good story if they don't do that. But *you* have to feel that space—you know you're in a library surrounded by books, but that space becomes wherever you want it to be. From week to week that space becomes more than just a library with a carpet and large open space.

These recollections of having to "work at" making the story happen in their heads and simultaneously make that psychological or imagined space could be indication that listeners experienced flow during story listening.

Because Stallings and Sturm were unable to identify the factors that could trigger S-LT to occur with regularity, they came to the conclusion that story-listening trance (we would say flow) isn't easily or commonly realized, but did happen occasionally (Stallings 1993, p. 21). However, we found that the unique psychological state while listening to stories, whether it was story-listening trance, transportation, or flow, was achieved regularly in recollections of UCLS librarian-tellers and our interviewees.

This could be due to the age of our students. Five-to-eight-year-olds are particularly prone to being entranced, and Stallings does point to research that suggests children under the age of six are capable of slipping into trance states more easily than adults (Stallings 1993, p. 14). But we believe that the regular occurrence of flow during story listening has to do with additional elements that weren't present often enough in Sturm's and Stallings's studies: context, familiarity, and repetition of experience.

Story times at UCLS were set up the same way each time they were held. Sessions took part in a special part of the library, the students entered the space through a door only used for story time, and they were told the stories without interruption. Informants remembered lining up to go to the library, going through the door, sitting down on the rug, and the emotions aroused by these actions—but not the story or the teller. Many talked of the rug as being the last thing they recalled before the story started, and then "waking up thirty minutes later with rug marks on my hands." One listener recalled:

> I remember lining up and going to the library. I remember sitting on the rug and then the story would start. It was like....5 – 4 – 3 – 2 – 1- blast off. I was in another world.

He was transported into the story, leaving place and time behind.

It appears an element of routine and repetition, as well as familiarity with the storyteller and the social context and environment, contributes to the altered states connected to narrative. Much like meditation, once you know how to get into a meditative state, you can do it regularly. The repetition needs to be frequent for the habit to form. This also suggests it helps to have a storyteller who is a familiar figure interacting regularly with listeners. A teacher, librarian, or family member sharing stories with children in a comfortable setting is more likely to find listeners entranced. Folklorist Carl Lindahl saw this in Appalachian storytelling. He observed that in traditional storytelling, when a kind of reverie happened it only resulted within closely knit groups in intimate settings (Lindahl 2001, 2018). He described storytelling as a "shy tradition," something not meant for mass consumption at festivals and story slams. Kuyvenhoven saw something similar with her fourth/fifth graders (Kuyvenhoven 2005).

Our informants indicated that because this ritualized altered mental state happened so frequently when they were told stories, once they learned how to read with fluency it was easy for them to recreate the experience for themselves. They said they continue to find that state as adults, by reading for pleasure and listening to podcasts and talk-radio, making libraries and book shops their favorite haunts, and seeking careers where they got to hear and share stories with colleagues and clients. One of our informants said that even now she couldn't listen to podcasts or talking-books while she was driving because she would "disappear" into the story.

THE ROLE OF NARRATIVE AND FLOW IN METACOGNITION AND THEORY OF MIND

Having defined story-listening trance, transportation, and flow, and delineated how they manifest, we wanted to examine what significance these psychological states play in child development and learning. Does regular experience of these states produce academic or social benefits? Wendy Suzuki and other neuroscientists recognize that storytelling "engages and even entrains our brains in reproducible ways" (Suzuki et al. 2018, p. 9470). What does storytelling "entrain" (in terms of incorporating ways of thinking) that can be reproduced? Earlier we established, through the work of Mark Turner and Barbara Hardy, that narrative imagining is a primary act of the mind, something fundamental for thought. Others, such as Charles Fernyhough, Jerome Bruner, Kendall Haven, and Susan Engel, have also asserted connections between narrative and how one organizes internal speech and thinking.

Does the story listening experience significantly affect how listeners organize their own thoughts? Many of the former UCLS students were certain that story listening was a solitary experience, just for them, even though they listened in a group of two classes (around forty to fifty children). These informants recalled feeling that the librarian told the stories directly to them and no other. Part of the joy of listening came from a sense of attachment to the teller, the feeling that the story was being told just to them—once they were "into" the story (experiencing S-LT or flow), the others in the room became irrelevant. Fellow students, and any off-task behavior by them (a rarity during stories) disappeared. One young woman recalled it this way:

> Once I got to the library I was totally distracted from those sorts of things. I thought I was there by myself. I thought it was personal. It was my chance to hear that story and I got to take it with me. We were in a group, yeah, but

> I didn't pay attention to the other kids during the story. Then it was being told to me and I got to take it and go.

Others expressed the same sentiment.

> Emotionally, I think I was really there by myself. I knew there were other people around me, but I wasn't concerned for them when I was listening to a story. It was a neutral time for me. I didn't have to compete with anyone. · You know, you can't compete when you're just listening.

Could memories of an impression that the librarian told directly and only to them, and the sense they were "alone" and "lost" in the story, be an unselfconscious metaphorical expression for being focused on their individual thoughts?

Cultural critics and psychologists believe well-crafted stories, whether told, heard, or read, prompt us to reflect on our own thinking and the thinking of others (Oatley 2011, pp. 81–106; Gold 2002, pp. 42–44, 61–62; Symons et al. 2005, p. 99). Cognitive psychologists refer to this as metacognition and/or the related theory of mind (ToM). (Both were mentioned earlier, in discussions of executive function skills and focus.) While metacognition is an awareness of one's own thought processes, theory of mind is the ability to attribute mental states to oneself *and to others*. Reader response experts and cognitive scientists have frequently considered these two processes in discussions on narrative thinking.

Keith Oatley states that around the age of four children begin understanding what others think and feel, and that this ability develops throughout adulthood.

> It is an essential human skill. And we do impute thoughts and feelings to others, based on what we know of ourselves. At the same time, we believe that people act for reasons. The very fact of explaining things by narrative depends on this idea. (Oatley 2011, p. 45)

He is supported in this by Charles Fernyhough, who describes the young child's mind being shaped by rhythms and unpredictabilities in social life (Fernyhough 2008, pp. 130–131). Stories give us enough information to engage our theory of mind processes, so we anticipate and analyze what characters do. In stories readers and listeners experience viewpoints different from their own: they observe new ways of reacting to life's situations.

Vicarious experiences drawn from the actions and emotions in a narrative add to listeners' knowledge of life experience. In *Why We Read Fiction*, Lisa Zunshine proposes all fiction is about finding out why humans behave as they do (Zunshine 2006, pp. 6–7.; Oatley 2011, p. 45). We enjoy listening to stories from a very young age, we are basically designed to do so (Engel 1995, pp. 4–22; Fernyhough 2008, pp. 165–180). This is also when our brains are set to absorb information on the way things work, the way people react and behave. The more we listen to stories about how people interact, problem solve, support the good, and punish the bad, the more we learn about the world that surrounds us. We are learning how to "think."

Cognitive psychology (and classical philosophy) asserts that figuring out ourselves and others are two sides of a coin and agree that we learn to do this kind of reckoning through stories. "Jerome Bruner has argued that while we may learn about the physical world through logical rules and abstract principles, we learn about the social world through narratives" (Engel 1995, p. 9). A sense of self "arises out of our capacity to reflect upon our own acts by the operation of 'metacognition'," as Bruner observed. He went on to say:

> metacognitive activity (self-monitoring and self-correction) is very unevenly distributed, varies according to cultural background, and, perhaps most important, can be taught successfully as a skill. (Bruner 1986, p. 67)

His key books on this—*Actual Minds, Possible Worlds* and *Acts of Meaning*—as well as numerous articles explore narrative as a distinct mode of thought and also the role of narrative thinking in child development. He argues that adults, not tools or technology, are indispensable for narrative thinking to transform children's learning experiences. The metacognitive mind develops through adult and child interactions, particularly when sharing stories. Bruner asserted that the narrative mind is what drives science, art, and a sense of self (Bruner 1986, pp. 44–45, 103–104, 1990, pp. 33–67).

To develop theory of mind we all must acquire an understanding of people through social and cultural experiences, made meaningful through interpretation. Bruner and others suggest all narrative is an interpretation, a version, of experience (Bruner 1988, pp. 575, 582; Fernyhough 2008, pp. 86–87; Engel 1995, p. 119). "As children take in the stories they hear all around them, they also take a particular interpretation of events and experience. People experience their lives as a series of overlapping and fluctuating stories" (Engel 1995, p. 9). Such acquired knowledge, or experience, allows us to continually make assumptions of people and events, real and fictional, which we use in developing a sense of self and to know how to act. Stories and the characters in them allow us to do this. When we hear a story we can safely infer and presume with far more "people" and life experiences than we could ever encounter in real life, especially as children.

Or as another of our informants put it:

> Stories have a huge impact on how children interact with each other. That's when you hear what you're supposed to do when you talk to other people. If—well, for example—I would probably think of myself as a character in a story when I was talking to someone else, see. I would look to the characters in a story to see how I should act with other people.

Synthesizing and making meaning of real-life events as story-structures (and vice-versa, synthesizing elements in stories into meaningful knowledge remembered and used in real life) is what makes narrative a mode of thought particularly important for children.

We have come to understand that reader response theorists and cognitive psychologists see narrative thinking as a way to develop a sense of self and learn to "read" others through cognitive mechanisms like metacognition and theory of mind. Reader response theory sees narratives tricking those mechanisms into working. Cognitive psychology sees both metacognition and ToM developing innately along with language. Like language, they require generational interaction through social and cultural activities like storytelling and story listening.

MENTAL STATE DISCOURSE WHEN LISTENING

One cognitive study by Douglas K. Symons and his colleagues demonstrated how sharing stories contributes to metacognitive and ToM development. They looked at mental-state discourse during shared reading and picture book storytelling tasks. In what Bruner referred to as "book reading routines" (Bruner 1986, pp. 76–77), they observed that adults perceived opportunities to elaborate, question, or describe what went on in the text and illustrations. As parents read or paraphrased a picture book story, they often interrupted the narrative to ask or suggest to their young child what characters were thinking and feeling. This became a model that child listeners imitated.

With frequent, regular shared reading children began to speculate spontaneously about what characters thought and felt. Although unable to decode, children repeated or created narratives from clues in illustrations or their memories of parents or nursery teachers reading to them; at the same time they ran a commentary on the characters and events (Symons et al. 2005, pp. 82, 99). Symons and other cognitive psychologists called this kind of speech "mental state discourse." To speculate about and report on characters' thoughts, feelings and actions children must reflect on their own thoughts and actions, and their sense of self. Adults modeled how to do this during the shared reading. In other words, this kind of storytelling experience models and rehearses metacognitive and ToM thinking.

There is a distinct difference between the "book reading routines" analyzed in Symons's study and the sort of storytelling and story listening experience we are describing. During UCLS story times children are encouraged, from the start, *not* to interrupt the story by asking the librarian-teller questions. And the librarian-teller doesn't interrupt a story with comments or questions about the characters' mental states: folk and fairy tales have little or no character development or internal monologue, as might be found in modern literature. Those characteristics are not part of the simple conversational style of storytelling we practice for young listeners. So how might metacognition and theory of mind develop through the kind of story listening experience (which includes S-LT/T and flow) that we advocate?

Previously we stated that Csikszentmihalyi viewed school activities as an external imposition, causing a decline of children's curiosity and attention. From one viewpoint, the UCLS and other formal story times are imposed. But because of the elements we've identified that grab listeners' focus, initiate visualization and imagining, and trigger flow, an adult telling stories is not perceived as an external imposition by the students. Exactly the opposite—the adult teller disappears from the story and the listener is acting on their own within the story. Csikszentmihalyi observed:

Often children ... need external incentives to take the first steps in an activity that requires a difficult restructuring of attention. Most enjoyable activities are not natural: they demand effort that initially one is reluctant to make.

But once the interaction starts to provide feedback to the person's skills it usually begins to be intrinsically rewarding. (Csikszentmihalyi 1990, p. 68)

The story, the actions of the storyteller, and the social and environmental context all combine causing children to focus and enter a state of absorption that provides pleasure, a kind that is almost addictive. These are the external incentives that restructure attention and, we believe, make the links between their thinking and the thinking of others. As Professor Manuel Martín-Loeches, a psychobiologist, and his colleagues observed, "Text reading or listening to a speech is highly immersive activity, by virtue of which the comprehender immerses himself into the narrative, thereby activating brain regions related to the content of the text" (Martín-Loeches et al. 2008, p. 621).

Bruner and other cognitive psychologists saw this, believing "Language is...a way of sorting out one's thoughts about things" (Bruner 1986, p. 72). Drawing on psychologist Lev Vygotsky's idea of the zone of proximal development, cognitive psychologists observed that parents and teachers provide activities (including physical and linguistic play) they labeled scaffolding. Such activities support the child's intellectual, emotional, or social development by modeling or demonstrating something slightly challenging. With storytelling, the parent or teacher, familiar with the child's abilities and interests, uses language and narrative content demanding linguistic and comprehension skills just a bit beyond those the child already commands, but not beyond her reach.

Earlier we spoke of research into motivation for learning, and better student engagement. David Shernoff, with others, looked at flow within education and what it might achieve. Exploring the psychology of optimal experience, happiness, and creativity, they conducted experiments with older students to learn what creates flow in both educational and recreational settings. They found engagement depends on developing activities students find challenging and relevant while simultaneously making them feel in control of their learning and confident in their abilities (Shernoff et al. 2003, p. 173). Working independently as individuals or in small groups is more likely to establish flow than approaches relying on lectures and rote-learning. As might be expected, sports, the arts, and computer studies frequently generate flow but so too can traditional academic subjects when meeting the criteria described above (Shernoff and Vandell 2007). Although these studies looked at dozens of subject areas and enrichment activities, storytelling and story listening were not examined.

The activities in older grades that Csikszentmihalyi, Shernoff, and others looked to for signs of flow may seem far removed from young children's story times. But a zone of proximal development also exists for older students' learning, as does reliance on narrative thinking, metacognition, and using language to sort out thought. Flow experiences developing a more complex sense of self happen at any age. Much research into the psychology of optimal experience seeks to address persistent educational challenges such as underachievement and behavioral and emotional problems. These challenges are not only in middle and high school, and we could argue their foundations are in early childhood. If story listening in early childhood does engage flow on a regular basis, as we believe, then it is worth much more attention to help us identify any enduring effects it may have.

AWAY WITH THE FAIRIES

Most specialists looking at child development, learning, and teaching of literacy remain unfamiliar with oral story listening and its impact. But the idea that being lost in a story does "entrain" the brain with lasting effects is not a new one. Irish folklore has long recognized it. Where Americans might joke about an absent-minded person being a "space-cadet," the Irish describe day-dreamers as being "away with the fairies." Many Irish stories tell of a backward, unassuming character with few abilities, who encounters the fairies. The "Good People" literally lift this protagonist into the air, dropping them somewhere unknown, where they're expected to do impossible things never done by them before (like playing a fiddle, or conducting brain surgery). The surprised protagonist accomplishes the tasks, to his or her own amazement. The fairies celebrate the feats achieved and then whisk the hero back to where they started, where no time has passed. Forever afterward that individual is a talented and beloved musician, or storyteller or poet, whom everyone knows was "lifted" or "touched" by the fairies. It's become common parlance, a sign of respect, to describe a musician or writer with wonderful talent as having been "lifted." We all need time "away with the fairies," taken there by stories, poems, or music (or conviviality), in order to grow and develop—or just to keep our sanity. Perhaps this "folk-science" is something people recognized and named in the past and we now call it flow.

Csikszentmihalyi and his colleagues uncovered evidence of the benefits of such experiences. Through observations, interviews, and experiments they found that adults who developed coherent, satisfied, happy lives shared one thing in common:

> When told by a loving adult whom one trusts, fairy tales, biblical stories, heroic historical deeds, and poignant family events are often the first intimations of meaningful order a person gleans from experience of the past. In contrast, we found in our studies that individuals who never focus on any goal, or accept unquestioningly from the society around them, tend not to remember their parents having read or told stories to them as children. Saturday morning kiddie shows on television, with their pointless sensationalism, are unlikely to achieve the same purpose. (Csikszentmihalyi 1990, pp. 235–236)

Over decades we have witnessed story listeners enter what appeared to be a type of trance state, which we now believe to be motivational. We observed that students became instilled with what Dewey said was true education—self-motivation to repeat the experience, to go on learning. Maya Angelou is attributed with saying, "I've learnt that people will forget what you said, people will forget what you did, but people will never forget how you made them feel." This sums up what informants told us in multiple interviews. As adults they never really remembered which librarian told them stories, and few remembered the specific stories, but they all recalled the feeling listening to stories gave them. The desire to later recreate that feeling independently led them into habits that have endured throughout their lives.

References

Bruner, J. 1986. *Actual Minds, Possible Worlds.* Cambridge, MA and London, UK: Harvard University Press.

Bruner, J. 1988. Research Currents: Life as Narrative. *Language Arts,* 45(6): 574–583. https://www.jstor.org/stable/41411426.

Bruner, J. 1990. *Acts of Meaning.* Cambridge, MA and London, UK: Harvard University Press.

Bus, A. G., van Ijzendoorn, M. H., and Pellegrini, A. D. 1995. Joint Book Reading Makes for Success in Learning to Read: A Meta-Analysis on Intergenerational Transmission of Literacy. *Review of Educational Research,* 65(1): 1–21. DOI: https://doi.org/10.3102/00346543065001001.

Bus, A. G. 2002. Joint-Caregiver—Child Storybook Reading: A Route to Literacy Development. In *Handbook of Early Literacy Research, Volume 1,* eds. Susan

B. Neuman and David K. Dickinson, 179–191. New York and London: The Guildford Press.

Chubb, P. 1902. *The Teaching of English in the Elementary and the Secondary School.* New York: The Macmillan Company.

Chubb, P. 1929. *The Teaching of English in the Elementary and the Secondary School, Revised and Largely Rewritten.* New York: The Macmillan Company.

Csikszentmihalyi, M. 1990. *Flow: The Psychology of Optimal Experience.* New York: Harper and Row.

Csikszentmihalyi, M. 2004. *Flow, the Secret to Happiness.* TedTalk. https://www.ted.com/talks/mihaly_csikszentmihalyi_flow_the_secret_to_happiness?language=en. Accessed February 12, 2020.

Davis, P. 2013. *Reading and the Reader.* Oxford: Oxford University Press.

Donaldson, M. 1978. *Children's Minds.* New York: W.W. Norton.

Engel, S. 1995. *The Stories Children Tell.* New York and Oxford: W. H. Freeman and Company

Engel, S. 2015. *The Hungry Mind, the Origins of Curiosity in Childhood.* Cambridge, MA and London, UK: Harvard University Press.

Fernyhough, C. 2008. *The Baby in the Mirror: A Child's World from Birth to Three.* London: Granata Books.

Galdone, J. and Galdone, P. 1979. *The Tailypo: A Ghost Story.* Tadworth: World's Work.

Gerrig, R. 1993. *Experiencing Narrative Worlds: On the Psychological Activities of Reading.* New Haven, CT: Yale University Press.

Gold, J. 2002. *The Story Species, Our Life-Literature Connection.* Markham; Ontario; and Allston, MA: Fitzhenry and Whiteside.

Jackson, P. W. 1968. *Life in Classrooms.* New York; Chicago; San Francisco, Atlanta; Dallas; Toronto; Montreal; and London: Holt, Rinehart and Winston, Inc.

Kuyvenhoven, J. 2005. *In the Presence of Each Other: A Pedagogy of Storytelling.* Doctoral Dissertation, University of British Columbia. https://open.library.ubc.ca/cIRcle/collections/ubctheses/831/items/1.0055624. Accessed July 10, 2020.

Kuyvenhoven, J. 2007. "What Happens Inside Your Head When You Are Listening to a Story?" Children Talk About Their Experience During a Storytelling. *Storytelling, Self and Society: An Interdisciplinary Journal of Storytelling Studies,* 3(2): 95–114. DOI: https://doi.org/10.1080/15505340701282755.

Lindahl, C. 2001. Surrounding a Shy Tradition: Oral and Written Styles of American Mountain Märchen. In *Perspectives on the Jack Tales and Other North American Märchen,* eds. Carl Lindahl, 68–98. Indiana University Bloomington, The Folklore Institute.

Lindahl, C. 2018. Dream Some More: Storytelling as Therapy. *Folklore,* 129(3): 221–236. DOI: https://doi.org/10.1080/0015587X.2018.1473109.

Martín-Loeches, M., Casado, P., Hernández-Tamames, J., and Álverez-Linear, J. 2008. Brain Activation in Discourse Comprehension: A 3t fMRI Study. *NeuroImage*, 41(2): 614–622. DOI: https://doi.org/10.1016/j.neuroimage.2008.02.047.

Mol, S. E., Bus, A. G., de Jong, M. T., Smeets, D. J. H. 2008. Added Value of Dialogic Parent-Child Book Readings: A Meta-Analysis. *Early Education and Development*, 19(1): 7–26. DOI: https://doi.org/10.1080/1040928 0701838603.

Murphy, K. 2020. *You're Not Listening. What You're Missing and Why It Matters*. London: Vintage Digital.

Nell, V. 1988. *Lost in a Book. The Psychology of Reading for Pleasure*. New Haven, CT and London: Yale University Press.

Oatley, K. 2011. *Such Stuff as Dreams, the Psychology of Fiction*. Malden, MA; Oxford; Chichester, and West Sussex: Wiley-Blackwell.

Parkinson, R. 2011. *Storytelling and Imagination. Beyond Basic Literacy*. London and New York: Routledge.

Postgate, D. 1998. *The Hairy Toe: A Traditional American Tale*. London: Walker Books.

Roberts, J. E. and Burchinal, M. R. 2002. The Complex Interplay between Biology and Environment: Otitis Media and Mediating Effects on Early Literacy Development. In *Handbook of Early Literacy Research, Volume 1*, eds. Susan B. Neuman and David K. Dickinson, 232–241. New York and London: The Guildford Press.

Ryan, P. 2007. Once Upon a Time Into Altered States: Temporal Space, Liminality, and Flow. In *Time Everlasting: Representations of Past, Present and Future in Children's Literature*, ed. Pat Pinsent, 36–44. NCRCL Papers 13. Shenstone, Lichfield, Staffs: Pied Piper Publishing Ltd.

Shernoff, D. J., Csikszentmihalyi, M., Schneider, B., and Shernoff, E. S. 2003. Student Engagement in High School Classrooms from the Perspective of Flow Theory. *School Psychology Quarterly*, 18(2): 158–176. DOI: https://doi.org/10.1007/978-94-017-9094-9_24.

Shernoff, D. J. and Vandell, D. L. 2007. Engagement in After-School Program Activities: Quality of Experience from the Perspective of Participants. *Journal of Youth and Adolescence*, 36: 891–903. DOI: https://doi.org/10.1007/s10964-007-9183-5.

Stallings, F. 1988. The Web of Silence: Storytelling's Power to Hypnotize. *The National Storytelling Journal*, Spring/Summer: 6–19. https://www.franstallings.com/Publications. Accessed November 22, 2019.

Stallings, F. 1993. Journey Into Darkness: The Story-Listening Trance. https://www.franstallings.com/uploads/Fran/Jouney.pdf. Accessed November 22, 2019.

Stevens-Guille, E. M. and Boersma, F. J. 1992. Fairy Tales as Trance Experience: Possible Therapeutic Uses. *American Journal of Clinical Hypnosis*, 34(4): 245–254. DOI: https://doi.org/10.1080/00029157.1992.10402854.

Sturm, B. 2000. The "Storylistening" Trance Experience. *The Journal of American Folklore*, 113(449): 287–304. DOI: https://doi.org/10.2307/542104.

Suzuki, W. A., Feliú, M. I., Uri, H., Yehuda, R., and Zarate, J. M. 2018. The Science and Power of Storytelling. *The Journal of Neuroscience*, 38(44): 9468–9470. DOI: https://doi.org/10.1523/JNEUROSCI.1942-18.2018.

Symons, D. K., Peterson, C. D., Slaughter, V., Roche, J., and Doyle, E. 2005. Theory of Mind and Mental State Discourse During Book Reading and Storytelling Tasks. *British Journal of Developmental Psychology*, 23(1): 81–102. DOI: https://doi.org/10.1348/026151004X21080.

Thorne-Thomsen, G. 1901. Reading in the Third Grade. *Elementary School Teacher and Course of Study*, 2(3): 227–235.

Van Allsburg, C. 1979. *The Garden of Abdul Gasazi*. Boston: Houghton Mifflin.

Van Laer, T., De Ruyter, K., Visconti, L. M., and Wetzels, M. 2014. The Extended Transportation-Imagery Model: A Meta-Analysis of the Antecedents and Consequences of Consumers' Narrative Transportation. *Journal of Consumer Research*, 40(5): 797–817. DOI: https://doi.org/10.1086/673383.

Weir, L. 1995. *Boom Chicka Boom: A Book of Stories and Rhymes to Share*. Dublin: O'Brien Press.

Whitehurst, G. J. and Lonigan, C. J. 1998. Child Development and Emergent Literacy. *Child Development*, 69(2): 848–872.

Whitehurst, G. J. and Lonigan, C. J. 2002. Emergent Literacy: Development from Prereaders to Readers. In *Handbook of Early Literacy Research, Volume 1*, eds. Susan B. Neuman and David K. Dickinson, 11–29. New York and London: The Guildford Press.

Zweig, P. 1974. *The Adventurer*. London: Dent.

Zunshine, L. 2006. *Why We Read Fiction, Theory of Mind and the Novel*. Columbus, OH: Ohio State University Press.

CHAPTER 5

"Damn, I wish I still had story time." *The social effects of story listening experience*

Deeper meaning resides in the fairy tales told me in my childhood than in any truth that is taught in life. (Friedrich Schiller)

In previous chapters we have discussed, and hopefully shown, the beneficial outcomes that have direct effects on the listener with repeated exposure to oral story. Now we'd like to examine a group of outcomes arising from story listening that have a lasting civic and social affect. Specifically, we want to look at attachment, empathy, and cultural understanding. As Jackson has said, within the transformative tradition teachers "are actually trying to bring about changes in their students…that make them better in the sense of being closer to what humans are capable of becoming—more virtuous, fuller participants in an evolving moral order" (Jackson 1986, p. 127). We will show you the role oral story listening plays in that development.

STORIES LET YOU WALK IN SOMEONE ELSE'S SHOES: EMPATHY

Empathy is the sense of understanding other people and of vicariously experiencing another's emotional state (Immordino-Yang 2016, p. 156). It is a learned behavior emerging in early childhood. Developmental psychologist Alison Gopnik has shown that empathy is already in evidence by fifteen months and continues to develop over time (Gopnik 2011, 2012). It is born out of an ability to "read" others' thoughts and feelings (ToM). The "companionable experience" of sharing stories has been shown to cultivate empathy (Haven 2007, p. 11; Oatley 2011; Gurdon 2019, p. xiv). This is particularly so with narrative experiences involving children and adults with whom they have close ties: parents, older siblings, other relatives, caregivers, and teachers and librarians (Gurdon 2019, pp. xiv, 84–86; Sturm and Nelson 2016, p. 15; Chambers 1991, pp. 57–58).

Reflecting on their story listening experiences a number of UCLS alumni remembered an awareness of story details and physical sensations that sparked cognizance of and interest in other people's feelings and thoughts. One informant recalled a revelation he had while listening in which he realized that the wolf he "saw" in the tale he had just heard didn't look like the wolf others envisioned.

> I think the storytelling helped me feel that everybody has something unique that they can pass to one another that wasn't material. I think from an early age, I had an idea that one kid's story was different from another kid's story. Because the way I visualized the spoken word would be different from the way another kid would visualize the spoken word. I mean, just because how I thought I saw what a wolf would look like, versus the way the other kids' wolf looked like, and that concept undoubtedly followed me through.

This made him want to know what others saw and thought, an interest that stuck with him. Others spoke in a similar way, telling us it led to choosing careers where they could hear different people's stories or helped them when encountering people or ideas that were different from their own. They felt they were able to accept different points of view and even look for them throughout their lives.

A response to one of Patrick's stories exemplifies this. He loves telling *Molly Whuppie*, a variant of *Jack and the Beanstalk* but with a confident, brave, and fabulously clever heroine. A rollicking adventure, Molly outwits the giant and becomes queen. One day, after telling this tale to third graders, a boy came up bursting with excitement, clearly having shared each tight spot with the protagonist. Astounded, he declared, "That Molly, she's so clever, and she's so brave and she's so much fun!" Patrick spontaneously responded, "Yeah! Girls really are clever and brave and loads of fun!" For a moment that skeptical look young boys often display regarding girls started to show itself, then suddenly his eyes sparkled with revelation. "Oh, yeah!" he replied thoughtfully, walking off in a daze.

People who read more are more sympathetic to the situations of others (Oatley 2011, pp. 81–106; Carey 2005, pp. 208–210; Gold 2002, pp. 42–44). This has been said about oral stories too, but not empirically studied. Jane Addams believed telling stories to Irish immigrants allowed them to see that people from other cultures shared similar lives (Addams 1912, pp. 358–561; Pellowski 1977, p. 94). In stories "we engage with issues because they are emotionally important to us, having to do with people, intentions, and with outcomes. The emotions we experience are not primarily those of the characters, they are our own, in the contexts we imagine" (Oatley 2011, p. 115). Becoming cognizant that we share emotions with other humans makes us empathic.

Various elements of story listening experience encourage empathy. Story content and structure prompt perspective-taking, "a highly complex social-cognitive process that entails what someone else might be seeing, thinking or feeling" (Edmiston 1990, p. 106). Young listeners apply memories and imagination to make meanings regarding what characters say, sense, think, and do, and of the actions and events. This causes them to take multiple perspectives and shift viewpoints, leading to better comprehension but also better understanding of one's self and others (Wilhelm 2008, pp. 81–82; Benton and Fox 1985).

Ways of telling orally, combined with the social setting and interaction (between teller and listeners, and listeners with each other), also contribute to awareness of and sensitivity to others, especially when physically and emotionally close in a safe, comfortable environment (Chambers 1991, pp. 57–58; Gurdon 2019, pp. 46–48). A professional storyteller reflecting on audience responses in classroom settings reported how astonished she was by the degree of compassion and empathy child listeners displayed toward the characters: they spontaneously shared personal accounts matching emotions or experiences of protagonists (Nelson 1989, p. 387). A pedagogical experiment in early years and primary school classes combined philosophy, oral discourse, and literacy. It found story listening was a way of "belonging together" which developed personal qualities like the need to listen, to respect others, and self-confidence to speak one's mind, challenge others and correct one's self (Fisher 2001, p. 69). Such traits indicate an ability to understand and empathize with other people.

When discussing situation modeling (visualization), we indicated listeners use all their senses to experience vicariously, perhaps also viscerally, events in a story, including characters' feelings. Specialists have recognized physical and physiological responses occurring during socio-cultural contexts for story listening, believing these contribute to lasting empathy. Gudrun supports this idea by quoting mental health practitioner Hilarie Cash and psychologist Susan Pinker, both of whom claim humans produce a range of neurochemicals in socio-cultural settings. They assert families produce such neurochemicals when sitting together informally to share stories. Cash, Pinker, and Gurdon believe this "chemical bouquet" that families create engenders trust, shared purpose, and mutual understanding (Gurdon 2019, pp. 46–49). Murphy related views of sociologist Michael Blau and philosopher Emmanuel Levinas, both of whom attributed the formation of empathy happening simply through physical and social acts of listening (Murphy 2020, pp. 201–202).

Murphy and Gurdon both summarized neurological findings that revealed listening to narratives causes the brains of the speaker and listeners to synchronize. They suggest this explains or helps the development of perspective-taking (empathy). Neuroscientists have conducted studies exploring whether "verbal communication is a joint activity where interlocutors share information" (Stephens et al. 2010, p. 14,425). Linguists, philosophers, cognitive psychologists, social psychologists, and neurophysiologists have long proposed a "theory of interactive linguistic alignment" in the brains of speakers and listeners, where "production and comprehension become tightly aligned on many different levels during verbal communication" (Stephens et al. 2010, pp. 14,428–14,429).

Zadbood, Hasson, and other neuroscientists looking at neural coupling in communication have also studied this hypothesis. (Murphy 2020, pp. 132–133, 173; Zadbood et al. 2017; Yeshurun et al. 2017). Their fMRI studies demonstrated that storytellers' and listeners' brains are "in synch" during story listening, because "the speaker's brain activity during production is spatially and temporally coupled with the brain activity measured across listeners during comprehension" (Stephens et al. 2010, p. 14,425). The greater the overlap between a storyteller's brain activity and a listener's, the better the communication, understanding, and connection. Comparable studies found similar brain activity during conversations between friends, and when people shared thoughts about a movie they had viewed separately (Zadbood et al. 2017). We're all familiar with close friends or families who finish each other's sentences. They are understanding, even anticipating, what the other person is thinking and feeling: they are empathic with each other.

Experienced storytellers see something similar in children's responses or interactions. As we've now often mentioned, the children predict what's coming next, what a character will say, or shout a warning displaying an understanding of how the protagonist thinks and feels. In other words, empathizing with that character or situation. And they take delight in all this. So this ability to see others' points of view, and enjoy the experience of doing so, generalizes beyond the story and endures. One informant talked of story listening experiences that really last, which he seeks out in his adult life.

It's hard to tell if it comes from childhood, but I have a broader concept of story than what other people have. I feel like I go looking for stories more than the average person my age. Telling stories, listening to stories, wanting stories—it's all a process, a concept that is reinforced over the years. I think the story times at Lab were a seed that was fed for over twenty-four years. My friends and I definitely do tell stories. I can't tell you how many evenings we spend just telling the same stories over and over and over again. I mean it's great. It's a barrel of laughs every time. When we're having dinner, it's who has a story to tell? Who's got the newest yarn to spin? Everything we talk about evokes some story about the past. I start the day listening to podcasts that are stories...any kind of story.

Stories communicate not just facts, but also emotions and perceptions, and expressions of attachment. If scientists are correct, viewing narrative communication as a joint activity where speakers and listeners share information, we must remember that in live oral storytelling shared information is not conveyed solely by words. As we've mentioned, eye contact, gestures, posture and body language, and the tone of voice and how the voice is used—nonverbal expressions *by both teller and listener*—are how the entire story listening experience is created. And the creativity

is shared between teller and audience. The teller creates the story line and delivers it orally to the listeners, who then create mental images and deliver back to the teller reactions to the story line. The reaction, in turn, affects the teller's choice of words, emphasis on plot development, and style of delivery. This co-creative interchange...continues for the entirety of the story. (Roney 1996, p. 7)

Thus story listening experience provides unique benefits that shared reading, and audio and video recorded narrative experiences, cannot.

STORIES CONNECT YOU: ATTACHMENT

Attachment to the teller and other listeners is another important change that develops out of the same cognitive, emotional, and physiological experiences with oral narrative that help promote empathy. Listening to and telling stories help children develop emotional connections that make sense of their world (Engel 1995, pp. 37–45). Some psychologists even view storytelling as a critical "attachment building behavior" because story listening and establishing attachments share elements like joint attention, turn-taking, affect attunement (shared emotional experiences), and inter-subjectivity (Killick and Frude 2009, p. 853; Engel 1995).

Informants recalled that listening to stories together on a regular basis created a sense of closeness, between them and the librarian, and between their fellow students:

> When it was just our class it was more personal. The librarians would con-centrate on just telling the story to a small group. I really think that the stories helped us connect as children. It helped us connect to each other because we all heard the same stories and also because we connected to the adults because they told us the stories.

Another former student confirmed this:

> There was an interaction between the librarian and the students. I loved that. Well it felt (*quietly*) special (*giggle*). Just because of that I always had a good bond with the librarians.

These students were talking about *attachment.*

Attachment is recognized as vital for healthy child development and success in education (Howes and Ritchie 2002; Killick and Boffey 2012). Clinical psychologist and storyteller Steven Killick described the link between attachment and storytelling:

> Attachment theory is about how humans develop relationships, how we make the bonds of attachment with others and how our relationships affect how we see the world. Storytelling can be an important way of building and strengthening the affectional bonds. After all, what we do most often, with those we are close to, is a kind of storytelling. We are always telling and lis-tening to the on-going stories of our lives, our problems, successes and failures. When we tell these stories and have heard them "validated" or

accepted they become ways that we make sense of and affirm our experience. (Killick and Boffey 2012, p. 21)

Normal attachment grows gradually, consisting of physical, emotional, and intellectual features, and usually "children become attached to their important adult caregivers, including teachers" (Howes and Ritchie 2002, p. 13).

Attachment happens not just with pupils and teachers, but also between classmates. The work of Mary Immordino-Yang, neuroscientist, psychologist, and former teacher, and fellow psychologists asserts that emotion and cognition are intertwined, simultaneously involving body and mind, in what they term social processing. Social processing happens when subjective interpretations of other peoples' beliefs, goals, feelings, and actions are internalized.

Many emotions are social, and anyone involved in educating children...knows that social learning is a major force in children's development. Typical children watch and engage with other people, imitate other people's actions (including mental actions and beliefs), and look to trusted adults and peers for emotional and other feedback on their behavior. They imagine how other people feel and think, and those thoughts in turn influence how they feel and think. (Immordino-Yang 2009, p. 8)

This social processing leads to group cohesion—as one of the informants said, the kids all "connected" because of listening to stories together. Empathically experiencing and then remembering the emotions and thinking created by someone else's circumstances causes children "to use empathic experiences to guide [their] attachment and learning" (Immordino-Yang 2009, pp. 10–11). The social processing comes from experiencing both real-life and fictional characters, actions, and settings.

Shared emotions and mental stimulation—caused by the story, event, and social setting provided by the teacher or librarian—transform everyone. "Children sit close, often hugged to you. They relax and become absorbed. As they listen they enjoy the security of belonging" (Chambers 1991, p. 57). Signs of attachment can appear quickly. Listeners unselfconsciously scoot closer until practically sitting on the teller's shoes or pulling her clothes, or as Donna experienced with a young German boy, rubbing her legs. Patrick has had instances where even on a first visit, nursery and kindergarten listeners became so attached through stories that when he said good-bye and got up to leave, they tried to grab hold of his legs or block the way out. They wanted more stories.

Connecting with the teacher or librarian through story listening leads listeners to rely on her in congruent experiences: not only other story times, but also when introducing new activities or concepts, helping with questions or sorting out any doubts, disputes or anxieties that arise (Howes and Ritchie 2002, p. 20; Emmerson 1959, pp. 31–32; Watts 2008). By listening to and telling stories children build "the trusting relationships that are the glue of democratic classroom communities. By listening to stories of others, children get to know each other" (Mardell and Kucirkova 2017, p. 172).

Psychologists and educators have found that an empathic and attached child has a high chance of educational success. Such traits also appear to support critical thinking and academic achievement (Symons et al. 2005; Lecce et al. 2017; Howes and Ritchie 2002). When attachment doesn't occur the consequences are a major concern. Difficulties forming attachment relationships prior to formal education become clear as pupils start school. Such children can have feelings of loss, anger, and perhaps confused emotions. As their schooling progresses, educators may see related outcomes arising from insecure attachment:

- Language difficulties.
- An inability to take perspectives of others (lack of empathy).
- Being overwhelmed by strong emotions, unable to calm.
- Poor attention and concentration.
- Poor emotional regulation and impulse control, which can lead to behavior problems.

(Killick and Boffey 2012, p. 20)

Discussion of these same behaviors came up in earlier discussions around focus.

Some see storytelling as one possible approach to addressing these problems, pointing to moral lessons in folk tales: good versus evil (with good always winning), and rewarding patience, kindness, fairness, hard work, and cleverness. But relying on fairy tales in this way usually is counterproductive, with the teller sounding preachy and pedantic. If told to teach a lesson, stories can sound stiff. The teller isn't particularly a fan of the story, just of the lesson. These tellings can fall on deaf ears.

Some Lancashire students were asked what they thought of professional soccer players and librarians telling them stories that were "just stories" on a library visit. One replied:

> Here, you learn stuff, because you're havin' a laugh. It's well better than school. When you're in school, it's like you don't really listen to what the people are saying. But when you're here learning with them library people and footballers it's fun and enjoyable so it doesn't just go in one ear and come straight out t'other and you're not like (*rolls his eyes and mouths disgust*). Because when you're at school you're just sitting there doing nothin'. (National Literacy Trust 2008)

Wilhelm found that telling stories that didn't moralize, but engaged and enticed—that evoked flow—resulted in the desired outcomes that "telling moral stories" tried for but didn't attain. To consider listening or telling a story as "just for the fun of it" is a misinterpretation. Story listening can be transformative by gradually developing trust in, reliance on, and respect and even affection for a teacher. Once present, problems with language, inhibition, and control, and regulating emotions and improved relationships with classmates all have a better chance of being resolved (Wilhelm 2008, p. 93; Wilhelm 2007, pp. 1, 2; Howes and Ritchie 2002, pp. 29–32).

We are not saying story listening is a panacea for all problems in modern education and contemporary life. But our experiences have led us to realize that stories can hold even a troubled child's attention and emotional attachment. Patrick has worked in special schools for students excluded for uncontrolled emotional or violent behavior, as well as at young offender units and prisons with boys and young men. All these institutions had individuals displaying profound learning and emotional needs, with trust and attachment often lacking. Yet no matter what disturbances or threatening attitudes were perceived at the start, once the stories began, he was never interrupted. Frequent responses as stories finished were requests for more stories, a demand to be taught to retell what they just heard, or a chance to share their life-narratives. In one project at a young offender unit, the boys took delight in retelling stories all night to their guards, especially ghost stories that made inmates and "screws" jump and laugh together (Ryan 2001, pp. 42–44). They enjoyed it so much that they started recounting stories about each other's reactions when Patrick visited for the next workshop. From sullen, silent young men who couldn't make eye contact to talking a mile-a-minute over each other to get a story out first was quite a transformation.

THE RE-SET BUTTON: STORY LISTENING WITH REGARD
TO CLASSROOM COMMUNITY AND MANAGEMENT

Because of the joy it gives, storytelling is one of the most effective ways of quickening the powers of perception and of directing the interests of children. (American Library Association 1929, p. 32)

What was true in 1929 remains true now. Collateral learning outcomes can be difficult to measure, usually revealed only years later, but some come to light sooner, within the first months in the classroom. Two are classroom management and building a classroom community (Rosen 1988; Cuffaro, H. K. 1995). Alumni never mentioned these, except peripherally when they alluded to wanting to please librarians and spend time in the library because of the stories. However, most storytellers are aware of their ability to hold attention and redirect focus with any new group. Beyond that we also saw story listening bring children closer via new interests and practices when we observed them in free time and fantasy play.

Donna came across some listeners playing at "being storytellers" during recess. They took turns imitating her, sitting in a chair and recalling the story she had told them a few days before, matching her intonation and gestures, even to the point of crossing their legs in a manner she wasn't aware of doing while she narrated. When she asked them if she crossed and uncrossed her legs often when telling stories, they said, "all the time." Equally impressive was how they not only mimicked but internalized new vocabulary and verbal expressions from the story, repeating them when role-playing but also in conversations and games.

As a fourth-grade teacher and also in year-long school residencies as a storyteller, Patrick observed similar outcomes. Catch phrases, expressions, and highly descriptive or evocative words from his stories migrated into his pupil's creative writing. Older children, whom he taught to tell stories to younger ones, mimicked his language when sharing tales, but also in their jokes and friendly conversation. Patrick often described characters as "taller than you can tell me and taller than I can tell you" or "more beautiful than you can tell me and more beautiful than I can tell you"; more than one student picked this up, joking "you've given me more homework than you can tell me and more homework than I can tell you."

Early education scholars describe such moments as "a community of minds," a theoretical framework based on ToM to better understand social-cognitive development during early childhood (Nelson et al. 2003). This "narrative view of child development presents an experiential child who explores the social, cultural, and physical world in search of meaning in collaboration with social guides and companions" (Nelson 2010, p. 42). This appears to be a restatement of Dewey's ideas. Through stories children intentionally participate in an adult "community of minds...where knowledge is shared, experiences are given meaning, and communities and cultural traditions evolve through discourse and joint action" (Faulkner 2017, p. 94).

In many ways, story listening is a "meeting of minds." Storytelling makes experiences pleasurable and relaxing, and encourages intense focus, perfect for managing a class. Donna's sons often use storytelling with their own children on a long car ride or when they've been stuck in the house on a rainy day to focus their children's attention or calm them down. Frequently, educators intuitively do the same. "We all have days as teachers when it feels like nothing is working the way we'd planned. On those days when we're frazzled or the children are particularly unfocused, we turn to a story. A quick story energizes the whole community. It acts as a re-set button" (MacDonald et al. 2013, p. 27). Folklorist, author, and academic Betsy Hearne came to the Lab School to speak to the eighth-grade students about writing. When she realized the students were not particularly attentive, she turned to them and said, "I'm going to tell you a story." She quietly began telling a ghost story. Suddenly the students were attentive and still. She finished the story and returned to her talk on writing. The students had no trouble staying on topic after that.

Telling a story can become an incidental reward by the teacher or librarian casually mentioning, "when we finish doing ... I'll tell you a story." Or a means to get everyone to focus. And because you are the one delivering this particular delight, and you are looking at each person as you tell, each listener wants to please you, to get you to tell again. This happens with *cumulative* and *congruent* experiences. With *frequent, regular story listening experience*, the tranquil self-control and ability to direct interest during story listening becomes habituated and transferred to other activities. That's why Betsy Hearne's story was able to quiet the eighth graders. *They had grown up hearing stories.*

This is not new information. Again, a century ago teachers realized story listening relaxed mental and nervous tensions: storytelling established a sympathetic relationship, formed habits of attention, and served as a disciplinary measure (Emerson 1959, p. 24). Julia Darrow Cowles said that

> through storytelling a teacher may come into so close and happy a relationship with her pupils that they will respond to her suggestions and be molded by her influence to a degree not easily attainable by any other means. A story may be told as a means of restoring order in a roomful of restless children, or when some untoward occurrence has brought the tension of the school discipline dangerously near to the breaking point. This use of the timely, the appropriate, story is worthy of consideration by teachers far beyond the primary grades. (Cowles 1916, p. 17)

When story time behaviors transfer to other classroom activities, some then identify the resulting practices and classroom atmosphere as a storytelling classroom or school (Egan 1988, 2005; Wajnryb 2003). As Wilson put it, schools incorporating regular storytelling have a palpable "culture of storytelling": not everyone tells stories, but all are aware of stories and storytelling and their potential uses and outcomes in education (Ryan 1997, p. 15; Wilson 2006, p. 103).

Achieving a storytelling classroom means storytelling is constant and cumulative: "constant because a positive classroom dynamic is not produced by any one specific act but requires constant nourishment and exercise; and cumulative in that shared experiences, including shared stories, gradually constructs a 'storied' class" (Wajnryb 2003, p. 17). A storytelling classroom's consistent "feel good" factor cements a community. "[A] class of happy smiling faces, of responsive, spontaneous and friendly people, sends a message of personal success to the teacher. And it is a two-way thing, a symbiotic relationship, in which teachers and students resonate in and energise each other" (Wajnryb 2003, p. 157).

Anthropologists and folklorists often describe communities using storytelling to teach and discipline the young. Doucleff and Greenhalgh reported on Jean Briggs's and others' accounts of life with Inuit families. When a child acts inappropriately Inuit parents tell that child a story relating to "bad" behavior, acting it out dramatically and playfully. Relating what happened raises questions, and through playing, they find answers. The child learns and internalizes what is acceptable and expected (Doucleff and Greenhalgh 2019; Briggs 1971). This is practiced by many cultures, particularly among First Nation and Native American families, and other non-European societies. Hugh Yellowman, a Navajo storyteller and leader, said, "If my children hear the stories, they will grow up to be good people; if they don't hear them, they will turn out to be bad" (Toelken 1976, p. 155, 1998; Pellowski 1977, p. 48).

Storytelling is like a magic charm with a powerful hold. In the Lab School the weekly storytelling begins with kindergarten classes and continues through second grade. When the third graders come to the library their first week of a new school year, they are reminded that now they will not be coming for storytelling time; their librarian will tell them stories only occasionally. Even though they were informed of this at the end of second grade, it suddenly becomes real. The librarians have had students crying, protesting how unfair that is, and begging for stories during their regular library time. Librarians often found third graders "looking for research materials" when younger children were listening to stories.

When we asked our second-grade informant what would happen if there were no more stories in the world, she considered it for a moment and replied:

> That would be very sad for me. Like, if there was a law against people telling stories. Stories usually calm people down.

She protested vehemently when she got to third grade.

Virtues, character traits, interests, attitudes, values: Collateral learning outcomes from story listening

Virtues, character traits, interests, attitudes, values—as educational goals all of them fall within the moral realm of the "right" or "proper" or "just." Now when we ask about the function or purpose of narrative, one answer (some might say the only one) is: to moralise. Narratives present us with stories about how to live or how not to live our lives (Jackson 1986, pp. 124–125).

All societies use stories to teach and challenge cultural norms, and many kinds of traditional tales have lessons and morals. Stories and narrative events both relate actions, based on sentiments, that divulge values, beliefs, and prejudices, and "every time we tell ... a story, we are marking out those values that we wish to share" (Daniel 2012, p. 86).

Consciously or subconsciously listeners analyze or judge characters and their actions, anticipating many different outcomes that might arise from situations in the narrative. This "promotes the idea that someone can choose how to react to circumstances—and that different responses produce different outcomes that are worth thinking about beforehand—either as goals worth being pursued or as fates best avoided" (Spaulding 2004, p. 11). Some stories seem designed to provoke on purpose.

One example is the open-ended folktale, a genre categorized as "endless" or "circular." (A well-known one: "It was a dark and stormy night. And the captain said, 'Tell us a story!' So his first mate began, 'It was a dark and stormy night. And the captain said...'") Open-ended stories can pose moral dilemmas. A Nigerian-American student shared such a story with Patrick:

> Two friends stole yams because they were starving; when one friend stole the other's share, they fought over it. An old man invited them into his house to help resolve the argument. Being poor and hungry, the man whispered to his son to steal the yams. Advised to share equally, the friends agreed but then realized the host had stolen their yams, protested, and left, still angry and starving. The old man called his son for the yams, only to be asked, "Yams? What yams?"

The story ends with the question,

> Who was the worst? Those who stole from the farmer, the friend who stole from a friend, the host who stole from guests, or the son who stole from his father?

Stories that leave the listeners with no clear resolution stay with the listener. Although this is a moral tale, it lacks a conclusive "right" answer. Listening to a story like this provokes an experience that leads to having real thoughts and emotions involved in difficult decision making, and in considering concepts about right and wrong, fairness and justice. Patrick has witnessed pupils react to *The Yams Story* by nearly bursting with frustration trying to convince classmates their opinion is correct, while others calmly and rationally attempt a good argument for their point of view (and often end up contradicting themselves). Listeners predict and reflect as if they have lived this situation themselves. It allows them to see similar situations with the same critical eye. Sometimes listeners will say that they would never react the way a character did in these stories. Which is exactly the reaction society is hoping for.

Another genre provoking such thinking is the trickster tale. In trickster tales the protagonist is always a crafty creature who uses cunning to get what he wants or just cause mayhem. A famous American trickster is Brer Rabbit (cousin to Anansi, whose stories originated in Ghana and traveled through West Africa to the Caribbean). Brer Rabbit made quite an impression on one former student:

> I did remember Brer Rabbit. It made me really uncomfortable because it was trickier [ibid] and I wasn't sure you were supposed to be tricking anyone. The morality of it really bothered me. The stories that involved deception or trickery, I felt were wrong. I felt like I was a kid and knew better. I understood that someone was...I just wasn't sure if it was ok. I wasn't sure if deception was ok.

The interviewee doesn't reveal how or if he resolved this discomfort. But the potential transformative effect seems evident to us. Continuing to carry that unease as an adult could help in life dilemmas, like how to vote in an election, what to trust in the news, and choosing business partners or making financial decisions.

G. K. Chesterton said that in fairy tales "one idea runs from one end to the other—the idea that peace and happiness can only exist on some condition. This idea, which is the core of ethics, is the core of the nursery-tales" (Chesterton 1908, p. 253). Therefore fairy tales "have a key role to play in children's social cognition" (Fisher 2001, p. 20) and seem pretty straightforward in representing morals: clear good and evil, with virtues rewarded. But absorbing such values doesn't happen simply through pointing out good guys win and bad ones get punished. In actuality, a child listener's reaction to a fairy tale can reveal their understanding that right and wrong are not always clear cut.

As an example, Donna's grandson Everett had an intense reaction when he heard her telling of *Alexandra the Rock Eater* (Van Woerkom 1978). He was tremendously concerned every time Alexandra tricked the baby dragon and his mother. Everett thought it was very mean and unfair of her—even though in this story Alexandra is clearly good. She is just trying to get food for her one hundred hungry children and the dragons steal animals and gold from others. Developmentally it is quite natural for a five-year-old to struggle with gray areas of morality. Everett kept asking his father if it was okay for Alexandra to trick the dragons. After much discussion, he decided it *was* okay because the dragons were basically mean, and Alexandra was basically good. A difficult lesson made easier with a story.

Librarian-storyteller Amy Spaulding believed that:

> One of the greatest gifts someone can give to future generations is values: kindness, generosity, integrity, and the value of hard work, in particular, which can be carried on, regardless of individual situation. Inculcating this belief is what traditional stories have been so good at. (Spaulding 2011, p. 134)

Folk and fairy tales do this by challenging reason, knowledge, and the natural order. Regular exposure provokes children to challenge both stories and the narrator. Is it true? Is it real? Did that really happen? They often try to figure out how fantastic things in stories occur, creating explanations and their own versions of the story. This helps develop critical literacy. "Critical literacy is the ability to analyse the presentation of information and identify how the presentation influences listeners' and readers' understanding of the information" (Zipes 2004, p. 53; pp. 71–71). Questioning what they hear or read, finding answers, developing explanations, and their own versions of stories heard transform students' thinking.

We both tell fairy tales and find they provoke children to question and strike out independently to find "the truth." Patrick once told second graders an Irish story about a fairy thorn tree—hawthorn trees where one encounters fairies. Irish fairies don't have gauzy wings and magic wands, and cause mayhem by being mildly mischievous to downright dangerous. As soon as he finished the usual barrage of questions hit: "Is that true? Did it really happen?" He reported he wasn't certain, he knew people in Ireland who believed it, and that information about such things was in books and online. Next morning three second graders reported finding photographs of fairy thorn trees on the Internet and books about them. They solemnly informed him that only *some* hawthorn trees are fairy thorn trees, *most* are *not*. Stories tell which really are, so everyone stays clear (which results in staying safe and protecting nature—not bad values to have).

Psychologists and cultural critics have considered connections between the mind and fairy tales. Bettelheim analyzed them from a Freudian perspective, describing their emotional, symbolic, and therapeutic importance for children (Bettelheim 1976). He explained that magical and darker elements represent children's fears and anxieties. Listening to these stories with trusted caregivers, children learn to cope with strong emotions while simultaneously being acculturated into society's mores.

Taking another approach, Jack Zipes proposed fairy tales "stick" and have effect because once humans

> developed the cognitive capacity to recognize, refine, and retain specific narratives that spoke to the conditions in their environment about survival, they began to...shape diverse stories artistically to make better and more efficient use of them. (Zipes 2006, p. 13)

He asserts that fairy tales create a paradox, creating disorder to create order while simultaneously expressing utopian desires. Representing instinctual drives and social conflicts, communicating information, and questioning social codes, fairy tales lead listeners to think critically (Zipes 2006, p. 15). Or as he puts it in lectures and conversations, a fairy tale—or any story—should get children and adults asking, "What is this story about? Why is this person telling it to me? What do they want? Most importantly, how can I make this story my own?" Thoughtful questioning, silent or spoken, is part of how values become inculcated through story listening. Not from films and versions by adults presenting sentimental, simple renditions preaching that everyone who's good gets a happy ending.

STORY LISTENING EXPERIENCE AND DIVERSITY

Vivian Paley believed that story "is the essential culture builder and learning tool of any society or family or classroom" (Paley 1995, p. 93), and MacDonald stated:

> Students need to see themselves in the curriculum and also need to have a way of learning that others are different from themselves in their customs and traditions. Stories are the perfect vehicle for this. They can function as a mirror to see their own culture reflected, or as a window through which they can view the cultures of others. (MacDonald et al. 2013, p. 97)

Both are correct. In theory, hearing a story can give a sense of how it feels to be in another's skin, of the similarities and differences the characters have with listeners, allowing them to view and accept others' situations and cultures. But in reality, this can become too simplistic if educators rely on it happening because children hear one or a few "multicultural" stories a year. As we've enumerated, story listening experience must be cumulative to have affect. A London storyteller and theater director with whom Patrick works, Arti Prashar, once wittily observed, "Multiculturalism isn't just a once-a-year event with a storyteller coming dressed in a sari to tell stories while everyone eats samosas."

Teacher and consultant Debbie Diller pointed out, "the numbers of African-American, Hispanic, and Asian students in the U.S. public schools are steadily increasing. Yet the teaching force remains predominantly white, middle class, and female" (Diller 1999, p. 820). The theory of cultural discontinuity, describing possible mismatches between school and home culture because of how teachers and school systems interact with and ask students to work, is one challenge arising from diversity that has been addressed by storytelling (Diller 1999, p. 821; Dyson and Geneshi 1994; Groce 2004).

Our argument for more storytelling in classrooms stems from our belief, and professional experience, that the benefits of story listening experience outlined so far transform all students, of any ability or background. Whether they are of a minority, have special needs that are physical, intellectual, emotional, or behavioral, speak a home language different from the teaching language at school, or come from a lower socioeconomic environment, stories have potential to catch all listeners' attention, taking them into experiences resulting in the subsequent positive outcomes we've described. The variance in practice comes in how the teacher or librarian-storyteller prepares and adapts the storytelling for the needs of specific groups.

To do this Dorothy Strickland advises that:

> Teachers who work with these children should enter the classroom informed as much as possible about the broader population from which these children come—both from reading the relevant literature and from first-hand experiences with others who belong to that population. They should also learn as much as they can about the immediate community and the families of these children. They should use what they learn as a framework for understanding who and where their learners are. (Strickland 1994, p. 330)

Strickland is speaking about African American students, and her advice is echoed by many educators specializing in tackling injustice and failure in contemporary education (Bell 2003; Groce 2004; Diller 1999; Quintero and Rummel 2015). "With the growing number of culturally and linguistically diverse students, curricula must move," and the answer, Humes says, is "representing the cultural and linguistic experiences and learning styles of these students" (Humes 2016, p. 6).

Groce and Diller, in separate studies, described teaching colleagues, students, and parents from different racial, ethnic, or linguistic backgrounds to engage with each other. They listened to each other's personal, family, and traditional stories, and read children's and adult literature by authors from backgrounds different than their own. We should all do this more often. Storytelling is a social art so use it to socialize: there's no rule stopping teachers, parents, and kids swapping stories. In both Groce's and Diller's studies teachers familiarized themselves with the history and context of stories from other traditions and languages in their communities, learning that "storytelling and counter-storytelling are powerful tools to create urban learning environments" (Humes 2016, p. 13).

In the modern educational and cultural contexts, counter-stories are those especially created by writers and tellers, and by teachers and students, to confront stereotypes and injustice (Humes 2016). Counter-storytelling and traditional stories both subtly challenge power and unquestioned social norms (Humes 2016; Delpit 1992; Bell 2003). Some folk tales indirectly do this (such as the open-ended and trickster stories). Much folklore comes from oppressed individuals and communities, and speaks truth to power, expresses injustices, and shows how to cope with adversity (Warner 1994, 1998; Zipes 1983, 2007). Within educational contexts, counter-stories play a role in both developing and expressing critical literacy, but also in strengthening ties or addressing problems within a community.

While a "narrative style of teaching can collect a great diversity of people under a common umbrella of understanding" (Paley 1995, p. 96), there are risks of relying unintentionally on generalizations and stereotyping (Humes 2016; Strickland 1994; Diller 1999; Delpit 1992). Zipes warned that multiculturalism, by emphasizing cultural differences, can conceal class differences and how class operates within ethnic groups (Zipes 2004, p. 246), which can result in failure to increase learning attainment for all. Active engagement with other people and their cultural traditions, and using counter-stories, avoids the tokenistic multiculturism described above. It means a better chance that diverse needs are met.

We can see the results of considered, well-developed approaches to storytelling. Patrick and other tellers like Liz Weir and Arti Prashar come across classrooms where students and their teachers really know little about each other's backgrounds. They have met teachers who have not heard the different languages that fellow teachers or their own students use at home. They rarely shared with each other any stories from their respective backgrounds. As visiting tellers, all three encourage teachers and children to start swapping stories, across all languages.

An exception to this, and a good example of how active cultural engagement through storytelling works, came from middle school teacher Betty Rosen. She told stories every week to her eleven- and twelve-year-old students, and insisted on including non-English speakers. Rosen encouraged these pupils to tell or write their stories in Turkish, Greek Cypriot, Urdu, or whatever their preferred language was. Then colleagues and parents helped to translate the tales which she shared with the entire class (Rosen 1988, pp. 29–38). Her school was in an economically deprived part of London, with associated behavioral and academic challenges. Sharing students' stories saw considerably positive outcomes, not only in academic attainment but in creating a school community based on respect and mutual understanding.

As Rosen told it, her students "made rich stories. And while making those stories together, they made friendships. And they also made peace. And none of it was nonsense" (Rosen 1988, p. 162). This is just how Bruner saw education as serving changing societies.

> Such groups provide not only a locus for instruction, but a focus for identity and mutual work. [...] The balance between individuality and mutual effectiveness gets worked out within the culture of the group; so, too, the balancing of ethnic or racial identities and the sense of the larger community of which they are a part. (Bruner 1996, pp. 81–82)

ENDURING EFFECTS: LISTENING TO THE LISTENERS

As practitioners, we have long recognized that change occurs when children listen to stories. We believe that change is a form of transformative or collateral learning that endures over time. Studies in other fields have provided insight on this, but as we have mentioned before, story listening outcomes are not easily measured and few have been measured directly. We sincerely hope we've identified some enduring effects that are currently being, or will become, subject to scientific enquiry. But some may never be quantified in empirical studies.

Even so qualitative and subjective evidence remains valuable. Professor Hamish Fyfe pointed out anecdotes and stories are testimony. In societies prioritizing standardization, testing, and measured outcomes, stories may appear irrelevant but "testimony" still has impact (Fyfe et al. 2009; Llewellyn et al. 2017). He's supported by Francesca Polletta who observed personal stories can still "open the way to construct more truly universal standards" (Polletta 2006, pp. 82–83). Keeping this in mind, we'd like to consider a few more "testimonials" from our informants.

The effects enumerated in previous chapters have been within individuals, while this chapter discussed those having relevance in the wider community. From the Progressive Era to recent times, librarians, teachers, and professional storytellers have made sweeping claims regarding the influences of storytelling. Story listening led to appreciation of "good" literature and a life-long habit of reading for pleasure (Thorne-Thomsen 1901, 1903; Chubb 1902, 1929). It developed the well-rounded, healthy and informed individuals necessary for a democratic society (Chubb 1902, 1929). As stated, these claims are difficult to measure, especially over a lifetime.

But what some alumni said, without our prompting, points to effects that they believe have lasted from childhood into their adult lives. Two suggested their experience of hearing stories while young contributed to their decisions regarding how to take part in and contribute to society. One we quoted at the end of the first chapter, the young woman who intended to train as an elementary school teacher because experiencing storytelling in primary grades made her want to do the same, to "pass that along." The other believed story listening experience made him a better lawyer, and explained how he saw it working:

> I look for stories at work, too. Representing people who are trying to get on disability, I get caught up in their personal story. I think storytelling is persuasive. I think stories make an emotional connection and if you communicate it to the judge, it can help you. And so I try to learn their story in order to try to express it both through our written memorandum to the judge and through testimony. I end up talking with my boss thirty minutes a day about the story of one client as opposed to the story of another client, and I just don't see other people seeking those sorts of things out.

Many mentioned story listening experience contributing to their love of stories and reading. Like the flow they experienced when hearing stories, reading for pleasure became addictive.

> It's funny, I get stuck in bookstores and libraries. I don't just go to a bookstore to look at one book, unless I'm going to get someone a present. Even then I go to look for a book that someone might like *and* look at books I'll like. I go looking for stories more than other people.

> I've studied writing in college, so I've been in a lot of classes with very pretentious English students and they criticized genre fiction quite heavily. And yet what I like about genre fiction…is that they explore the same topics, the same dramas that great literature explores…. For some reason, to me, that is a more powerful way to evaluate these motives, hang-ups, and fights than discussing them in an everyday context. Which is what a lot of people miss about genre fiction.

> If you didn't have a story, you got hungry for one. I missed it. I make time to read, to find stories. Now I know it's meditative, because I have trouble sleeping if I don't read before I go to bed. But I just thought it was something we were supposed to do and not like "eat your spinach" supposed to do. You're supposed to have a story, like you're supposed to have lunch. Period. If you don't, you get hungry.

Our informants clearly and emphatically see the outcomes of listening as being deeply ingrained in who they now are. What story listening did to them, and for them, remains with them to this day.

One young woman summed it up perfectly:

> It was just that at school, during that time of the day, you were supposed to have a story. And then you get older, and you say, "Damn. I wish I had story time."

THREE APPLES FELL FROM THE SKY: ONE FOR THE STORYTELLER, ONE FOR THE LISTENER, AND ONE FOR WHOEVER UNDERSTANDS

Rather than summarize this chapter by listing the social effects discussed, we trust the point has been made. There's ample anecdotal and qualitative evidence supporting the claim that storytelling in education produces results. Questions arising from what we've learned regarding story listening experience present scholars in education, literacy, psychology, and neurology many starting points to initiate quantitative research on the topic. Whether viewed as collateral, experiential, transformative, or mimetic learning, story listening experience should be used in schools and libraries as a central part of the learning experience. Story listening experience should be examined. The outcomes of story listening should be recognized and incorporated into educational settings. The story of story listening needs to be heard.

We would like to finish with a true story—really, it happened. It's history.

Long ago in old Baghdad, the caliph gave a banquet celebrating the birth of his son. Many came bearing gifts. But a young teacher named Mehelled Abi arrived empty handed. Honoring the caliph, he explained, "Because the young prince will have many fine presents of gold and jewels, I will give something different. Every day I will come and tell him stories." Mehelled Abi kept his word and when the prince became a man, and then caliph, he was wise and much loved. Baghdad became one of the happiest, most enlightened civilizations the world has ever seen, famous for arts, sciences and mathematics, learning that benefits us to this day. In Europe the young caliph was known as Aaron the Upright, Aaron the Wise, and Aaron the Just. His real name was Haroun-al-Rashid. On his command *The Thousand and One Nights* was first written, because of his love of those stories and desire to share them with the world. In a museum in Budapest, a scroll tells this history, written by Mehelled Abi himself, who finishes his account by saying, "All this came to pass because of the seeds sown by the tales, told by a teacher."

References

Addams, Jane, *Twenty Years at Hull House* (New York, Boston, Chicago, San Francisco: The MacMillan Company, 1912), pp358–61.

American Library Association. 1929. *Children's Library Yearbook*. Chicago: American Library Association.

Bell, L. A. 2003. Telling Tales: what stories can teach about racism. *Race, Ethnicity and Education.* 6(1): 3–28. DOI: https://doi.org/10.108 0/1361332032000044567.

Benton, M. and Fox, G. 1985. *Teaching Literature 9–14.* Oxford: Oxford University Press.

Bettelheim, B. 1976. *The Uses of Enchantment, The meaning and importance of fairy tales.* New York: Alfred A. Knopf.

Briggs, J. 1971. *Never in Anger, portrait of an Eskimo family.* Cambridge, MA and London: Harvard University Press.

Bruner, J. 1996. *The Culture of Education.* Cambridge, MA: Harvard University Press.

Carey, J. 2005. *What Good Are the Arts?* London: Faber and Faber.

Chambers, A. 1991. *The Reading Environment. How adults help children enjoy books.* Avonset, Bath, England: The Thimble Press.

Chesterton, G. K. 1908. Fairy Tales. In *All Things Considered*, 253–272. London: Methuen and Co.

Chubb, P. 1902. *The Teaching of English in the Elementary and the Secondary School.* New York: The Macmillan Company.

Chubb, P. 1929. *The Teaching of English in the Elementary and the Secondary School, revised and largely rewritten.* New York: The Macmillan Company.

Cowles, J. Darrow. 1916. *The Art of Storytelling, with nearly half a hundred stories.* Chicago: A. C. McClurg and Co.

Cuffaro, H. K. 1995. *Experimenting with the World. John Dewey and the early childhood classroom.* New York and London: Teachers College Press.

Daniel, A. K. 2012. *Storytelling Across the Curriculum.* London and New York: Routledge.

Delpit, L.D. 1992. Education in a multicultural society: our future's greatest challenge. *The Journal of Negro Education* 6(3): 237–249. DOI: https://doi.org/10.2307/2295245.

Diller, D. 1999. Opening the dialogue: using culture as a tool in teaching young African American children. *The Reading Teacher.* 52(8): 810–828. jstor.org/stable/20204703.

Doucleff, M. and Greenhalgh, J. 2019. How Inuit Parents Teach Kids To Control Their Anger. https://www.npr.org/sections/goatsandsoda/2019/03/13/685533353/a-playful-way-to-teach-kids-to-control-their-anger?t=1598031048947. Accessed July 20, 2020.

Dyson, A. H. and Geneshi, C. (Eds). 1994. *The Need for Story: Cultural diversity in the classroom.* Urbana, IL: National Council of Teachers of English.

Edmiston (Enciso), P. 1990. *The Nature of Engagement in Reading: Profiles of three fifth-graders' engagement strategies and stances.* Doctoral Dissertation. Columbus: Ohio State University. https://etd.ohiolink.edu/!etd.send_file?accession=osu1487684245466824anddisposition=inline.   Accessed August 17, 2017.

Egan, K. 1988. *Teaching as Story Telling, An alternative approach to teaching and the curriculum.* London: Routledge.

Egan, K. 2005. *An Imaginative Approach to Teaching.* San Francisco: John Wiley and Sons, Inc.

Emerson, L. S. 1959. *Storytelling, the art and the purpose.* Grand Rapids, MI: Zondervan Publishing House.

Engel, S. 1995. *The Stories Children Tell.* New York, Oxford: W. H. Freeman and Company.

Faulkner, D. 2017. Young children as storytellers: collective meaning making and sociocultural transmission. In *Storytelling in Childhood. Enriching language, literacy and classroom culture* .Eds. Teresa Cremin, Rosie Flewitt, Ben Mardell, and Joan Swann. London and New York: Routledge.

Fisher, R. 2001. Philosophy in primary schools: fostering thinking skills and literacy. *Literacy,* 35(2): 67–73. DOI: https://doi.org/10.1111/1467-9345.00164.

Fyfe, H., Wilson, M., Pratt, S., Rose, M., Lewis, K. 2009. *A Public Voice: Access, digital story, and interactive narrative.* Pontypridd and Cardiff: University of Glamorgan (South Wales) and BBC Wales.

Gold, J. 2002 *The Story Species, our life-literature connection.* Markham, Ontario and Allston, MA: Fitzhenry and Whiteside.

Gopnik. A. 2011. What do babies think? TedTalk. https://www.ted.com/talks/alison_gopnik_what_do_babies_think/footnotes?language=en. Accessed August 1, 2020.

Gopnik, A. 2012. Scientific thinking in young children: Theoretical advances, empirical research, and policy implications. *Science* 337, 1623–1627. DOI: https://doi.org/10.1126/science.1223416.

Groce, R.D. 2004. An experiential study of elementary teachers with the storytelling process: interdisciplinary benefits associated with teacher training and classroom integration. *Reading Improvement.* 41(2): 122–128.

Gurdon, M. Cox. 2019. *The Enchanted Hour:* the miraculous power of reading aloud in the age of distraction. London : Piatkus.

Haven, K. 2007. *Story Proof: the science behind the startling power of story.* Westport, Ct.; London: Libraries Unlimited.

Howes, C. and Ritchie, S. 2002. *A Matter of Trust. Connecting teachers and learners in early childhood curriculum.* New York and London: Teachers' College Press.

Humes, L. 2016. *African American Storytelling: a vehicle for providing culturally relevant education in urban public schools in the United States.* St. John Fisher College: Doctoral .Dissertation.

Immordino-Yang, M. H. 2009. Our bodies, our minds, our selves: Social neuroscience and its application to education. In *The Neuropsychology of Emotional Disorders.* Eds. S. Feifer and G. Rattan Middletown, MD: School Neuropsychology Press

Immordino-Yang, M. H. 2016. *Emotions, Learning and the Brain. Exploring the educationalimplicationsofaffectiveneuroscience.*NewYork,London:W.W.Norton and Company.

Jackson, P. W. 1986. *The Practice of Teaching.* New York: Teachers' College Press.

Killick, S. and Boffey, M. 2012. *Building Relationships through Storytelling.* Cardiff: The Fostering Network / Rhwydwaith Maethu.

Killick, S. and Frude, N. 2009. The Teller, the tale, and the told. *The Psychologist.* 22(10): 850–853. https://thepsychologist.bps.org.uk/volume-22/edition-10/eye-fiction-teller-tale-and-told. Accessed June 10, 2020.

Lecce, S., Caputi, M., Pagnin, A., Banerjee, R. 2017. Theory of mind and school achievement: The mediating role of social competence. *Cognitive Development.* 44: 85–97. DOI: https://doi.org/10.1016/j.cogdev.2017.08.010.

Llewellyn, D. H., Rohse, M., Bere, J., Lewis, L. and Fyfe, H 2017. Transforming landscapes and identities in the south Wales valleys. *Landscape Research,* 44(7): 804 821. DOI: https://doi.org/10.1080/01426397.2017.1336208.

MacDonald, M. Read, Whitman, J. MacDonald, and Whitman N.F. 2013. *Teaching with Story, classroom connections to storytelling.* Atlanta, GA: August House.

Mardell, B. and Kucirkova, J. 2017. Promoting democratic classroom communities through storytelling and story acting. In *Storytelling in Early Childhood, Enriching language, literacy and classroom culture.* Eds. Teresa Cremin, Rosie Flewitt, Ben Mardell and Joan Swann. London and New York: Routledge.

Murphy, K. 2020. *You're Not Listening. What you're missing and why it matters.* London: Vintage Digital.

National Literacy Trust (2008). *Kick into Reading, promotional video.* https://www.youtube.com/watch?v=5_btrzKC0E4andt=71s. Accessed July 31, 2008.

Nelson, K., Plesa Skwerer D., Goldman S., Henseler S., Presler N., Fried Walkenfeld F. 2003. Entering a community of minds: An experiential approach to "Theory of Mind". *Human Development,* 46(1): 24–46. DOI: https://doi.org/10.1159/000067779.

Nelson, K. 2010. Developmental narratives of the experiencing child. *Child Development Perspectives.* 4(1): 42–47. DOI: https://doi.org/10.1111/j.1750-8606.2009.00116.x.

Nelson, O. 1989. Storytelling: Language experience for meaning making. *The Reading Teacher.* 42(6): 386–390. jstor.org/stable/20200160.

Oatley, K. 2011. *Such Stuff As Dreams, the Psychology of Fiction.* Malden, MA, Oxford, Chichester, W Sussex: Wiley-Blackwell.

Paley, V.G. 1995. Looking for magpie, another voice in the classroom. In *Narrative in Teaching, Learning and Research.* Eds. Hunter McEwan and Kieran Egan. New York: Teachers College Press.

Pellowski, A. 1977. *The World of Storytelling.* New York and London: R. R. Bowker Company.

Polletta, F. 2006. *It was Like a Fever. Storytelling in protest and politics.* Chicago and London: The University of Chicago Press.

Quintero, E. P., and Rummel, M. K. 2015. New York, Bern, Frankfurt, Berlin, Brussels, Vienna, Oxford, Warsaw: Peter Lang.

Roney, R. C. 1996. Storytelling in the classroom: some theoretical thoughts. *Storytelling World.* 9:7–9. ERIC Number: ED405589.

Rosen, B. 1988. *And None of It Was Nonsense: The power of storytelling in school.* London: Mary Glasgow Publications Ltd.

Ryan, P. 1997. *Word in Action: A report.* Derry/Londonderry: Verbal Arts Centre.

Ryan, P. 2001. Secure storytelling: Storytelling in prisons and young offenders' units. In *All Our Children, Library Services to Children at Risk.* Ed. Anne Marley, 42–44. London: CILIP (Charted Institute of Librarians and Information Professionals), Young Libraries Group (YLG) Publication.

Spaulding, A. 2004. *The Wisdom of Storytelling.* Lanham, Toronto, Oxford: The Scarecrow Press, Inc.

Spaulding, A. 2011. *The Art of Storytelling, Telling truths through telling stories.* Lanham, Toronto, Oxford: The Scarecrow Press, Inc.

Stephens, G. J., Silbert, L. J., Hasson, U. 2010. Speaker–listener neural coupling underlies Successful Communication. *Proceedings of the National Academy of Sciences of the United States of America.* 107(32): 14425–14430. DOI: https://doi.org/10.1073/pnas.1008662107.

Strickland, D. 1994. Education African-American learners at risk: Finding a better way. *Language Arts.* 71(5): 328–336. jstor.org/stable/41961974.

Sturm, B. W. and Nelson, S. B. 2016. With our own words: Librarians' perceptions of the values of storytelling in libraries. *Storytelling, Self, and Society* 12(1): 4–23. DOI: https://doi.org/10.13110/storselfsoci.12.1.0004.

Symons, D.K., Peterson, C.D., Slaughter, V., Roche, J., Doyle, E. 2005. Theory of mind and mental state discourse during book reading and storytelling tasks. *British Journal of Developmental Psychology.* 23(1): 81–102. DOI: https://doi.org/10.1348/026151004X21080.

Thorne-Thomsen, G. 1901. Reading in the third grade. *Elementary School Teacher and Course of Study,* 2(3): 227–35.

Thorne-Thomsen, G. 1903. The educational value of fairy-stories and myths. *Elementary School Teacher* 4(3): 161–7.

Toelken, B. 1976. The "pretty languages" of Yellowman: Genre, mode and texture in Navajo Coyote narratives. In *Folklore Genres.* Ed. Dan Ben-Amos, 93–123. Austin: University of Texas Press.

Toelken, B. 1998. The Yellowman Tapes, 1966–1997. *The Journal of American Folklore* 111(442): 381–91. DOI: https://doi.org/10.2307/541046.

Van Woerkom, D. 1978. *Alexandra the Rock Eater, an old Rumanian tale retold.* New York: Knopf, Random House.

Wajnryb, R. 2003. *Stories. Narrative activities in the language classroom.* Cambridge, England: Cambridge University Press.

Warner, M. 1994. *From the Beast to the Blonde. On fairy tales and their tellers.* London: Chatto and Windus.

Warner, M. 1998. *No Go the Bogeyman*. Scaring, lulling and making mock. London: Chatto and Windus.

Watts, J. 2008. Benefits of storytelling methodologies in fourth- and fifth-grade historical instruction. *Storytelling, Self, Society*, 4(3): 185–213 DOI: https://doi.org/10.1080/15505340802303519.

Wilhelm, J. D. 2007. "It's in our control" Engaging and teaching literacy to boys. *Middle Matters*. 15(4): 1–3. https://www.naesp.org/sites/default/files/resources/2/Middle_Matters/2007/MM2007v15n4a5.pdf.   Accessed August 20, 2017.

Wilhelm, J. D. 2008. *"You Gotta BE the Book": Teaching engaged and reflective reading with adolescents*. New York and London: Teachers College Press.

Wilson, M. 2006. *Storytelling and Theatre, contemporary storytellers and their* art. Houndmills, Basingstoke, Hampshire; Palgrave Macmillan.

Yeshurun, Y., Swanson, S., Simony, E., Chen, J., Lazaridi, C., Honey, C. J., Hasson, U. 2017. Same story, different story: The neural representation of interpretive frameworks. *Psychological Science*. 28(3):307–319. DOI: https://doi.org/10.1177/0956797616682029.

Zadbood, A., Chen, J., Leong, Y. C., Norman, K. A., and Hasson, U. 2017. How we transmit memories to other brains: Constructing shared neural representations via communication. *Cerebral Cortex* 27(10): 4988–5500. DOI: https://doi.org/10.1093/cercor/bhx202.

Zipes, J. 1983. *Fairy Tales and the Art of Subversion, The classical genre for children and the process of civilization*. New York: Wildman Press.

Zipes, J. 2004. *Speaking Out, storytelling and creative drama for children*. New York and London: Routledge.

Zipes, J. 2006. *Why Fairy Tales Stick. The evolution and relevance of a genre*. New York and London: Routledge.

Zipes, J. 2007. *When Dreams Came True, Classical fairy tales and their tradition*. New York and London: Routledge.

CHAPTER 6

"How often would you have to tell stories to your own children to have them get this experience?" *Reasons for investing time in storytelling and how to get started*

> When a storyteller and child meet, life is enriched for both by the sharing of a story. To have laughed together, shared excitement or sadness, experienced wonder and emotion, establishes a mutual feeling of warmth and comradeship, an experience worth all that it may cost in time and energy. (Colwell 1980a, p. 5)

To summarize what we've presented so far: When children are exposed to oral stories on a regular basis, story listening has the potential to support aspects of cognitive and neurological development. These include emergent literacy behaviors like narrative understanding, visualization and vocabulary, and executive function processes such as attention and inhibition. Frequent story listening has also been found to help form a sense of community in a classroom through the development of theory of mind, metacognition, and empathy. Such psychological processes affect attachment to the teacher and fellow students, which is helpful in classroom management while also developing self-confidence and mutual understanding and respect among students of diverse backgrounds and abilities. This latter use of storytelling can provide means of exploring identity and culture. Story listening also plays a role in establishing critical literacy and independent thinking. And as quantitative research into the effects of story listening expands, there may well be as yet undiscovered connections between story listening and learning outcomes.

© The Author(s), under exclusive license to Springer Nature Switzerland AG 2021
D. Schatt, P. Ryan, *Story Listening and Experience in Early Childhood*, https://doi.org/10.1007/978-3-030-65358-3_6

All of which explains why we want to encourage classroom teachers and school librarians, as well as administrators, to consider incorporating frequent oral storytelling to students in their charge. Frequent being the operative word. When storytelling is only an occasional school activity, whether presented by a teacher or visiting teller, you cannot expect to see the results we have previously discussed. Although a school visit from a professional storyteller is pleasant and entertaining, that type of experience does not produce the outcomes outlined throughout this book.

We know this is asking a lot. There are three basic hills to climb if you want to start a storytelling program. First of all, some policy makers and administrators see storytelling and other arts programs distracting teachers from mandatory curricula and testing. The opposite has been shown to be true. Dr. Linda H. Humes uncovered "overriding literature that affirms the benefits of storytelling...as a viable pedagogy for educating all students and supporting teachers," and went on to state "that when schools integrate the arts into the academic schedule, students fare better in all curricula areas" (Humes 2016, p. 83). Other reports confirmed that when teachers use any artform in their teaching, and were supported while learning to do so, many positive outcomes occur since "arts experiences enhanced all phases of schooling" (Garvis 2009, p. 25). Administrators noted considerable increase in teaching competence among teachers integrating any art form in their teaching habits, and teachers reported administrative encouragement for integrating arts in classroom practices refreshed their commitment to teaching (Longley 1999, pp. 12, 13).

We know that learning to tell stories is practicable and helps achieve curricular goals. We've seen it happen, as have countless authors and poets including John Masefield, Walter de la Mare, Pura Belpre, Elizabeth Cook, and Philip Pullman. These and other writers have collaborated with teachers and librarians to train them in storytelling. Professor Jack Zipes, who has had significant success and experience in creating a storytelling pedagogy delivered by teachers and artists in public schools, knows that

> teachers can become storytellers and assist students to become storytellers in a communal setting. Teaching is a collaborative effort among children, their families, and experimental programs. Storytelling is integral to teaching, and I want to stress that storytelling for me is not simply method or means. Storytelling involves a socio-political perspective that is closely bound to the experimental method of animating children to become storytellers of their own lives. (Zipes 2018, p. 41)

In addition, the self-confidence and emotional experience derived from story listening that we've described is not just something for your students. You'll be amazed at how fulfilling it is to tell and how different storytelling feels from reading a book to the children.

Secondly, we are aware that some school systems are concerned about adding storytelling as a classroom or school library practice because they say they don't have the money to put toward another program. But the truth is that storytelling is economically efficient. The primary costs consist of some basic training, and support for teachers or librarians as they are becoming tellers.

When it comes to training, we know from experience that an after-school workshop or a one-day training course aren't sufficient for any educator to establish a classroom storytelling habit. Evaluations of teacher training methods show short-term training can't embed any specialist skills. Leach and Conto point to "evidence that a brief in-service training workshop for teachers aimed at increasing specific instructional and managerial behaviors in their classrooms had only temporary effects on their performance" (Leach and Conto 1999, p. 461). Analysis of pre-service training for elementary school teachers shows small success in providing sufficient confidence or capability for them to effectively deliver specialist lessons like drawing, singing, drama, or storytelling (Garvis 2009, p. 23). Investment in initial storytelling training is worth it when what it produces is sustainable with minimal further costs.

The only way to ensure storytelling becomes a solid feature in a school is when there is regular support and encouragement *for a few months to a year after initial training*. This ensures that storytelling becomes a solid feature in a school (Leach and Conto 1999, pp. 459, 461; Longley 1999). Once stories and the skills to tell them are learned, it costs nothing to maintain the practice; it's self-sustaining. There is no hardware, software, or consumables to replace or update. You only need access to either a library with a folklore collection, or the Internet. Costs are minimal when compared to what can be achieved in the long term.

And lastly, we have observed that the absolute biggest obstacle to beginning a storytelling program in your class or at your school is telling your first story. So, this final chapter provides some basic tips for storytelling and encourages you to follow through on your own by sampling any of the story collections and storytelling manuals listed in Appendix B.

Every title has been used successfully by us or other librarians, teachers, or storytellers. We've also included stories in Appendix A which are models for you to study and use. And Appendix C provides case studies reporting how individuals, who never expected to tell stories, managed to establish storytelling practices and delighted in doing so.

Given all the benefits, and knowing the reasons why all the obstacles should be challenged, we hope you will take us up on telling your first story.

How to begin

> When I was in the business of helping students to become teachers, I used to urge them to tell stories in the classroom—not read them from a book, but stand up and tell them, face to face, with nothing to hide behind. The students were very nervous until they tried it; they thought that under the pressure of all those wide-open eyes, they'd melt into a puddle of self-consciousness. But some of them tried, and they always came back the next week and reported with amazement that it worked, they could do it. (Pullman 2002)

You can do it too. Begin by starting small. Don't bite off more than you can chew, especially if you are doing this on your own. A good way to begin is to choose a book or story that is already familiar. For instance, *The Three Billy Goats Gruff*, *The Three Little Pigs*, or *The Mitten*, or a story or book that was a childhood favorite. Many people start this way.

Our good friend, librarian, and storyteller Professor Janice Del Negro did. As a young librarian reading Paul Galdone's *The Three Billy Goats Gruff* for the umpteenth time to an assembly of twenty-five preschoolers in her public library, she noticed that the children were looking at her face, not the book. Realizing she knew every page from constant re-readings, Janice put the book down and told from memory. She discovered much by doing so.

> The complex and sometimes exasperating logistics of holding the book so everyone could see were eliminated; everyone could see without difficulty because now the pictures were in their imaginations. As the story went on the children scooted up toward my chair, until they were clustered closely around my feet, some even holding on to the hem of my pants. When we got to the end of the story, the cries [were] of "Again! Do it again!" (Del Negro 2014, pp. 2–3)

She uncovered not only the powerful effect story listening experience has but also, more importantly, how easily she could transition from read aloud to told stories. We all can do this.

Find a place where you can tell the story to yourself. Keep the book near in case you get stuck and can't remember what comes next in the story you're learning. Del Negro reminds us that there are as many ways and means to learn stories as there are storytellers. "Some tellers write a bullet list of plot points and phrases; some draw story maps with simple stick figures and lollipop trees to reflect the action; some use flash cards; some imagine the story as a movie in their heads" (Del Negro 2014, p. 69). Patrick loves long walks and has found the easiest way for him to rehearse a new story is in his head or by saying it aloud while walking along a beach or on nearby hills. When Donna first began to tell stories, she would get into the bath, run the water, and tell the stories to herself. It removed her from the chaos of young children running around and allowed her to be in a "safe place" to make mistakes or feel foolish. These many years later, she still finds it the best place to learn a new story.

Once you've found your preferred method and your "safe" spot, tell the story to yourself a few times. When you're starting out it's best not to stray too far from the original, but you should be comfortable with the language used and make it your own. Don't memorize the author's words. That way you won't freeze if you forget "the exact" wording. If there are repeated phrases (trip trap, trip trap), include those as written. But it doesn't matter if you say, "The name of all three goats was Gruff", or you say, "Gruff was what the goats were called." You get the idea.

When you are comfortable that you can tell the story well enough that you don't need the book—pick a time to tell it. Then you should DO IT. Have the children come to wherever it is you usually read to them. Kids are wonderful, kind listeners, and you will be amazed at how focused on your face and voice they will be, quickly taking in the story like a special treat. British author and teacher-trainer Elizabeth Clark said whatever story you tell isn't just any story. Once learned, it's yours, "and the children will meet us half-way and make it theirs too, be very sure of that" (Clark 1927, pp. 18–19). Explain to the children that you are going to TELL them a story. You can say that telling means there are no pictures to look at, only the pictures they see in their heads. Ask them to allow the storyteller (you) to tell the whole story before asking questions (this may be hard for very young children). And then begin. It is that simple and will change your world.

When inexperienced storytellers start telling they are often surprised by the students' response to their story. Many assume the children won't listen, or, as Philip Pullman admitted as a young teacher, think they might "melt into a puddle of self-consciousness" (Pullman 2002). In our experience you don't have to get very far into the story for even the more restless students to get sucked into the narrative and sit entranced. All the aspects of the story's content and the human act of narrating come into play, and you'll quickly sense which elements work best for you. You'll naturally absorb that knowledge, reincorporating it in later tellings. We've frequently mentioned how rhythm and repetition in the phrases and actions entice listeners to join in, whether they're instructed to or not. Some teacher- and librarian-storytellers can be startled by this. But relax, you'll soon be used to it and recognize it as a natural, even desired, reaction. It's a matter of finding the amount and type of audience participation which works best for you, which

> depends on the teller; the age, and the sophistication of their audience; and the teller's comfort level with ad libbing or improvising [....] Participation such as this can be a lot of fun for both the teller and the audience, but it doesn't always need to be this active or rambunctious! Sometimes it can be as subtle as eye contact between teller and audience members; soft audience chanting and small movements ... ; or chants during the telling of a nursery rhyme.... (Chasse 2009, pp. 54–55)

Eventually, as you get used to listeners' responses you will find their participation helps you pace and embellish your storytelling. It also increases your connection to the listener and enjoyment while telling.

When the story ends observe the students' reactions. When you tell it next (to the same group or a different one), take note of how that group acts. Every time will be slightly different. This is not only because each time you tell a story you change it a little, or because audiences are different. Librarian-storyteller Amy Spaulding observed that when she told the same story to different audiences, she had "gotten very different responses from hearers. ... None of those responses was wrong; each was right from the perspective of the hearer, for it was what had been evoked in them" (Spaulding 2011, p. 125). Even if your pupils heard you tell the story before, they will pick up something they missed the first time or find another meaning just from the changes that have occurred in them. And as we've already discussed, both you and the listener have had new experiences, heard new language, learned new things since the last time you told the story.

There was a third-grade student at Lab who had broken her leg. One day, instead of going on a class field trip, she stayed in the library. She observed Donna telling the same story to two different groups of students. Afterward the student asked Donna why she told a different story to each group. Donna had told the same story—but to the observer it seemed different. The first group had been calm when they entered the library while the second group had come in from recess and needed to be brought into the story; different classes, different personalities, dynamics, and energy levels. They responded differently to the stories and Donna responded by changing her cadence and the details of the story. That is what the student noticed and so she heard them as completely different tales.

When a story ends, children will give you feedback in different ways. Often they'll tell you that they liked the story and want to hear it again, immediately. Sometimes they'll cheer and clap as though you're an opera diva. But the most common response is one of calm, quiet satisfaction in how the story turns out. Academic and teacher-trainer Jacqueline Harrett told her storytelling classes:

> Often the end of a story is greeted by silence, which is something novice story-tellers may find unnerving. This silence, however, is simply indicating that the listeners have absorbed the story and they are bringing themselves back from fantasy to reality. Occasionally the end of a story is met by a universal sigh. Far from indicating disillusionment, this is a symptom of involvement with the fantasy world to such a degree that the participants, the listeners, have difficulty extraditing themselves from the fantasy world they have become so involved in. (Harrett 2004, p. 14)

Take that moment and appreciate the calm the story has created.

DEVELOPING A REPERTOIRE OF STORIES

When you are starting to build a repertoire, work through the stories you are already familiar with. That will give you a good base. But when ready to move onto other stories, start looking through the story books and digital resources listed in Appendix B. These provide hundreds of titles to choose from. The digital section includes links to recordings of storytellers telling tales you might enjoy enough to want to learn. Some people find it easier to discover a story they like by reading the material while others feel that hearing a story told fixes itself more readily in their memory. We suggest that if you're going to use the digital resources you may want to listen to but not watch the telling. This way you won't be tempted to mimic someone else's gestures or facial expressions. In Appendix B there are also websites with digitalized story collections. Many of these are earlier publications now out of print, but are worth consulting, especially for their stories.

Once you've looked through a few collections, choose a story that appeals to you. For reasons we've already discussed traditional folk and fairy tales are a good place to start. We suggest this because folk and fairy tales are composed of narrative elements easily remembered and designed for oral telling. Which partially explains why they have survived over time. Look for narratives with easily summarized plot and character elements, particularly variants of familiar favorites. You can easily retell these lesser-known versions your own way. Margaret Read MacDonald tells her students, "No two tellers present their tales in exactly the same way. Each new teller brings another perspective, another way of telling the tale. And all are useful." She goes on to confirm that "there is no correct version of a folktale, there are myriad retellings, each differing from the others" (MacDonald 1993, p. 11). *Jack and the Beanstalk* is a good example: you can quickly list the characters, rhyming verses, and main plot points, and retell it in your own way. Finding lesser-known versions of *Jack and the Beanstalk*, such as *Molly Whuppie* (Reeves 1954; Jacobs 1968b; Campbell 1890, 2009; Minard 1975a; Lurie 1980, 2005) or the Appalachian story *Jack and the Beantree* (Chase 2003a) will provide you with a "new" story that you already nearly know.

Look for stories with repetitive, rhythmic language, and repeated actions and events. These features are indicative of tales that are "tellable"; such features encourage participation and engage listeners, especially young ones. Another helpful element making folktales memorable and "tellable" are the minimal but evocative details for characters, objects, or settings (e.g., "white as snow and red as blood," "a house of gingerbread," "a steed of bells," or "east o' the sun and west o' the moon"). And it's all right to take two or three different versions of a tale, mixing together elements you like from each to create your own new story. "The more familiar you are with the available body of folktales for youth, the more expert and discriminating you will become at selecting stories for telling" (Del Negro 2014, p. 5).

When you've chosen your story or maybe even before, you should consider who you will be telling to. If young children are your main listeners, it probably would be best to not tell a *Bluebeard* type of tale, even if you love the story. Knowledge of what appeals to child listeners, and an understanding of their developmental stages is of great importance when selecting a story. Her first year at UCLS Donna chose to tell *Hansel and Gretel* to a first-grade class the first week of school. The children didn't know her at all and hardly knew their teachers. The school year had begun four days earlier and more than a few of the kids were probably feeling "abandoned." Half-way through the story two children were crying and one child had crawled into his teacher's lap and was covering his ears. Donna had to stop the story and calm the children down. If she had told that story six months later, the children would have trusted her to tell them a story that ended well, they would have been comfortable with their teachers and it would have been fine. Lesson learned. Know your audience!!

We have found that four- and five-year-olds love tales containing silly humor, particularly in which they anticipate an outcome before the protagonist. Stories like, *Soap, Soap, Soap* (Chase 2003b; Birdseye 1993; Dulemba 2009), *Epaminondas* (Merriam and Schart Hymen 1968; Bryant 1905; Maestro and Cabassa 2010; M. Valeri 1982), and *The Woman Who Flummoxed the Fairies* (Nic Leodhas 1962; Minard 1975c; Forest 2013) have worked well for us. On the other hand, all listeners respond to stories with clear, strong emotions they can identify with: good examples of such tales are *A Necklace of Raindrops* (Aiken 1968) and *Cap o' Rushes* (Williams-Ellis 1960; Minard 1975b; Jacobs 1968a; Ryan 2001; Ness 1995).

Although it will get easier over time, finding stories and building a repertoire is an extremely challenging task. Margaret Read MacDonald, in her manual *The Storyteller's Start-up Book*, provides great tips for learning a story in one hour (MacDonald 1993, pp. 17–22). Although that may be attainable, the problem for most beginners is finding a story in the first place. Eileen Colwell, another renowned librarian-teller, said selecting a story is hard "not because of a shortage of material but because there is so much to choose from" (Colwell 1980a, p. 13). Story selection requires reading through collections or listening to stories while at the same time developing the ability to recognize what story you can easily learn, remember, and tell effectively. Although you must be aware of your audience when telling, you must pay attention to yourself when choosing what to learn. If a teller does not love a story it will be difficult to tell the story with any enthusiasm. Any story you choose you will tell a lot, to yourself, out loud, to your audience. If you are lukewarm about it, you're going to hate that story after a while. Every storyteller has made this mistake, you don't want to make it often.

Stories are not universally appealing to all tellers. It has to do with a story's cadence, the cultural feeling of a story, and the general likes and dislikes of the storyteller. Donna is most comfortable telling stories from Eastern Europe, Asia, and Africa. She likes to tell stories that have tricksters or scare the listener, she also tells a few stories that leave her audience in tears. Patrick is most comfortable with stories from Ireland, Italy, Northern and Western Europe, and American folktales that derived from Ireland and Britain. He loves stories that are humorous or variants of well-known classic adventurous folk and fairy tales, and he, too, likes telling scary stories.

In time, you'll figure out what stories you are most comfortable telling. As Del Negro observed, becoming a storyteller is a process. "If you start telling stories today, you will know a great deal more a year from now about how stories work. Storytelling is a subtle passion that takes over your life; you will begin to see pattern and story wherever you go" (Del Negro 2014, pp. 153–154). At some point you will undoubtedly learn a story that you decide never to tell again after the first time. We've all done it. Luckily once you've learned a story that you do enjoy telling, you never lose it. And people love hearing the same stories again and again. And you'll love telling it.

The best and really the only way to learn to tell is to actually tell. We can't stress that enough. Learning stories, and developing a library or classroom storytelling practice, is initially time consuming. We recommend starting slowly—learning just one story a month will eventually lead to a wonderful personal repertoire. The more stories you learn and the more often you tell, the easier it becomes to learn and tell new stories you encounter. Once learned, the story becomes yours, and is never really lost.

WHAT TO LOOK FOR

Behind all storytelling is one basic essential, wide reading! …. This is not a tedious duty but a journey of delight in which new byways are constantly discovered, intriguing incidents which demand further investigation, new fields of interest. Even a large collection of stories may only yield one story that is just right for the occasion and about which we can feel enthusiasm. The kind of story we choose may differ for each one of us, but once shared with children, the telling becomes a memorable and pleasant experience for both the children and ourselves. (Colwell 1980b)

As we have previously said, traditional folk and fairy tales consist of narrative elements designed to be memorable, to be compelling, and to suit oral presentation. Because this narrative form does work so well, many picture books, including those relating an original story in a contemporary setting, maintain narrative features similar to folktales (see Chap. 3), making these picture book stories easy to learn and relay orally.

In recommending that you look to traditional folk and fairy tales for your repertoire, we're not unaware of criticisms regarding this genre.

The popularity of the traditional folktale for youth has swung back and forth throughout the history of children's literature: folktales are too violent for young listeners and readers; folktales are unrealistic and give children a skewed vision of the world; female characters in folktales are passive and boring; folktales published for youth are not culturally authentic. The pendulum swings: folktales help children develop their imaginations and creativity; heroines and heroes in folktales teach listeners to persevere and overcome obstacles; the narrative schema of traditional folktales can teach children basic story structure and assist in the acquisition of literacy skills; folktales can help children connect to their own and other cultures. (Del Negro 2014, p. 152)

Remember, these stories were originally meant for adult audiences, as we mentioned previously. There are traditional tales with elements we now acknowledge to be sexist, racist, too violent, or too sexual, largely because they reflect mores of a different time or culture. And remember what we said in the last chapter: seek advice on stories and talk with other storytellers with backgrounds and interests in story traditions different from your own. Understand and acknowledge the culture a story comes from, and don't adopt a story by relying on stereotypes or limited knowledge.

Three things to remember while acknowledging these undesirable aspects. First, there are countless versions of almost all folk tales. If the fairy tales you know best are the classic animated cartoon versions of *Cinderella*, *Snow White*, and *Sleeping Beauty*, you will be surprised at how strong, independently active, and intelligent female characters are in older versions or in variants of these stories from other cultures and languages.

The second thing to keep in mind is that you can always amend narratives to tell a story any way you wish: make changes, combine versions, and incorporate various details from different variants. Folktales come from "the folk." You can choose those stories that speak to your listeners' histories, the cadence of their speech, or that of your own. Folktales have carried the culture's mores and beliefs since before written language. Choose what you and your listeners will be comfortable with.

And as we've now said many times, it's important to tell a story you like, with which you are comfortable. There are plenty of stories to choose from. And remember, unlike written stories, oral stories are alive, they change with time, culture, the teller, the listeners, and dozens of other factors effecting the story as it is being told.

If you would like to read more about the history and criticism of folklore, it's worth looking at works by scholars such as Jack Zipes, Amy Spaulding, Kay Stone, Deanna Reder, Marina Warner, Trudier Harris, and Maria Tartar. They and many others have written fascinating studies on the evolution, meaning, and politics of folk and fairy tales. These can provide insight on how you can fashion stories and your overall repertoire to suit your own tastes and situation. Appendix B provides information on all kinds of sources for finding, learning, and interpreting stories, as well as for developing a storytelling practice within your and your institution's educational philosophy.

Managing a Story Time

Stories are everywhere, you tell them to your friends, children tell them to their parents, and strangers even exchange stories waiting for a bus or at parties. But to achieve the outcomes of story listening that we've identified, setting up a regular context and controlled environment will be most effective. It may seem obvious, but you need to think about the space where you share a story. It should be a quiet corner, comfortable enough for all of your group to sit, with few distractions such as background noises, passing traffic, or bright sunlight coming in from a window. The sort of space that allows good eye contact and a sense of inclusion or coziness. Most classrooms in nurseries and primary grades have a quiet carpeted corner with cushions, or something similar like an alcove or quiet room nearby. Libraries, too, usually have a corner or carpeted area designated for story times.

And like any classroom practice, when telling a story, things can go wrong for reasons beyond your control. When it happens, a novice story-teller's natural tendency is to assume they chose the wrong story, told it incorrectly, or used the space in some way not conducive for listening. Upon reflection you'll often find it wasn't what you did but some external factor. Liz Weir, the colleague we mentioned earlier working in Northern Ireland during the "The Troubles," likes to call these events "Disasters We Have Known and Loved" when teaching storytelling courses.

We all have such disasters. Liz often recalls how her story times took place in community centers. Volunteers running these summer camps loved having librarians come to tell stories but didn't always appreciate the need for quiet and keeping interruptions to a minimum. Now and then some adult caregiver would walk in during a story and shout, "Jimmy, you're wanted!" to fetch a child going home early. Or a well-meaning organizer would loudly interrupt to offer her a cup of tea just at the most dramatic part of a tale. The UCLS story program happened in a library corner surrounded by stacks holding much of the collection; it was under-stood those particular shelves were off limits during story times. Even so, one substitute teacher believed she could make herself invisible and crept behind the librarian-teller mid-story, crawling like a discombobulated cat burglar determined to find a book. One September when Patrick was teaching, the summer building renovations continued into the Fall term. Somehow the builders always seemed to work just outside his area at story times. He thought it was simply bad timing until one of the workers approached him in the faculty room to ask how the previous day's story finished, as he had left early so didn't hear the ending. It turned out the builders timed their work so they could hear the stories.

All sorts of incidents like these can briefly take away your listeners' attention or cause you to lose your place in a story. But don't take it per-sonally! Donna was once telling a Polish story entitled *Nine Crying Dolls*, adapted by Anne Pellowski (Pellowski 1980). The story involved crying dolls being secretly given to families that had new babies. Donna was say-ing the occupations of the families the dolls were being given to when "Priest" popped into her head and out of her mouth. Clearly the Priest did not have a new baby. Donna thought quickly and said he was on his way to visit his niece who had just had a new baby. No one, but Donna, noticed the mistake. The more you tell stories, the more your students will get used to listening and keep that intense focus, so they won't notice such distractions, or any mistakes you might make.

Again, many of the manuals we list in the second Appendix provide detailed advice on how to manage actual story times. *Storytelling: Art and Technique* provides excellent advice for everyone but especially for librarians in both school and public libraries (Greene and Del Negro 2010, pp. 95–109). Jacqueline Harrett's booklet *Tell Me Another...Speaking, Listening and Learning Through Storytelling* is great for teachers who want to start storytelling and aren't sure how to begin. And Alistair Daniel's *Storytelling Across the Primary Curriculum*, also aimed at teachers, gives a detailed and more academic set of guidelines (Daniel 2012, pp. 42–54). Another quite detailed guidebook is *Storytelling, Process and Practice* by Norma J. Livo and Sandra A. Rietz (Livo and Rietz 1986, pp. 92–117). *The Storyteller's Start-Up Book* (MacDonald 1993) and *Teaching with Story, classroom connections to storytelling* (MacDonald et al. 2013) both present a generic overview for establishing story time practices over an academic year. And there are plenty of other good resources.

DEVELOPING A STORYTELLING PRACTICE

Teachers and librarians will attend workshops on storytelling, leave with great enthusiasm and with all intentions of telling stories to their classes. We know it is not that easy to carry through with these intentions. We've provided scores of storytelling workshops and courses, training hundreds of educators, librarians, and others who work with children. We've recognized that at the end of these sessions, many are motivated and positive, and leave determined to start incorporating regular storytelling into their routines. And some do! But keeping in touch with those we train, we are aware that once people are back into the routine of their classroom, or library, these intentions may not be realized.

This is not a failure on anyone's part. Jeffrey Wilhelm, and Zeichner and Tabachnick (Zeichner and Tabachnik 1981), produced research showing that

> pre-service and in-service teachers who go back to school will articulate new theories and develop rich repertoires for implementing these new theories, but then quickly revert to teaching the way they were taught or in the ways they have taught before. Why? The pressures of traditional structures and expectations are difficult to overcome. (Wilhelm 2008, p. 34)

After a storytelling course you're on your own. Institutional habits, routines, and attitudes gradually come back and take over. Although it can be disconcerting, having other adults to tell to and learn stories with can be an important support.

In their respective studies on multicultural and African-American storytelling in education, Dr. Robin D. Grace and Dr. Linda H. Humes found that teachers in storytelling courses were uncomfortable telling stories before their peers, but they all loved listening to the stories told by all the other teachers in the class. By overcoming the discomfort, and then by sharing more stories from their own mixed backgrounds and learning from each other, the teachers found not only could they tell stories and use storytelling in their classrooms, they found material from cultural traditions outside of their own that they loved and could be comfortable sharing with students. (Groce 2004; Humes 2016). If you can find a way to be comfortable and maintain that sort of support, it's a great way to avoid the ennui which can come from working solo.

It is easy to be overwhelmed at the premise of telling stories weekly or even monthly, especially when you have never told a story. Particularly if you are the only person in your school or library doing this. As we've said, start with one story that you already are familiar with and love. Your listeners will benefit from whatever stories you tell them as you gradually build a storytelling habit for them and for yourself. Maybe at the end of a year you have three or four stories. Great! That's more stories than your students had up to now. Next year you start with those stories and learn a few more. And so it goes.

Some people starting with this gradual approach find by the second or third year they recall more stories from their youth which they can tell, or just find it easier and quicker to learn a new story. Patrick often saw this with the soccer project previously mentioned, where he trained professional players and coaches to tell stories to children. At first the athletes told just the stories he introduced in the training. But they quickly expanded their repertoires on their own initiative. In each case, it came from drawing on their own knowledge and experiences. Coaches at Manchester United soon recalled local ghost stories they'd heard as children and started including them in their story times. An education and community officer with Arsenal Football Club asked Patrick what he thought about *The Iliad* and *The Odyssey*. He'd studied Classics at Oxford University but hadn't considered relating those myths as part of his club's educational outreach work until the storytelling program had run awhile.

This sort of expansion of story repertoire happened repeatedly with players and coaches at other clubs.

Should a school, library system, or school district decide to support a large number of teachers, classroom assistants, librarians, and principals to develop their storytelling, our advice would be to consider an extended course, not an after-school workshop or one day of training on a teachers' institute day. Plenty of independent storytellers with education or library backgrounds can deliver such extended consultancy. Some locales have colleges or universities offering storytelling classes. We've found that an intensive three- or four-day course, all in one week or delivered one day a month, with three or four short follow-up digital meetings over the next six months, develops a sustainable storytelling practice among those faculty who get involved willingly.

Regular storytelling practices can be developed in a single class, or on a class-by-class, school-by-school, or district-wide basis. But an important part of that development is networking and coordination. When we've provided training, participants linked by the same administration have created support networks to build sustainable mutual practices. Participants keep in touch and meet a few times each semester, practicing their storytelling on each other and alerting each other to sources for new stories. Social media makes this even easier to do.

This is a tried and tested practice in public libraries. Amy Spaulding, former librarian-storyteller in New York Public Libraries, described this as "trading programs".

> Because it took considerable effort to learn several stories for a program, the storytellers would trade programs, going to different libraries to perform for a different audience. This made it more formal and also gave children the chance to hear different storytellers with different backgrounds and telling styles. (Spaulding 2004, p. 58)

A variation of this can happen within one school. Three or four people in one building can each agree to learn one story a month. Each week, one of the team tells the story they learned that month to their own and other classes, so all students hear a new story every week. And as an added plus, telling the same story several times to different groups over a short period is a terrific way to reinforce a new story in your repertoire. After two or three years, everyone has enough stories they can maintain a weekly story time on their own, should they wish.

When a number of people are telling stories to the same groups of students, good communication between all the tellers is imperative. You may think you can all keep track mentally of what's in your repertoire and what you've told to different classes, but when your repertoire becomes substantial that's easier said than done. It's one reason UCLS's storytelling program developed a record-keeping system that provided us with useful data for this book. Since the late 1940s, librarians have recorded the title of each story told, its source, who told it, and to whom it was told. They continue to do so today. It allows them to keep track of who has told what stories, so no one repeats a story to the same group without meaning to. The older records also provide information on tales that later librarian-tellers can revive when they want to refresh their repertoire.

At whatever stage of your development as a storyteller, record keeping allows a chance to reflect on how you're doing and on how the children respond. Livo and Rietz also encourage and provide advice on program planning and record keeping as a means of critiquing your practice to keep it fresh (Livo and Rietz 1986). Keeping records like this helps you assess your growth as a storyteller and also provides data for your peers, administrators, and parents to better understand the impact and role of something that's ephemeral and, to the untrained eye, can seem frivolous. And, as we are encouraging reading specialists and cognitive and neurological scientists to look more closely at the impact of the oral story listening experience, the more records teacher- and librarian-storytellers can provide the more fruitful such studies will be for us all.

Keep in mind that all this should be enjoyable for both you and the students. As Paddy Tunney, a wonderful old traditional Irish singer, storyteller, and poet, told Patrick once, "Doing a study on storytelling…that's not dull and boring, that's the most wonderful thing you could do to pass the time!" (Ryan 1995, p. 1). Have fun with it. Stories have been told since before written language developed. The beauty of it is that it is natural to us, captures our imagination, helps us learn and feel wonderful about the experience, and connects to those experiencing story listening with us. Make each story you learn yours, in your own unique way. The stories will change with your listeners. They will change as you develop as a teller. They will change how you and your listeners see the world.

SO THE STORY IS TOLD, AND HERE IT BEGINS: A CONCLUSION
AND PLEA TO CONTINUE

We started this book with the hope of opening our readers up to the idea that listening to oral stories is a vital educational tool that achieves more than just promoting an interest in books. Those achievements are found in the areas of cognitive, moral, and social development. Such gains require repeated story listening exposure and manifest over time. In Philip Jackson's book *Life in Classrooms*, he reminded educators that their main job "is to get the students to pay attention while engaged in activities judged to be of benefit to them. And that, as every teacher knows, is a large order" (Jackson 1968, p. 103). Storytelling grabs attention and provides a beneficial activity leading to plenty of follow-up activities, both formal and informal, making story listening real collateral learning.

In our opinion, and experience, with better understanding of the effects of story listening, educators can use storytelling in a way that makes them better teachers and helps them avoid the pedagogical fallacy of which Dewey speaks of when he stated, "the main point of a lesson may not be the most important thing learned and taken away" (Dewey 1938, p. 48). We hoped we could help you understand that the trend toward viewing storytelling as an entertaining "add-on," redundant of reading instruction and not essential in education, may very well be a misunderstanding of real benefits gained from the story listening experience.

We also believe there are great benefits to be gained in having academic researchers work with educational storytellers to design research directly measuring the outcomes attained from frequent story listening. These studies would allow policy makers relying on quantitative data to consider how best to include oral storytelling in early childhood education programs. If we know the effects of long-term story listening, we will be able to encourage educators to incorporate storytelling at the heart of their best practices.

One teacher-librarian, who developed her storytelling mid-career, sums it all up for us:

> Storytelling has changed my whole approach to my job as a teacher-librarian. I once attended a conference where a storyteller said if we, the teacher-librarians, aren't telling the stories, who will? I knew what he said was true, but I didn't have the confidence or understanding of how I could start telling stories to my students. Now I've learned not only how to tell stories but

also how easy it is to implement into my weekly routine. I have blossomed as a person and professional through the telling of stories. This past year the connections I've made to the students who come to the library have been stronger and I've marveled at how students of all ages are held captive merely by the power of the story. Before...I told on average two stories a year, and those not very well. Now, I tell at least two stories a week and I cannot imagine my job without this essential element.

REFERENCES

Aiken, J. 1968. *A Necklace of Raindrops: and other stories.* London: Cape.

Birdseye, T. 1993. *Soap, Soap, Don't Forget the Soap!* New York: Holiday House.

Bryant, S.C. 1905. The story of Epaminondas and his auntie. In *Stories to Tell to Children: fifty-one stories with some suggestions for telling*, 63–68. Boston and New York: Houghton Mifflin Company.

Campbell, J. F. 1890, 2009. Maol a Chliobain. In *Popular Tales in the West Highlands*, 244–248. Paisley and London: Alexander Gardner (1890) and London: Abela Publishing (2009).

Chase, R., Ed., compiled by Halpert, H. 2003a. Jack and the bean tree. In *The Jack Tales*, 29–35. Boston: Houghton Mifflin Harcourt.

Chase, R. 2003b. Soap, Soap, Soap! In *Grandfather Tales: American-English Folk Tales*, 115–132. Boston: Houghton Mifflin Harcourt.

Chasse, E. J. 2009. *Telling Tales, a guidebook.* New York: Neil-Shuman Publishers, Inc.

Clark, E. 1927. *Stories to Tell and How to Tell Them.* London: University of London Press Ltd.

Colwell, E. 1980a. *Storytelling.* London, Sydney, Toronto: The Bodley Head.

Colwell, E. 1980b Storytelling. Each one of us as a potential storyteller." *Books for Keeps.* 5. http://booksforkeeps.co.uk/issue/5/childrens-books/articles/other-articles/storytelling. Accessed March 1, 2020.

Daniel, A. K. 2012. *Storytelling Across the Curriculum.* London and New York: Routledge.

Del Negro, J. M. 2014. *Folktales Aloud, Practical Advice for Playful Storytelling.* Chicago: ALA Editions.

Dewey, J. 1938. *Experience and Education.* New York: Collier Book.

Dulemba, E.O. 2009. *Soap Soap Soap / Jabon Jabon Jabon*, Raven Tree Press.

Forest, H. 2013. *The Woman who Flummoxed the Fairies.* Atlanta, Georgia; August House.

Garvis, S. 2009. Improving the teaching of the arts: Pre-service teacher self-efficacy towards arts education. *US-China Education Review*, 6(12): 23–28. Eric Number; ED511176.

Greene, E. and Del Negro, J.M. 2010. *Storytelling: Art and Technique*. Santa Barbara, California, Denver, Colorado, Oxford, England: Libraries Unlimited.

Groce, R.D. 2004. An experiential study of elementary teachers with the storytelling process: interdisciplinary benefits associated with teacher training and classroom integration. *Reading Improvement*. 41(2): 122–128.

Harrett, J. 2004. *Tell Me Another…Speaking, listening and learning through storytelling*. Leicester, England: UKLA Minibook Series.

Humes, L. 2016. *African American Storytelling: a vehicle for providing culturally relevant education in urban public schools in the United States*. St. John Fisher College: Doctoral Dissertation.

Jackson, P. 1968. *Life in Classrooms*. New York, London: Holt Rinehart and Winston.

Jacobs, J. 1968a. Cap o' Rushes. *English Fairy Tales (English Fairy Tales and More English Fairy Tales)*, 34–37 London, Sydney, Toronto: The Bodley Head

Jacobs, 1968b. Molly Whuppie. In *English Fairy Tales (English Fairy Tales and More English Fairy Tales)* 79–82, London, Sydney, Toronto: The Bodley Head.

Leach, D. J. and Conto, H. 1999. The additional effects of process and outcome feedback following brief in-service teacher training. *Educational Psychology*, 19(4): 441–462. DOI: https://doi.org/10.1080/0144341990190405.

Livo, N. J. and Rietz, S. A. 1986. *Storytelling, Process and Practice*. Littleton Colorado: Libraries Unlimited, Inc.

Longley, L. (Ed.) 1999. *Gaining the Arts Advantage: Lessons from the school districts that value arts education*. Washington D.C.: Department of Education / National Endowment for the Arts.

Lurie, A. 1980, 2005. Molly Whuppie. In *Clever Gretchen and Other Forgotten Folktales*, 45–52. Lincoln, NE: iUniverse, Inc. (1980, 2005).

M. Valeri, E de and de Sesé. 1982, *Epaminondas*. Barcelona: La Galera, S.A. Editorial.

MacDonald, M. R. 1993. *The Storyteller's Start-up Book*. Little Rock, AR: August House, Inc.

MacDonald, M. R., Macdonald-Whitman, J., Whitman, N.F. 2013. *Teaching with Storytelling; classroom connections to storytelling*. Atlanta, Georgia: August House.

Maestro, P. and Cabassa, M. 2010. *Epaminondas* Madrid: Carretera.

Merriam, E. and Schart Hymen, T. 1968. *Epaminondas*. New York and London: Follet Publishing Co.

Minard, R. 1975a. Molly Whuppie. In *Womenfolk and Fairy Tales*, 20–29. Boston: Houghton Mifflin Company.

Minard, R. 1975b. Cap o' Rushes. In *Womenfolk and Fairy Tales*, 77–82. Boston: Houghton Mifflin Company.

Minard, R. 1975c. The woman who flummoxed the fairies. In *Womenfolk and Fairy Tales*, 135–145. Boston: Houghton Mifflin Company.

Ness, C. 1995. The king and his daughters, a Punjabi story. In *The Ocean of Story, a collection of magical folk tales,* 22–23. Hemel Hemstead, Herts: MacDonald Young Books.

Nic Leodhas, S. 1962. The Woman Who Flummoxed the Fairies. In *Heather and Broom, Tales and Scottish Highlands,* 35–43. New York: Holt, Reinhart and Winston. 35–44

Pellowski, A. 1980. *Nine Crying Dolls: a story from Poland.* New York: Philomel Books.

Pullman, Philip. 2002. Voluntary Service. *The Guardian,* December 28, https://www.theguardian.com/books/2002/dec/28/society.philippullman. accessed April 22, 2020.

Reeves, J. 1954. Molly Whuppie. In *English Fables and Fairy Stories.* Oxford, New York, Toronto, Melbourne: Oxford University Press.

Ryan P. 1995. *Storytelling in Ireland: A Re-Awakening.* Derry/Londonderry: The Verbal Arts Centre.

Ryan, P. 2001. Cap o' Rushes. In *Shakespeare's Storybook,* 62–67. Boston and Bath: Barefoot Books.

Spaulding, A. 2004. *The Wisdom of Storytelling.* Lanham, Toronto, Oxford: The Scarecrow Press, Inc.

Spaulding, A. E. 2011. *The Art of Storytelling, Telling Truths through Telling Stories.* Lanham, Toronto, Plymouth, UK: The Scarecrow Press Inc.

Wilhelm, J. 2008. *"You Gotta BE the Book": Teaching Engaged and Reflective Reading with Adolescents.* New York: Teachers College Press.

Williams-Ellis, A. 1960. Cap o' Rushes. In *Fairy Tales from the British Isles.* New York and London: Frederick Warne and Co., Inc.

Zeichner, K., and Tabachnick, B. 1981. Are the effects of university teacher education "washed out" by school experience? *Journal of Teacher Education.* 32(3): 7–11. DOI: https://doi.org/10.1177/002248718103200302.

Zipes, J. 2018. Once Upon a Time: Changing the World through Storytelling. *Storytelling, Self, and Society.* 13(1): 33–53. DOI: jstor.org/stable/10.13110/storselfsoci.13.1.0033.

Appendix A: Some sample stories

The following folkloric tales all have elements which make a story easy to learn, remember, and tell. Some have aspects which appeal to children as young as four-years-old. Each has repetitive, rhythmic language and repetition of actions and images that create story listening experiences. *The Name of the Tree* and *The Seven-Headed Dragon* come from non-English speaking traditions. It's important to respect their cultural and linguistic origins as discussed in Chap. 5.

Don't Wake the Baby: a participatory nursery story

A word of warning: children aged five and under often think this story is the best joke ever. When you share it, be prepared to tell it lots of times. They'll want to hear it repeatedly and will retell it to others every chance they get.

This story will need an introduction. Explain that you're going to tell a story, but it only works if everyone has good imaginations. Ask if your listeners are good at pretending, if they can see things that they aren't looking at—for instance can they close their eyes and see the moon. Listeners will claim they can pretend really well.

Now, hold up one hand and with your other point at its palm and say you brought your baby to story time, and the baby is sitting in the middle of your hand, where you're pointing. Ask if they can see the baby. There

D. Schatt, P. Ryan, *Story Listening and Experience in Early Childhood*, https://doi.org/10.1007/978-3-030-65358-3

will always be at least one who says no. Explain that you can't begin until everyone sees the baby; curiosity and peer pressure will cause the more reluctant to suddenly "see" the baby. Then you start. As you tell the story, point to a thumb or finger to represent different family members. (By the way, they can be any family members: step-dad, cousin, auntie, best friend, the pet dog or cat, etc., not just the ones we say here.)

Don't Wake the Baby!

There's the baby!

Can you see the baby? Oh, good. There's the baby. See the baby?

Yes? Great.

(*from here, point in turn to each finger of the hand you're holding up*)

Mommy says, "Don't wake the baby!"

Daddy says, "Don't wake the baby!"

Grandma says, "Don't wake the baby!"

Grandpa says, "Don't wake the baby!"

Big sister says, "Don't wake the baby!"
(*Now look around for a few seconds.*)

Oh no! This is terrible! I forgot where I put the baby, I've lost the baby! Oh my goodness, I don't remember where the baby is.

Does anyone here remember where I left the baby? Do you know where the baby is? Can someone help find the baby? Can you point to the baby?

(*invite one child to come up and point to the baby—they'll touch the middle of your palm.*)

Oh, thank you! You found the baby! BUT! OH NO!

You touched the baby and you woke the baby up, and we said,

DON'T WAKE THE BABY!!!!

(*There's a chance the child will think they really did something wrong—just quickly reassure them.*)

Uh, oh....did I play a trick on you?

Oh, you're a good sport to take part in the joke. Everyone give (*child volunteer's name*) a big, big clap for helping find the baby.

(*to volunteer:*) But you're not the only one who would touch the baby. I think all the other kids who volunteered would do that. And if you tell this story to your sisters and brothers, to your parents and grandparents, to your friends, even to the principal—do you think they'll touch the baby? They will! And you can play a trick on them.

Should I teach you to tell the story? Can we say it all together?

(*and repeat the story*)

Variants or alternatives

There are no other written versions of this story that we know of. However, there are many similar short nursery stories, often with rhymes or finger-play, which you can find in the collections and manuals listed in Appendix B.

THE NAME OF THE TREE: AN OLD AFRICAN FOLKTALE— POSSIBLY WITH BANTU OR SOUTH AFRICAN ORIGINS

This story was first published in 1923 by Edith Rickert, a University of Chicago professor of English. A world expert on Chaucer and modern literature, she also wrote children's books and worked for the American government as a cryptographer during World War I. This story has been told at Lab School since her time. Rickert said the story is an African folk tale but didn't say from what language or country. Other writers claim it comes from Bantu, Zulu, and South African traditions. The tree has many names. In Rickert's version it's named Bojabi, possibly an Arabic word meaning "most or plenty." In other versions the tree is named Ungalli, a Zulu word meaning "don't cry"; Zulu is a Bantu language. Or it's Uwungelema, which is Xhosa, a language in South Africa, and it means "you can't stop."

For the listeners the meaning of the tree's name doesn't matter so much. What they love is the sound and rhythm of it, and the nonsense and the rhymes that come from the story's repetitive elements, which also make it easy and fun to tell. Some storytellers find it fun to keep the name of the tree unsaid until the very end of the story; listeners like to guess what it will be. Depending on your audience feel free to shorten or lengthen any lists that are part of the story. Rickert's original version is much longer, with each animal having a cute name and doing funny actions. These elements in Rickert's telling delight audiences aged five and under, encouraging them to join in, and helping the storyteller remember the story.

If you're looking for other printed versions, try the following:

- Rickert, E. 1923. *The Bojabi Tree.* Garden City and New York: Doubleday, Page, and Company.
- Tooze, R. 1959. The Bojabi Tree, pp. in *Storytelling: How to Develop Skills in the Art of Telling Stories to Children,* ed., Ruth Tooze, 90–97. Englewood Cliffs, NJ: Prentice-Hall.
- Lottridge, C. B. 1989. *The Name of the Tree, a Bantu Folktale.* Toronto: Douglas and McIntyre.
- Friedman, A. and Johnson, M. 2004. *Uwungelema, A South African Tale. https://www.uexpress.com/tell-me-a-story/2004/11/28/uwungelema-a-southern-african-tale* (accessed July 10, 2020).
- Fairy-Tale Info. 2005. *Uwungelema, A South African Tale.* https://www.fairy-tale.info/index.php/action_show_id_NTJ8PDwmPj58NTJ8PDwmPj58.html (accessed July 10, 2020).
- World of Stories. 2006. *Uwungelema.*https://emcn.ab.ca/corporate/media_assets/world_of_story/uwungelema/Uwungelema.pdf (accessed July 10, 2020).
- Hofmeyr, D. and Grobler, P. 2014. *The Magic Bojabi Tree.* London: Frances Lincoln Children's Books.

The Name of the Tree

A long time ago, in the land where all the animals lived, there was a great terrible hunger. All the animals were hungry, there was no food to eat. Every day they got up and they went here and there looking for food, but all they could find were sticks and roots. So, they ate those. But goat and gazelle, pig and rat, hare and mongoose, monkey and tortoise, springbok and buffalo, zebra and giraffe, crocodile and hippo, rhinoceros and elephant, they were all so very hungry.

Well one day when looking for food, the animals found a tree they had never ever seen before. It was a great big tree, and there was beautiful fruit hanging from that tree. The fruit looked and smelled delicious! The fruit LOOKED like

mangoappleorangemelonpearpomegranateplumbanana.

And the fruit SMELLED like

bananaplumpomegranatepearmelonorangeapplemango.

The animals all gathered around and they began to talk.

"What are we going to do? Look at this tree! That fruit looks delicious! But what is the name of this tree? What is the name of the fruit? Is it safe to eat? What are we going to do? What are we going to do?"

Finally, crocodile said, "I know what to do. Let's send rat to lion. The rat is quick, and the king of animals is wise. Rat can ask lion about this tree."

Yes! All the animals agreed that this was a wonderful idea.

So, rat took a piece of the fruit and ran and ran, and jumped and leapt, and leapt and jumped, and ran and ran until he came to lion, the king of animals.

Lion was really happy to have a visitor. Hardly anybody came to see him.

"Welcome rat, my friend!" growled lion. "Why have you come? Do you have a question to ask me?"

"Oh! I do," said rat. "King lion, all the animals are hungry, and we found a tree with this fruit. But we don't know the name of the tree or the name of the fruit, and whether or not we can eat it."

Well, lion looked at the fruit and said, "Hmmm...it LOOKS like a

mangoappleorangemelonpearpomegranateplumbanana.

Then he smelled it. "And it SMELLS like a

bananaplumpomegranatepearmelonorangeapplemango.

"I know what this is," said lion. "The name of this fruit and the name of that tree is Bojabi. And this is a fine fruit to eat."

"Oh, thank you," said rat, leaving the fruit with lion.

And rat was away, quick as he could he ran and ran, and jumped and leapt, and leapt and jumped, and ran and ran all the way back to the animals. And all the time he was dreaming of how delicious the fruit would be to eat.

And when the animals saw him coming, they shouted, "Rat! What's the name of the tree? What's the name of the fruit?"

The rat caught his breath and opened his mouth and said "Ummm....the name of the fruit..." It was on the tip of his tongue. "The name of the tree..." He couldn't remember!" "Ugh, said rat, "The lion told me, but I forgot!"

"You forgot!!! You forgot the name of the fruit???" The animals couldn't believe it. They howled and they screamed and they screamed and they howled and they growled and they grunted and they shrieked and they squealed, each in their own particular voices.

"Never mind!" harrumphed the elephant. "We must ask the lion again. Hare and gazelle and springbok are very fast—let them go! Maybe between the three of them they'll remember what the king of animals says!"

All the animals agreed that this was a wonderful idea.

So, hare and gazelle and springbok each took a piece of the fruit and they ran and ran, and jumped and leapt, and leapt and jumped, and ran and ran until they came to lion, the king of animals.

Lion was happy again to have more visitors. But he was a bit surprised to see so many so soon.

"Welcome good friends!" growled lion. "Welcome hare and gazelle and springbok. Why have you come? Do you have a question?"

"We do, we do!" they shouted. "King lion, all the animals are hungry, and we found a tree with this fruit. But we don't know the name of the tree or the name of the fruit."

The hare said, "It LOOKS like a

mangoappleorangemelonpearpomegranateplumbanana.

And the gazelle said. "And it SMELLS like a

bananaplumpomegranatepearmelonorangeapplemango.

And the springbok asked, "But can we eat it?"

Lion sighed. "All right," said the king of animals "I already told Rat. But I'll tell you, too. The name of the tree and the name of the fruit is Bojabi. And it is safe to eat."

"Thank you," shouted hare and gazelle and springbok.

And with that hare and gazelle and springbok left the fruit with lion. And they ran and ran, and jumped and leapt, and leapt and jumped, and ran and ran until they came back to the other animals.

Again, when the animals saw them coming, they shouted, "Springbok! Gazelle! Hare! What's the name of the tree? What's the name of the fruit"

"Oh!" gasped the hare.

"Um..." stuttered the gazelle.

"Ergh...." choked the springbok.

"We forgot!" they cried. "Lion told us, but we forgot!"

"You forgot the name of the fruit and the tree?" said the animals. They were starving! "How could you do that?"

They howled and they screamed and they screamed and they howled and they growled and they grunted and they shrieked and they squealed, each in their own particular voices.

Well, there was nothing else to do. They HAD to know the name of the fruit, they HAD to know the name of the tree, and HAD to know if the fruit was safe to eat.

So the biggest or the fastest or the strongest animal each took a turn to go and ask lion. Goat and pig, mongoose and monkey, zebra and giraffe and buffalo, crocodile and hippo, rhinoceros and elephant, they all went and asked the lion. But none of them could remember the name of the tree or the name of the fruit or if they could eat it!

And lion got very angry with so many visitors asking him the same question and never remembering what he said!

Well the animals were so, so, so, so very hungry and they wondered what to do.

Suddenly from below their legs came a quiet little voice that said, "I'll go! I'll ask lion, what the name of the tree is."

Everyone looked down and saw it was tortoise speaking. The smallest, slowest, quietest animal of all. Then they laughed and laughed and laughed.

"You're too small!" said elephant and giraffe.

"You're too slow!" said hare and gazelle and springbok.

"You're not strong enough!" said buffalo and hippo and rhinoceros.

"You're not smart enough!" said all the other animals.

"Never mind. I'll go anyway," said tortoise. And he did. He didn't run and he didn't leap and he didn't jump. He ambled slowly, step by step and inch by inch, and inch by inch and step by step but didn't stop and at last he came to lion.

Well, lion was NOT happy to see another visitor. Not happy at all. His head shook back and forth and his tail swished side to side and he showed his sharp teeth when he growled.

"Tortoise!" said lion. "Why have you come? Do you have a question?"

"Yes," tortoise replied.

The lion said, "Is it about the tree with the fruit that LOOKS like

mangoappleorangemelonpearpomegranateplumbanana.

and SMELLS like a

bananaplumpomegranatepearmelonorangeapplemango?"

"Yes," tortoise answered.

The lion roared in anger. And he said, "Tortoise! I told rat, and I told hare, and I told gazelle and springbok, and I told mongoose and monkey, I told crocodile and hippo and elephant and rhinoceros and buffalo, I told them ALL and I AM NOT GOING TO TELL YOU that the name of the fruit and the name of the tree is Bojabi and it's safe to eat! Now get out of here!"

"Bojabi!" Tortoise whispered to himself. "Bojabi!"

"Thank you!" Tortoise said, and he turned around and started walking back to the other animals. Tortoise didn't run and he didn't leap and he didn't jump. He ambled slowly, step by step and inch by inch, and inch by inch and step by step. And all the time he walked and stepped he sang to himself:

Bojabi Bojabi Bojabi Bojabi. Bojabi Bojabi Bojabi Bojabi.
Rat and pig what will you eat? Bojabi Bojabi Bojabi.
Hare and monkey what will you eat? Bojabi Bojabi Bojabi.
Elephant and hippo what will you eat? Bojabi Bojabi Bojabi.
Mongoose and springbok what will you eat? Bojabi Bojabi Bojabi.
Giraffe and rhinoceros what will you eat? Bojabi Bojabi Bojabi.
Gazelle and buffalo what will you eat? Bojabi Bojabi Bojabi.
Animals, animals, what will you eat? Bojabi Bojabi Bojabi.

He sang Bojabi over and over and over again, because that was what great-grandmother tortoise had taught him to do long, long ago. When you want to remember something, say it and sing it, again and again and again and again. So he did. And tortoise didn't stop until finally he came to where all the animals were, standing underneath the beautiful wonderful magical tree.

Goat and gazelle, pig and rat, hare and mongoose and monkey, springbok and buffalo, zebra and giraffe, crocodile and hippo, rhinoceros and elephant, they were all so very hungry. They looked at tortoise and the animals all cried, "What is the name? What is the name?"

And the tortoise said, "BOJABI"

And as tortoise spoke, the fruit fell from the Bojabi tree. And the animals ate and ate and ate. It was so delicious. The fruit LOOKED like

mangoappleorangemelonpearpomegranateplumbanana.

But it TASTED like

bananaplumpomegranatepearmelonorangeapplemango.

and everyone ate it until they were full. But the little tortoise ate the most!

And the animals cheered and danced and sang. And from then on, they never made fun of the tortoise again. For the smallest and slowest of them all had saved their lives.

EPAMINONDAS: A FOLK TALE, WITH BLACK AMERICAN AND SOUTHERN APPALACHIAN VARIANTS, AS WELL AS MANY ALTERNATIVE VERSIONS FROM EUROPEAN TRADITIONS

Epaminondas has been popular with teacher- and librarian-storytellers for over a hundred years. Folklorists label it as a "what should I have done?" tale. Such stories relate misadventures of fools, numbskulls, and noodle-heads. This version does so in a gentle way while depicting the love between a young child and his mother. The story was first written down by Sarah Cone Bryant, a teacher-storyteller during the Progressive Era. She referred to it as a comical story from the Southern United States, and it has been identified both as an African American story and Southern Appalachian tale. There are many similar versions throughout Europe, and also variants from Latin American countries.

Other versions, and variants of this story:

- Bryant, S. C. 1905. Epaminondas. In *Stories to Tell to Children: Fifty One Stories with Some Suggestions for Telling*. Boston and New York: Houghton Mifflin Company.
- Merriam, E. and Schart Hyman, T. 1968. *Epaminondas*. New York and London: Follet Publishing Co.
- Valeri, de M. Eulàlia. 1982 *Epaminondas*. Illustrated by de Sesé. Barcelona: La Galera, S.A. Editorial.
- Maestro, Pepe. 2010. *Epaminondas*. Illustrated by Mariona Cabassa. Madrid: Carretera.

- Birdseye, T. 1993. *Soap, Soap, Don't Forget the Soap!* New York: Holiday House.
- Chase, R. 1948. Soap, Soap, Soap! In *Grandfather Tales*. Boston: Houghton Books.
- Dulemba, E. O. 2009. *Soap Soap Soap/Jabon Jabon Jabon*. Raven Tree Press.
- Jacobs, J. 1993. Lazy Jack. In *English Fairy Tales*. London: Everyman's Library Children's Classics.
- Ross, T. 1985. *Lazy Jack*. London: Andersen Press.

Epaminondas

There was once a boy named Epaminondas. He and his mother lived on one side of a brook and his grandmother lived on the other side. Once a week Epaminondas would visit his grandmother and whenever Epaminondas visited his grandmother, she would give him something to bring home.

One day when Epaminondas was leaving his grandmother's house, she told him that she had a piece of freshly baked yellow cake for him to bring home and share with his mother. Epaminondas thanked his grandmother, gave her a kiss and put the freshly baked yellow cake in his hands and closed his fingers tightly around it and began to walk home. As he walked his fingers got tighter and tighter, making sure that he didn't drop the cake.

When his mother saw him coming, she said, "Epaminondas what do you have in your hands?"

"Cake, Mama" said Epaminondas and he opened his hands. But he had squeezed the cake so hard there was nothing left but crumbs.

"Oh Epaminondas" said his mother, "you don't have the sense you were born with. That's not the way you carry cake. The way you carry cake is to wrap the cake in some leaves and then put the cake on your head under your hat and holding your head up high you walk slowly home. Will you remember that Epaminondas?"

Yes Mama" said Epaminondas. "I'll remember that."

The next week when Epaminondas was leaving his grandmother's house, she told him that she had some freshly churned creamy butter for him to bring home and share with his mother. Epaminondas thanked his grandmother, gave her a kiss, and took the freshly churned creamy butter in his hands. He remembered what his mother had said. He wrapped the butter in some leaves and then put the butter under his hat and carrying his head high he walked slowly home. Now it was a hot day and the sun was beating down on Epaminondas. Soon the butter began to melt and Epaminondas, with his head held high, felt the butter running down his forehead, and down his nose and under his chin and down his shirt. But he held his head high the way his mother had told him to.

When his mother saw him coming, she said, "Epaminondas what have you got all over your face?"

Epaminondas took off his hat and showed his Mama the little bit of freshly churned creamy butter that hadn't melted, "Fresh creamy butter, Mama."

"Oh Epaminondas" said his mother, "you don't have the sense you were born with. That's not the way you carry butter. The way you carry butter is to wrap it in some leaves and then bring it down to the brook and cool it in the water and cool it in the water and cool it in the water. Then you take it in your hands and gently carry it home. Will you remember that, Epaminondas?"

"Yes Mama" said Epaminondas. "I'll remember that."

The next week when Epaminondas was leaving his grandmother's house, she told him she had a surprise for him to bring home and she gave him a frisky little puppy. Epaminondas thanked his grandmother, gave her a big kiss and picked up the puppy. The puppy wiggled in his hands and licked and nipped his face. And Epaminondas remembered what his mother said. He wrapped the puppy in leaves and then brought the puppy down to the brook and cooled him in the water and cooled him in the water and cooled him in the water and then put him in his hands to carry him home.

When his Mama saw him coming, she said, "Epaminondas what have you got in your hands?"

"A frisky puppy, Mama. I carried him home the way you said, but he's not frisky now, he's shivering."

"Oh Epaminondas" said his mother, warming the puppy in a blanket, "for sure, you don't have the sense you were born with. That's not the way you bring home a puppy. The way you bring home a puppy is to tie a piece of string around his neck and you take the other end of the string in your hand and lead him home. Will you remember that, Epaminondas?

"Yes Mama" said Epaminondas. "I'll remember that."

The next week when Epaminondas was leaving his grandmother's house, she told him she had baked a loaf of brown crusty bread for him to bring home and share with his mother. Epaminondas thanked his grandmother, gave her a kiss, picked up the bread, and remembered what his mother said.

He tied one end of a string around the bread and took the other end of the string in his hand and pulled the loaf of bread behind him. The bread bounced on the ground and bumped into rocks and dirt and puddles.

When his mother saw him coming, she said, "Epaminondas what is that dirty thing you have at the end of that string?"

"It's a loaf of bread, Mama.

"Oh Epaminondas" said his mother, "for sure and certain, you don't have the sense you were born with. That's not the way you carry bread home, but I'm not going to tell you any more ways to carry things home from Grandma's house. I'm going to go see Grandma myself."

"Now, Epaminondas, listen carefully. I've just baked six pies and they are cooling on the back steps. While I'm gone, I want you to be careful how you step on those pies. Can you remember that, Epaminondas?"

"Yes Mama" said Epaminondas. "I'll remember that."

And as soon as his mother left Epaminondas went to the back steps and he was very careful how he stepped on those pies. He stepped right in the middle of each one.

When his mother got home, he showed her how he had been careful of how he stepped on those pies.

His mother shook her head, she began to laugh and she said "Epaminondas, you don't have the sense you were born with, you never had the sense you were born with and you never will have the sense you were born with. But I will always love you anyway."

She kissed Epaminondas and said, "Will you remember THAT?"

"Yes, Mama. I'll remember THAT!" said Epaminondas. And he always did.

The Seven-Headed Dragon: a retelling
of a Mexican folk tale that has related variants
across Central and South America and Europe

This retelling of a Mexican folktale has many versions in Latin American traditions. Most of these tell of a dragon-slayer who is a girl or young woman. Variants of this story are also all over Europe, the Middle East, and North Africa, but those versions mostly have a boy or young man as the protagonist. When we developed this version we consulted a number of friends: one from the region in Mexico where this story was often collected, another who is a native Spanish speaker, and a Native American storyteller and scholar who could contextualize the philosophy and practices of some of the folklorists associated with earlier forms of the tale. We did this so our rendition could be a respectful translation and adaptation. This is a much more complex story to tell compared to the other samples, but we wanted to include a story that would challenge our readers.

For other versions and variants of this story check out the following:

- Bierhorst, J. 2002. *Latin American Folktales: Stories from Hispanic and Indian Traditions.* New York and London: Penguin Random House.
- Elswit, S. B. 2015. *The Latin American Story Finder: A Guide to 470 Tales from Mexico, Central America and South America, Listing Subjects and Sources.* Jefferson, NC: McFarland Company, Inc., Publishers.
- Hernandez, J. 2017. *The Dragon Slayer: Folktales from Latin America.* New York: TOON Books.
- Wheeler, H. T. 1943. Mostro de Siete Cabezas. In *Tales from Jalisco Mexico.* Philadelphia: American Folk-Lore Society.

The Seven-Headed Dragon
You know, there was once a girl named Amarilla. Poor Amarilla—this young woman had no family. I don't know what happened to them, but she had no parents or brothers or sisters, or anyone else. She was alone in this world, but what could she do? She travelled through life as best she could, and she was always very kind to everyone and worked hard when given the chance. The people she met liked Amarilla very much, and knew she was a good person.

One day she had to beg for food. There was no work to earn it. Amarilla was so very hungry. A man who ran a *tortilleria* felt sorry for her, and so, he gave her some tortillas. She was ever so grateful. She ate one and saved the other for later.

Then Amarilla headed onto the road, to travel to another place where there might be work. She walked and walked and walked, until the road took her into a dark green forest. After many more miles of walking, Amarilla sat down under a big tree to rest, and to eat the last tortilla. Because, of course, she was hungry again.

But just as she sat down to eat, an old woman dressed in rags came up to Amarilla. "*Buenos días,* friend," the woman said. "Can't you give me that tortilla? I tell you for two days I have walked without eating a thing, and I'm almost starved."

Amarilla replied with a smile. "Well, yes, old woman, take this tortilla. I am very sorry that I have no more to give you." And although Amarilla was hungry herself, she gave her last tortilla to the old woman.

"*Gracias,* you are a good girl." And the old woman returned her smile and ate the tortilla. After she finished, she asked, "Amarilla, do you want work?"

Astonished, Amarilla said, "Well, yes, old woman, I want work. If don't find it, I'm going to starve."

So, the old woman gave her this advice. "Very far away is the land of Quiquiriqui, where the king is most powerful. And there, in his palace, you will surely find work with no trouble."

"Then I'll go straight there," Amarilla decided.

"Wait," said the woman. "You gave me something, so now I give something to you."

And the old woman reached into a raggedy pocket and took out a stick of wood no more than a twig. She handed it to Amarilla.

"What's this?" asked the girl.

"*La varita mágica,*" the old woman told her, "A magic wand. When you want to know something, or have something done, use the wand this way. Hold it before you and say:

> *Little magic stick of wood*
> *Full of kindness, full of good*

"And then ask a question or say what you want. You will be told your answer or see that thing done immediately!"

Amarilla thanked her and said *adiós* and hid the magic wand in her own pocket. Then, again, she walked and walked and walked, and at last arrived in the land of Quiquiriqui.

Once there, she went right up to the king's palace and asked for a job. They put her to work in the king's kitchen. Amarilla worked so very hard scrubbing and cleaning, and fetching and carrying, and stirring and chopping, and frying and baking and boiling and roasting, and doing all she was told to do. She was so happy to have the work!

But you know Amarilla was kind and thoughtful, and after a time she noticed that everyone in that place was always sad. And the powerful king of Quiquiriqui was the saddest of all, for he often wept and hardly ever spoke.

Curious to know the reason for all this, one day when no one was looking, Amarilla decided to see if her magic wand could help her find out why everyone was so sad. So, she took the magic wand from her pocket and said,

> *Little magic stick of wood*
> *Full of kindness, full of good*
> *I want to know*
> *Why is the king so sad?*

Well, the magic wand told her, of course.

> *The king is sad, the news is bad:*
> *The dragon with the seven heads,*
> *It wants to devour this king*
> *And then eat all the people of Quiquiriqui.*

So now Amarilla knew why everyone was sad, especially the king. She wondered what to do.

It just so happened that not long after, the king made a big proclamation. He was too scared to go and fight the dragon himself. So, the king announced that whoever killed the dragon with the seven heads would have any wish they wanted. Whatever the dragon slayer asked for, the king would grant. That was a promise! Many knights and soldiers went off to slay the dragon, but none could! Either the dragon ate them, or they got scared and ran away.

Well now. Amarilla heard about the king's proclamation, and his promise to grant a wish. And seeing that no one else could do the job, Amarilla decided to kill the dragon herself. Better to be a dragon-slayer than a kitchen maid, she thought. And, so, as soon as she was alone, Amarilla pulled the magic wand from her pocket and asked,

> *Little magic stick of wood*
> *Full of kindness, full of good*
> *I want to know*
> *Can this dragon be killed?*

And she got an answer. The magic wand told Amarilla where to go and what to do.

Early the next morning Amarilla set out to slay the dragon. She walked and walked until she came to the dragon's cave. Now she got there just at midday and that seven-headed monster was fast asleep, his seven heads snoring away. It was all just as the magic wand had told her it would be!

Amarilla held up the magic wand and asked.

Little magic stick of wood
Full of kindness, full of good
I want to know
How do I kill this dragon?

And the twig told her,

With this magic stick of wood
Full and kindness, full of good
Tap the dragon's tail three times
But not one head!
Then the dragon's dead!

So quietly and carefully, Amarilla tiptoed around the seven sleeping heads of the dragon, until she came to the dragon's tail, all coiled up at the back of the cave. And ever so quietly and carefully, Amarilla waved the wand around and around. And ever so quietly and carefully, she then tapped the tail with the magic wand three times with all her might.

And that was the end of the wicked seven-headed dragon! The magic wand made music and sang, and Amarilla danced for joy.

Then the magic wand told Amarilla to do something very odd, and very strange.

Amarilla, quick quick quick,
Cut off each tongue with this stick
And put them in your pocket.

This seemed a funny thing to do, but Amarilla did as told. She went around the dragon, opened the mouth of each head, and cut off the seven slimy tongues and put them in her pocket.

Then she quickly walked back to the palace of the king of Quiquiriqui.

As soon as she arrived at the palace, Amarilla ran to the king and shouted, "Great Majesty, great news! I have killed the seven-headed dragon!"

When he heard this, the king laughed and laughed and laughed. He could barely speak! "Don't be silly, Amarilla. How could you kill this terrible monster? Don't tell lies! Go back to the kitchen where you belong."

But Amarilla insisted, "No, great majesty. I really did the job! I am the true dragon-slayer."

"Oh pooh pooh, I don't believe you!" the king replied. He was now quite angry. "If you killed the dragon, where's the proof?"

And then Amarilla understood why the magic wand had told her to take the tongues from the dragon. She reached into her pocket and took out the dragon's seven tongues.

Amarilla grinned and said, "I am the one who killed the monster, and to prove it, here are the dragon's seven tongues."

And she showed them to the king.

"You truly are the dragon slayer!" cried the king. "You killed this monster! Good job. Now, what do you want for your work?"

Amarilla smiled once more and said her wish, "I want to be queen and rule this land!"

"NO!" The king screamed. He started shouting and yelling all over. "How can a kitchen maid be a queen?"

"But a king does not go back on his word," Amarilla reminded him. "And that is my wish!"

Well now, the king was not only a coward, afraid to face the dragon himself. He was a cheat! He never kept his word!

"Whoa, whoa, whoa," said the king. "Not so fast. I still say a kitchen girl can't be queen. You don't look like a queen. Dressed in rags, with bare feet and nothing on your head! Where are your beautiful clothes? Where is your crown?"

"Oh. I have none of those things," admitted Amarilla. "I only have the clothing I wear for work."

"That's so true!" smiled the wicked king, who saw a chance to keep his job. "Raggedy Amarilla, when you look like a queen, then you can be the queen."

And laughing at his own cleverness, the king ordered Amarilla to go back to the kitchen and to wash the pots and pans.

Well, the girl who was a dragon slayer was NOT going to do THAT! As soon as she was alone, Amarilla raised the wand and asked,

Little magic stick of wood
Full of kindness, full of good
I want to know
Can you make me look like a queen?

Now, you know, of course the magic wand told Amarilla what to do and where to go.

One more time, she turned around and walked and walked and walked until she came to the most beautiful garden. Flowers blossomed and bloomed all around, and bees buzzed and birds sang among the fruit trees. And in the middle of the garden was the biggest most beautiful tree. And beneath the tree was a huge wooden chest.

The beautiful garden was all just like the magic wand had said that it would be.

Amarilla opened the chest with the magic wand. Inside it was filled with beautiful clothes and a pair of silver slippers. And on top of the clothing was a golden crown. Soon, she was dressed as a queen from the tip of her toes to the top of her head.

Amarilla turned around and went back to Quiquiriqui every bit like a queen. She entered the palace and stood there for all to see, in her silver slippers and gown made of gold and jewels, with the golden crown on her head.

Everyone gasped to see such beauty—even the mean cowardly king!

Amarilla now looked so rich and beautiful that it caused the king to do a silly thing. The king suddenly fell in love with her and wanted to marry her!

Now you know, Amarilla was really fed up with this foolish cowardly mean old man.

"Enough!" she said. "Why would I marry a mean cowardly king who doesn't keep his promises? You're like a greedy fat pig, and I wish that you were one!"

Perhaps the magic wand was still listening, or maybe it was the crown that was magic and heard her wish. I don't know. But as soon as Amarilla made her second wish, the king turned into a plump pink pig!

So Amarilla became queen of Quiquiriqui. That was quite a good job for her—and hadn't the old woman said she'd find work in the palace? It all came true.

Besides all that, Queen Amarilla also now had a plump pink pig for a pet. A pink pig that danced whenever that magic wand played music.

Queen Amarilla lived for many years and was so kind and good that everyone in that land was happy. And Queen Amarilla had many parties in her palace, and I was invited to them all, and that's how I heard this story.

Appendix B: Resources

Publications

Anthologies of folk and fairy tales, myths, and legends

What follows is a short sample of traditional folk and fairy tale anthologies. Various traditions, cultures, and languages are represented. By no means is this list exhaustive, it's just to get you started. All the collections have stories that we, other teacher- and librarian-storytellers, and professional storytellers, have often told, so they are tried and tested.

Afanasyev, Alexander. *Russian Fairy Tales*
Asbjørnsen, Peter Christen. *East of the Sun and West of the Moon—Old Tales from the North*
Bashevis Singer, Isaac. *Naftali the Storyteller and his Horse Sus: And Other Stories*
Bashevis Singer, Isaac. *Zlateh the Goat and Other Stories*
Carter, Angela. *Angela Carter's Book of Fairy Tales*
DeSpain, Pleasant and Lamo-Jiménez, Mario. *The Emerald Lizard. Fifteen Latin American Tales to Tell in English and Spanish*
Dockery-Young, Richard and Judy. *African-American Folktales for Young Readers*
Doyle, Malachy. *Tales from Old Ireland*

155
D. Schatt, P. Ryan, *Story Listening and Experience in Early Childhood*, https://doi.org/10.1007/978-3-030-65358-3

Forest, Heather. *Wisdom Tales from Around the World*
Forest, Heather. *Wonder Tales from Around the World*
Gavin, Jamilla. *The School for Princes, Stories from the Panchatantra*
Gelfand, Shoshana Boyd. *The Barefoot Book of Jewish Folk Tales*
Gunderson, Jessica. *Little Red Riding Hood Stories Around the World: 3 Beloved Tales*
Hallworth, Grace. *Sing Me a Story, Song and Dance Tales from the Caribbean*
Hamilton, Martha and Weiss, Mitch. *40 Fun Fables, Tales That Trick, Tickle, and Teach*
Hamilton, Virginia. *Her Stories: African American Folktales, Fairy Tales, and True Tales*
Harrison, Annette. *Easy-to-Tell Stories for Young Children*
Holt, David and Mooney, Bill, eds. *Ready-to-Tell Tales, Sure-fire Stories from America's Favourite Storytellers*
Holt, David and Mooney, Bill, eds. *More Ready-to-Tell Tales, from Around the World*
Husain, Sharukh. *The Wise Fool, fables form the Islamic World*
Jungman, Anne. *The Prince Who Thought He Was a Rooster and other Jewish Stories*
Laird, Elizabeth. *The Ogress and the Snake and Other Stories from Somalia*
Laird, Elizabeth. *A Fistful of Pearls, and other tales from Iraq*
Lester, Julius. *The Tales of Uncle Remus, the adventures of Brer Rabbit*
Lunge-Larsen. *The Troll With No Heart in his Body, and Other Tales of Trolls from Norway.*
Lupton, Hugh. *Tales of Mystery and Magic*
Lupton, Hugh. *The Story Tree*
Lupton, Hugh. *Tales of Wisdom and Wonder*
Lurie, Alison. *Clever Gretchen and Other Forgotten Folktales*
MacDonald, Margaret Read. *Shake-It-Up Tales! Stories to Sing, Dance, Drum and Act Out*
Massie, Eithne. *Best-Loved Irish Legends*
McAllister, Angela. *A Year Full of Stories*
McCall-Smith, Alexan. *The Girl Who Married a Lion: And Other Tales from Africa*
Meister, Cari. *Cinderella Stories Around the World: 4 Beloved Tales*
Meister, Cari. *Rapunzel Stories Around the World: 3 Beloved Tales*
Mhlophe, Gcina. *African Folktales*
Minard, Rosemary. *Womenfolk and Fairy Tales*
Mitchell, Adrian. *Shapeshifters—Tales from Ovid's Metamorphoses*

Monte, Richard. *The Dragon of Krakow and Other Polish Stories*
Naidoo, Beverly. *Aesop's Fables*
Nanji, Shenaaz. *Indian Tales*
Nmir, Sonia. *Ghaddar the Ghoul and Other Palestinian Stories*
Nunes, Shiho S. *Chinese Fables: The Dragon Slayer and Oher Timeless Tales of Wisdom*
O'Brien, Edna. *Tales for Telling: Irish Folk and Fairy Tales*
Pullman, Philip. *Grimm Tales for Young and Old*
Sherman, Josepha. *Trickster Tales, Forty Folk Stories from Around the World*
Tarnowska, Wafa. *The Arabian Nights*
Weir, Liz. *Boom-Chicka-Boom*
Weir, Liz. *Here, There and Everywhere, Stories from Many Lands*
Williamson, Duncan. *The Coming of the Unicorn: Scottish Folk Tales for Children*
Williamson, Duncan. *The Flight of the Golden Bird: Scottish Folk Tales for Children*
Wolkstein, Diana. *The Magic Orange Tree and Other Haitian Folk Tales*
Zipes, Jack. *The Great Fairy Tale Tradition, from Straparola and Basile to the Brothers Grimm*
Zipes, Jack. *The Original Folk and Fairy Tales of the Brothers Grimm: The Complete First Edition*

Picture book and literary stories

There are hundreds, if not thousands, of picture books retelling individual folk or fairy tales. These often represent cultural traditions from throughout the world, not just the classic well-known European stories that many think of as picture book fairy tales. Some are literary tales woven out of traditional folk and fairy tale motifs. Here are a few examples:

Aardema, Verna. *Why Mosquitoes Buzz in People's Ears*
Agard, John. *Brer Rabbit, The Great Tug-O-War*
Behan, Brendan and Lynch, P. J. *The King of Ireland's Son*
Doyle, Malachy. *Una and the Sea-Cloak*
Galdone, Joanna C. *Tailypo: A Ghost Story*
Haley, Gail E. *A Story a Story*
Isador, Rachel. *Rapunzel*
Jones, Andy. *The Queen of Paradise's Garden*
McCissack, Patrick. *Flossie and the Fox*
McGovern, Ann and Taback, Simms. *Too Much Noise*
Steptoe, John. *Mufaro's Beautiful Daughters*

Taback, Simms. *Joseph Had a Little Overcoat*
Young, Ed. *Lon Po Po: A Red Riding Hood Story from China*
Zelinsky, Paul O. and Grimm, Brothers. *Rapunzel*
Zemach, Harve and Margot. *Duffy and the Devil, a Cornish Tale Retold*

Often picture books relate original stories that, as we mentioned, have repetition, rhythm, and tropes making their structure similar to a folk tale. This makes them easier to tell and appealing to child listeners. A few that we know work well as stories told from memory include:

Allard, Harry and Marshall, James. *Miss Nelson is Missing!*
Brown, Peter. *My Teacher is a Monster*
Browne, Anthony. *Willy the Wizard*
Dodd, Lynley. *Hairy MacLary from Donaldson's Dairy*
Doyle, Malachy and Whitson, Andrew. *Molly and the Stormy Sea*
Hutchins, Pat. *The Doorbell Rang*
Roberts, Dave. *Dirty Bertie*
Smath, Jerry. *But No Elephants*
Storr, Catherine. *Clever Polly and the Stupid Wolf*
Sutton, Eve. *My Cat Likes to Hide in Boxes*
Waddell, Martin. *Owl Babies*

For literary fairy tales, we suggest trying short stories written for children by the authors we mentioned in various chapters: Joan Aiken, Eleanor Farjeon, Hans Christian Andersen, Rudyard Kipling, and Chris Van Allsburg. Others to consider are stories by James Thurber, Carl Sandburg, Florence Parry Heide, and Roald Dahl. Walter de la Mare's *Told Again: Old Tales Told Again* has been reissued in the *Oddly Modern Fairy Tales* series published by Princeton University Press. It includes some well-known and not so well-known fairy tales rewritten in a literary style that have been popular with librarian-tellers for nearly a century.

Once you get a sense of the types of stories you like to tell, and start looking around public libraries and bookshops, you'll find plenty of these kinds of books. Don't forget to ask librarians and other storytellers for suggestions, they can usually point you in the right direction.

Manuals and guides on how to tell stories

The following are books that provide advice on how to find, learn, practice, and tell stories. Some include recommendations for using storytelling to deliver the curriculum, or suggest stories and activities for library programming. Many also include folk and fairy tales to tell.

Chasse, Emily S. *Telling Tales, a Guidebook*
Collins, Reeves and Cooper, Pamela J. *The Power of Story, Teaching Through Storytelling*
Colwell, Eileen. *Storytelling*
Daniel, Alistair K. *Storytelling Across the Primary Curriculum*
Del Negro, Janice M. *Folktales Aloud, Practical Advice for Playful Storytelling*
Elswit, Sharon Barcon. *The Latin American Story Finder: A Guide to 470 Tales from Mexico, Central America and South America, Listing Subjects and Sources*
Greene, E. and Del Negro, J. M. *Storytelling: Art and Technique* (4th Edition)
Harrett, Jacqueline. *Tell Me Another...Speaking, Listening and Learning Through Storytelling*
Heathfield, David. *Storytelling with Our Students, Techniques for Telling Tales from Around the World*
Livo, Norma J. and Rietz, Sandra A. *Storytelling, Process and Practice*
MacDonald, Margaret Read. *The Storyteller's Start-Up Book, Finding, Learning, Performing, and Using Folktales*
MacDonald, Margaret Read. *The Parents' Guide to Storytelling, How to Make Up New Stories and Retell old Favorites*
MacDonald, Margaret Read, MacDonald Whitman, Jennifer and Forrest Whitman, Nathaniel. *Teaching with Story, Classroom Connections to Storytelling*
Mooney, Bill and Holt, David. *The Storyteller's Guide, Storytellers Share Advice for Classroom, Boardroom, Showroom, Podium, Pulpit, and Center Stage*
Moore, Robin. *Creating a Family Storytelling Tradition, Awakening the Hidden Storyteller*
Parkinson, Rob. *Storytelling and Imagination. Beyond Basic Literacy 8-14*
Pellowski, Anne. *The Family Storytelling Handbook, How to Use Stories, Anecdotes, Rhymes, Handkerchiefs, Paper, and Other Objects to Enrich Your Family Traditions*
Pellowski, Anne. *The Storytelling Handbook, A Young People's Collection of Unusual Tales and Helpful Hints on How to Tell Them*
Schimmel, Nancy. *Just Enough to Make a Story*
Zipes, Jack. *Creative Storytelling, Building Community, Changing Lives*
Zipes, Jack. *Speaking Out, Storytelling and Creative Drama for Children*

Theory, history, and cultural critiques

These academic publications provide in-depth discussions on educational theory and storytelling, or on the history and background of traditional folk tales and literary fairy tales, or on the aesthetics or psychology of storytelling and of traditional stories.

Cremin, Teresa, Flewitt, Rosie, Mardell, Ben, and Swann, Joan. *Storytelling in Early Childhood, Enriching Language, Literacy, and Culture*
Egan, Kieran. *Teaching as Storytelling*
Harris, Trudier. *The Power of the Porch: The Storyteller's Craft in Zora Neale Hurston, Gloria Naylor, and Randall Kenan*
Hodges, Gabriell Clif, Drummond, Mary Jane, and Styles, Morag. *Tales, Tellers and Texts*
Lüthi, Max. *Once Upon a Time: On the Nature of Fairy Tales*
Lüthi, Max. *The Fairy Tale as Art Form and Portrait of Man*
McEwan, Hunter and Egan, Kieran (eds.), *Narrative in Teaching, Learning and Research*
Opie, Iona and Peter. *The Classic Fairy Tales*
Paley, Vivian Gussin. *The Boy Who Would Be a Helicopter. The Uses of Storytelling in the Classroom*
Paley, Vivian Gussin. *A Child's Work. The Importance of Fantasy Play*
Pullman, Philip. *Daemon Voices, Essays on Storytelling*
Reder, Deanna and Morra, Linda M. *Troubling Tricksters: Revisioning Critical Conversations*
Reder, Deanna and Morra, Linda M. *Learn, Teach, Challenge: Approaching Indigenous Literatures*
Rodari, Gianni. *The Grammar of Fantasy*
Spaulding, Amy E. *The Wisdom of Storytelling in an Information Age*
Spaulding, Amy E. *The Art of Storytelling, telling Truths through Telling Stories*
Tatar, Maria. *Off With Their Heads! Fairy Tales and the Culture of Childhood*
Tatar, Maria. *The Cambridge Companion to Fairy Tales*
Turner, Mark. *The Literary Mind, The Origins of Thought and Language*
Warner, Marina. *From the Beast to the Blonde, On Fairy Tales and their Tellers*
Warner, Marina. *No Go the Bogeyman: Scaring, Lulling, and Making Mock*
Wilson, Michael. *Storytelling and Theatre, Contemporary Storytellers and their Art*
Yolen, Jane *Touch Magic, Fantasy, Faerie and Folklore in the Literature of Childhood*

Zipes, Jack. *Breaking the Magic Spell, Radical Theories of Folk and Fairy Tales*

Zipes, Jack. *Sticks and Stones, The Troublesome Success of Children's Literature from Slovenly Peter to Harry Potter*

Zipes, Jack. *Why Fairy Tales Stick, The Evolution and Relevance of a Genre*

DIGITAL RESOURCES

Texts of stories and digitalized storytelling books and anthologies that are out of print

Professor D. L. Ashliman, a folklorist scholar, published a website: *Folklinks, as a companion to Folk and Fairy Tales: a Handbook.* This site links to complete texts of folk and fairy tales from around the world. They are organized according to major collections, and also according to "tale type" or "motif." This means, for example, you can use the index and navigate a search for *Snow White* or another well-known tale and find variants of the story from numerous cultures and traditions. Many of the texts are taken from nineteenth- and early twentieth-century folklore studies, so some stories are meant for adults or will contain elements unsuitable for today, but a large number of tales are easily adaptable and work well with young elementary school children.

http://www.pitt.edu/~dash/folktexts.html
http://www.pitt.edu/~dash/ashliman.html
http://www.pitt.edu/~dash/folklinks.html

Folk and fairy tale anthologies published during the Progressive Era, specifically for use by librarian- and teacher-storytellers, have been digitalized and can be found online. A few include:

Jacobs, Joseph. *English Fairy Tales.* http://www2.hn.psu.edu/faculty/jmanis/joseph-jacobs/English-Fairy-Tales.pdf

Jacobs, Joseph. *Celtic Fairy Tales.* https://archive.org/details/morecelticfairyt00jaco

Lang, Andrew. *The Fairy Books. http://www.gutenberg.org/files/30580/30580-h/30580-h.htm*

Thorne-Thomsen, Gudrun. *East o' the Sun and West o' the Moon with Other Norwegian. Folk Tales.* http://www.gutenberg.org/ebooks/8653

There are also websites with many digitalized folk and fairy tale anthologies. Again, these collections from the late nineteenth and early twentieth centuries have stories that don't always work as material for children. If looking for different variants of stories, to see how you can combine them to make a story suitable to your style of telling and audience, these are useful websites. Those we suggest have slightly "New Age" connotations, but consist of dozens of facsimiles of complete book collections with folk and fairy tales from all over the world.

Sacred Texts. http://www.sacred-texts.com/neu/index.htm
SurLaLune Fairy Tales. http://www.surlalunefairytales.com/ebooksindex.html

Some storytelling books from the Progressive Era have been digitalized and made freely available. While the language may seem quaint or old fashioned, the tips and suggestions provided remain relevant to those wanting to learn to tell stories. Many also include stories for telling.

Bryant, Sara Cone. *How to Tell Stories to Children.* http://www.gutenberg.org/files/474/474-h/474-h.htm
Cowles, Julia Darrow. *The Art of Storytelling, With Nearly Half a Hundred Stories.* https://babel.hathitrust.org/cgi/pt?id=mdp.39015011695742andview=1upandseq=5
Shedlock, Marie. *The Art of the Storyteller.* http://www.gutenberg.org/ebooks/5957

Storytelling websites

These websites link to recordings of storytellers performing traditional and literacy tales. A search will find many others online. Included are recordings from *Stories Told By Heart*, mentioned in Appendix C, which are stories told by the librarian-storytellers at Lab School, and Maria Carriel, and Donna and Patrick.

Anancy and the Magic Pot, told by Sandra Agard. https://www.bl.uk/childrens-books/videos/anancy-and-the-magic-pot

Barney McCabe, told by David Holt. https://www.youtube.com/watch?v=JKocM1_fhK0andlist=PL2y09g3x9RN1g-j0eZ3vmzq5Z61Csa1Y5andindex=3

The Devil and Wicked John, told by Anne Shimojimo. https://www.youtube.com/watch?v=2i_jZSxro1candt=36s

The Giant's Causeway, told by Paul Rubinstein. https://www.bl.uk/childrens-books/videos/the-giants-causeway

The Golden Arm, told by Jackie Torrence https://www.youtube.com/watch?v=DTJJajXPZV8

Molly Whuppie, told by Francis Clarke Sayers https://archive.org/details/frances_sayers-molly_whuppie_1977

The Naughty Dog, an Aesop Fable, told by Sandra Agard. https://www.bl.uk/childrens-books/videos/the-naughty-dog

The Rathlin Fairy Thorn Tree Story, told by Liz Weir. https://www.youtube.com/watch?v=btqSm7qvefU

Stories Told by Heart stories told by the librarian-storytellers at Lab School, and Maria Carriel, Donna Schatt and Ryan, Patrick. https://www.youtube.com/channel/UCwM6xM5iO7lrPD4SNlfbO0g
[Stories Told: *Alexandra the Rock Eater; Bye Bye Turtle; The Cat and the Parrot; A Dark Dark Walk; Elephant's Child; Epaminondas* (in Spanish and English); *The Fairy Thorn Tree; The Fortunate Shoemaker; The Iron Man; Kayvan the Brave; The Magic Boat; The Magic Stove; The Mitten* (in Spanish and English); *Mr. Semolina Semolinus; The Name of the Tree; The Old Woman and the Willy Nilly Man; Phoebe and the Boat; Pickin' Peas; Ruby Red Lips; The Runaway Pancake; Silly Jack; Soap, Soap, Soap* (in Spanish and English); *Two Crabs and the Moonlight; Two of Everything; The White Cat; The Woman Who Flummoxed the Fairies*]

Tailybone. told by David Holt. https://www.youtube.com/watch?v=CBVkSJcU6TQandlist=PL2y09g3x9RN1g-j0eZ3vmzq5Z61Csa1Y5andindex=2andt=0s

A Trickster Tale, told by Jackie Torrence. https://www.youtube.com/watch?v=c1S7uFcAnwY

The Wave, told by Anne Shimojimo. https://www.youtube.com/watch?v=uxdPBW7cbTA

The White Horse Girl and the Blue Wind Boy, told by Francis Clarke Sayers. https://www.youtube.com/watch?v=oyv%2D%2DpDMdjY
Wiley and the Hairyman, told by David Holt. https://www.youtube.com/watch?v=aAunm142vzUandlist=PL2y09g3x9RN1g-j0eZ3vmzq5Z61CsA1Y5andindex=2

Appendix C: Case Studies

Case Study 1

"Kick into reading": teaching professional sports people to tell stories

Kick into Reading (*KiR*) was a program aimed at children eight-to-eleven years old that used the combination of sport and storytelling to promote reading for pleasure and the greater use of public libraries. From 1999 through 2011, professional athletes and coaches (mostly from soccer clubs, but sometimes from other sports) were trained to deliver story times for school groups invited to public libraries.

The project was highly successful, achieving more than originally planned. It received positive feedback from all participants, with sports clubs and libraries asking to take part multiple times. Ongoing assessment of *KiR* indicated consistent gains in the number of children reading for pleasure and using the libraries. What wasn't anticipated, although warmly welcomed, was that participating sports people sustained storytelling practices *long after the project finished*.

The following is a summary of the training used in *KiR*, analyzing what made it successful. *KiR* demonstrated that individuals, thought unlikely to have an interest or ability to tell stories, when given training and

© The Author(s), under exclusive license to Springer Nature
Switzerland AG 2021
D. Schatt, P. Ryan, *Story Listening and Experience in Early Childhood*, https://doi.org/10.1007/978-3-030-65358-3

encouragement, could excel at and delight in the experience. Hopefully this case study will encourage others to replicate this work.

Unlike the US where most sports programs for children are organized by parent volunteers or gym teachers in schools, Britain, by-and-large, has professionally trained coaches teaching children sports in community and educational settings. Qualified and overseen by national sports bodies, such as the Football Association (the FA) in the case of soccer, community coaches work directly for the FA or, more commonly, professional football clubs, where they are hired and given training to teach soccer in schools, parks, and community centers.

In Europe professional players are recruited through these community coaching programs. High school and college sport aren't usual entries into sporting careers. Girls and boys showing talent in community programs are "signed up" around the age of twelve to be given extra coaching in a club's football academy, which works with the children's schools to assure their education and well-being. At sixteen, those showing promise are offered contracts to work fulltime as "academy players," a kind of apprenticeship, with coaches and qualified teachers at the club's academy.

KiR mostly worked with professional community coaches, academy players, and a few "first-team" players (a club's full-time professional footballers). Male and female coaches and players joined *KiR*, but the majority offering to take part were men. Most clubs' participants ranged in age from sixteen through to their mid-forties. The National Literacy Trust (NLT), *KiR*'s sponsor, coordinated the program overall. Not a single participant failed to develop knowledge and skills necessary for effective story times. *KiR* often ran for three or four years in each club, in around thirty clubs across England, Wales, and Northern Ireland. *KiR* storytellers developed individual styles reflecting their club's local culture and dialect, displaying a wonderful variety of stories and ways of sharing them.

There was one day of storytelling training that took place a week or two before *KiR* tellers started telling stories in local libraries. The workshop covered oral storytelling, reading aloud picture books, poetry recitation, and riddles and word play. Each training session started the same way. Coaches' and footballers' body language communicated their nervousness and skepticism. Having briefly introduced himself and *KiR*, the course leader would share a specific story to demonstrate what the project required. Patrick had learned a humorous tale from Peter Rhoades-Brown (Rosie), a retired Chelsea footballer and coach for Oxford United, who instigated the first *KiR* program and was well-known and liked by football people all over the country. Starting with his story and explaining that this crazy project was originally all Rosie's idea allowed coaches and players to relax. The story was so simple, funny, and effective, with a neat trick, that everyone wanted to retell it. A common response was, "Is that what you want us to do? Is that all? Sure, we can do that!"

From that point, each training day found everyone enthusiastically trying out different stories, and sharing picture books, poems, and word-play. After Rosie's story came riddles, leading into visualization exercises modeling how to imagine and recreate a story, rather than memorize it. Over the day, the facilitator shared half a dozen easily learned folk tales. Between the stories came participatory exercises teaching participants how to learn, remember and tell stories, share picture books, recite poems, and involve listeners in riddles and word play. Paired group work to rehearse everything introduced made up the bulk of the day.

A range of activities was modeled so participants could find what gave them confidence and suited them best in terms of interest and ability. Sharing picture books aloud was included because research confirmed that practice supported the project's objectives to encourage children to read more and use their library. Another reason was that shy or less-confident sports people engaged more readily with picture books and, from these, developed oral storytelling later. Similarly, riddles and word play provided variety in a story time, but also provided a repertoire reluctant beginners were more comfortable starting with. The training day also looked at practicalities—how the project would run, the need for football staff to organize and practice their material and running order for each story time, and information on the schedule and venues for the story times.

Generally, over half the participants told oral stories, either the demonstrated folk tales or personal stories evolved out of workshop activities. Personal stories, usually from memories of football adventures, often took on a folkloric structure. Around a third preferred reading aloud picture books, and one or two per club recited poetry. NLT supplied anthologies of easily learned folktales, picture books appealing to the targeted age groups, and collections of football and sports poems. Everyone was happy to learn and use riddles and word games.

A week after training, a team of three to five coaches and players visited libraries, where each had at least one story or poem ready, usually more. What Patrick found interesting was how quickly players developed their own voices, that is, a style of their own. Many beginner storytellers imitate gestures and vocal patterns of tellers they learn from. This is natural, beginners usually retell stories learned from their mentor. But from the start *KiR* storytellers shaped Patrick's stories to tell them in a way that made the tales entirely new.

Patrick and other facilitators on the project noticed that coaches and players had more confidence to tell in front of each other, and to take and give criticism. This is not normally the case among other adults starting out as storytellers. Most people hate practicing stories or speeches in front of anyone, especially when learning something new. Teachers and librarians are also normally reluctant to give or take any sort of feedback with colleagues. Neither was the case with *KiR* participants.

It became clear *KiR* storytellers' willingness to practice in front of and accept criticism from peers arose out of personal experiences. As professional athletes, repeated practice and drill to achieve success was a big part of the "day job." So they conscientiously rehearsed their stories, accepting a need to do so almost out of habit. Making it professionally meant being brutally honest about their own physical accomplishments and accepting criticism regarding their skills and attitudes. By the time *KiR* came along, they automatically made use of any feedback. Their methods for imagining stories also appeared less as a visual and more as a kinesthetic or spatial way of thinking. Discussions revealed that many strategized learning and remembering stories in the same way they calculated moves during team practices and football matches. None of the *KiR* storytellers consciously "acted out" or "mimed" actions in their stories. But much of the material they shared featured football. When narrating moves like dribbling, heading, diving, and blasting, anyone observing them could see a hint of unconscious muscle movement connected to these actions, suggested by their stance or gestures, a sort of muscle memory. And as sports people they enjoyed and eagerly participated in friendly competition. A desire to tell the story *differently* to get a bigger or better response out of listeners pushed them to find their own way to relate the tales.

The learning-process continued beyond the one training day. The library story times had at least three to five representatives from the participating football club, along with the storyteller who led the training serving as an "Emcee". Sitting together as a "storytelling team" in front of invited classes, the Emcee introduced everyone and told a story to start the session. Then each footballer or coach took a couple of turns at telling or reading a story or sharing riddles and word play. As a "team" there was lots of interaction, gentle teasing, joking, and banter between adults, and between adults and listeners, all adding to the fun.

The Emcee told stories not heard on the training day, so footballers could pick up additional tales. He also made sure to say less each day, since as coaches and footballers gained confidence, their repertoires expanded, and they wanted more time to share new material. Three story hours a day over five days provided ample time to experiment, learn more, and develop confidence. Since most clubs repeated the project over three or four years, new staff picked up storytelling and joined the project, and returning football staff refreshed or expanded their skills and learned more stories.

Eventually each club had a team of tellers, and integrated storytelling into other community outreach work. Storytelling continued long after *Kick into Reading* ended. Academy and first-team players' contracts require that they do regular community service, such as visiting sick children in hospital, or senior citizens in nursing homes, or giving talks at school assemblies or charity events. Some found these visits a challenge, but as experienced storytellers, outreach work became easier, more meaningful, and more enjoyable.

Community coaches had sometimes included activities like other games, bounce houses, and face painting alongside teaching football at soccer camps run over school vacations. Storytelling easily slotted in as a soccer camp pastime. If kids got too excited and over-heated from physical activities, instead of shouting to get attention, coaches simply mentioned, "Hey, it's time for a story, let's go meet under that tree." Then children ran eagerly to a cool shady spot, and while one coach told a story, others passed water bottles around for everyone to re-hydrate. Once the story finished, with the group calm and refreshed, coaches could quietly explain what was to happen next. Not only did stories add to the fun and build a better connection between adults and young footballers, they proved a great way to manage, instruct, and motivate kids.

Many clubs also have coaches work in local schools, to enrich the PE curriculum or to help with playground supervision. Coaches started including story time activities for school visits. On dreaded rainy days, when pupils and teachers feared soccer being canceled, coaches surprised them by asking if a room or library was available, offering to spend the soccer hour telling stories.

To summarize, consider these takeaway points:

- When starting out, it's normal to be shy and nervous. Look to have fun in the learning, and don't take it too seriously, experiment. Learning with a supportive group that takes delight in what each one does helps, a lot.

- Repeated experience really makes storytelling easier and better. As you learn new material, if you share stories with other adults, and observe other adults who regularly share stories with children, you can pick up great ideas and habits.
- Children's "favorite" storytellers are the people they know best. NLT frequently gathered surveys to evaluate *KiR*. On students' questionnaires, children were asked whose stories they liked best. Always they indicated the footballers' and coaches' stories were their favorites. Because the coaches ran their soccer camps or school PE lessons, and they saw their footballers play in local matches, children knew them in the way they knew their parents, teachers, and librarians, so they saw the stories as being especially for them, from people they loved in their community.

If you want to know more about *Kick into Reading*, the following lists publications and videos regarding the project.

Articles and book chapters

1. National Literacy Trust Archives. 2004. *Kick into Reading Report, Hounslow*; 2005. *Kick into Reading Report*; 2008. *Kick into Reading/ Reading is Fundamental, Access to Art: Final Report. (https://literacytrust.org.uk)*
2. Ryan, P. 2002. A Beautiful Game: Oral narrative and Soccer. *Children's Literature in Education*, 30(2): 149–164
3. Ryan, P. 2009. Talking the Game: A Case Study of an Oral Narrative Project with Professional Footballers. *Arts and Communities*, 1(1): 79–92
4. Ryan, P. 2010. Storytelling in Libraries and Schools in the United Kingdom and Ireland in *Storytelling: Art and Technique* (4th Edition), 249–269, eds. Ellin Greene, E. and Janice M. Del Negro. Santa Barbara, CA; Denver, CO; and Oxford, UK: Libraries Unlimited
5. Ryan, P. 2012. Junior Reading Champions: Adolescent Storytellers as Role Models for Reading in Sport and Literacy. *English 4-11*. 44
6. Tottenham Hotspur FC News Archive. https://www.tottenhamhotspur.com/news-archive-1/kick-into-reading/

Videos

1. RTG (Reading the Game)/PFA (Professional Footballers' Association),
   Kick into Reading, 2007, https://www.youtube.com/
   watch?v=5_btrzKC0E4
2. Cardiff City FC: Kick into Reading, a BBC documentary for BBC2
   (terrestrial TV channel), 2009. https://www.bbc.co.uk/pro-
   grammes/b00kdtqd

CASE STUDY 2

In-service storytelling: course for teachers and librarians

Patrick and Donna were asked to deliver a storytelling course for the
Summer Institute at the International School of Brussels (ISB). Patrick
had worked for ISB as storyteller-in-residence several times over previous
years. Besides telling stories to students in all grade levels, nursery through
high school, he also developed workshops teaching storytelling and creative writing for early childhood and elementary school classes. Jeffrey
Brewster, the librarian coordinating Patrick's visits, believed teachers
could do more storytelling themselves, and incorporate more of Patrick's
workshop activities in their own teaching. Jeffrey also felt the library
wasn't being utilized enough by teachers. They agreed an extended storytelling course could lead to increased storytelling and teachers making
greater use of resources in the ISB library.

Patrick and Donna proposed co-teaching the course, basing it on
research gathered for this book. Together they had previously presented
conference papers and written articles based on their study. As individual
workshop facilitators, each had trained adults working with children to tell
stories. This provided an opportunity to pool knowledge and teaching
styles, and test which methods were effective in getting educators new to
it confident in their storytelling and capable of sustaining this newly
acquired skill. They both knew of many storytelling workshops that had
generated great enthusiasm but acting on that enthusiasm was difficult for
participants once the course was over. Usually such training was a one-off,
lasting a couple of hours after school or at a conference. Patrick had delivered projects that incorporated storytelling training through several meetings over an extended period. These had been more successful at seeing

teachers and librarians implement storytelling in classrooms and libraries. It was hoped an intensive course co-taught over a short period could yield similar outcomes.

The devised three-day storytelling course for the Summer Institute was part of a week-long program preceding the start of the academic year. ISB offered several classes and workshops supporting teachers' continuing professional development. The aims of the storytelling course were two-fold: to get faculty telling stories regularly; and to build their awareness of the library's folk and fairy tale anthologies and picture books, along with the professional books supporting teachers.

Eleven faculty members took part, a mix of early childhood and middle school teachers, school librarians, and college interns working as class-room assistants. The group shared an interest in storytelling but lacked confidence and means to practice. Some knew about oral storytelling, others were more familiar with shared reading of picture books (in early childhood) and of literary novels and short stories (for older elementary and middle school classes).

Over three days Donna and Patrick modeled storytelling for partici-pants, discussed recent research on the effects of oral story listening from cognitive development and literacy perspectives, and had the group par-ticipate in activities to develop storytelling skills and confidence. Emphasis was placed on finding and learning stories, and managing regular, frequent story times. The school library provided a comfortable and well-resourced environment, with both listening and practice spaces.

Donna and Patrick interspersed their storytelling between presenta-tions, activities, and discussions. They told seven stories the first day, some participatory (including *Don't Wake the Baby* in Appendix A), others slightly longer folk or fairy tales. Most took ten minutes or less to tell. Jeffrey introduced the folk and fairy tale collection, and professional books and journals reserved for faculty. Participants were given opportunities to browse both sets of materials. Toward the end of that first day participants, with a partner, were asked to practice and then tell each other one of the seven stories heard that morning. It was okay to make mistakes, forget parts, or change the story. The important thing was to say a story out loud, from start to finish, to prove to themselves they could do it. Before leaving, everyone was encouraged to start thinking of a story to tell the final day.

The second day, similar to the first, included Patrick and Donna sharing more stories. With many similar tales in their repertoires, they made a point of telling the same story in turn. This was an early and not well-known version of *Snow White*. Two tellers telling the same tale twice demonstrated how a story can be told differently, each teller having a distinctive style and interpretation. It showed participants it's all right to tell a story your own way and isn't about memorizing or imitating in an exact manner. Further activities that day provided more tips on finding, learning, and practicing stories. Much of the day was given to participants practicing what they planned to tell on the final day.

The morning of the third day, after given the chance to practice, participants then each took their turn telling their stories to the entire group. Normally novice tellers stumble, are shy, and/or are underprepared, so the experience becomes both challenging and unsatisfying. This time, however, everyone's performance was strong, each relating a story unique to them and their style. Many tales were new to Donna and Patrick. The experience was exciting and powerful for both tellers and listeners.

Confidence and enthusiasm for storytelling blossomed during the course. An unexpected development was that the participants decided to form a storytelling group. This was to support each other so they could institute and develop storytelling practices in their classrooms, from the early childhood department through elementary and middle schools. They met monthly after-school, practicing stories they discovered, sharing experiences, telling stories in each other's classrooms, and establishing a process to keep track of stories they found as well as all the stories told during the school year, along with tips and suggestions. The librarians, supported by the teachers, built a database providing evidence of the course's impact and sustainability.

Both librarians upped the frequency of their storytelling: one told stories weekly to third and fifth grades (that entailed learning a minimum of thirty stories over the year), another spent five weeks telling *pourquoi* tales which supported grade two's narrative writing program. The librarians also used opportunities to introduce storytelling to additional classroom teachers, choosing tales connected to what students were studying. Teachers were encouraged to integrate storytelling into their curriculums and not to view storytelling as "yet one more thing for which they had to find time." Both librarians shared stories regularly at pre-school and grades four and six assemblies.

Teachers enrolled in the course also started regular storytelling sessions. One devoted time for storytelling every Friday after lunch/recess, and a retired teacher came in weekly to tell stories. A middle school teacher trained her ESL students to share stories with students in second-grade classes. They told stories in English and in the students' home languages. Interns, encouraged first to read aloud picture books, soon transitioned to regular telling.

The networking developed *by participants* as the course came to an end was one of the most important outcomes for the success ISB faculty had at introducing and maintaining storytelling in the school. It seems obvious now, but it reminded Patrick and Donna and the course participants of the importance of taking ownership of any teaching practice, making it your own so it's relevant to your teaching situation. In a survey and final report evaluating the course, Jeffrey confirmed that "it's essential to have an onsite person, or two, to keep the group going, providing encouragement, and communicate with expert advisers." Both Patrick and Donna provided support through Skype discussions at some group meetings and when Patrick was in residence to tell stories and lead creative writing workshops at ISB later in that academic year.

The ISB Summer Institute storytelling course demonstrated an intensive short-course can achieve a sustainable, schoolwide storytelling program. On reflection, we realized common elements shared by this course with earlier successful storytelling programs that Patrick and Donna had run as individuals (in schools and libraries, but also with organizations supporting early childhood development, literacy, or reading for pleasure). Establishing enduring, workable storytelling practices in schools and libraries are successful when:

- Structured, meaningful activities follow on from initial training.
- Course participants hear the same stories told by *different*, experienced storytellers.
- Making sure anyone new to storytelling develops a sense of owning the stories and their storytelling.
- Ensuring a warm, safe, welcoming environment so participants develop trust and an ability to practice constructive criticism.
- Working as a team, to spread the effort needed to find and learn stories, and keep records on what stories are told, who tells them, and who hears them.
- Holding regular enjoyable meetings and use of social networking and shared documents to support storytelling long after the course finishes.

CASE STUDY 3

Research project: teaching an individual to tell stories

Dr Ece Ozlem Demir-Lira at the University of Iowa and Donna designed a research project hypothesizing that oral story could be used as an intervention to promote visualization in young children. For the University of Iowa study Donna would train an undergraduate student to tell stories. This student would then train others in a cascade-type training. Donna would do the training over Skype, with subsequent training done in person. They had no idea how prescient this new form of training would turn out to be. Donna had never trained anyone over Skype, and Maria, the pre-med undergraduate student who was chosen to be the lead research assistant on the project, had never told a story. She had no idea that storytelling was different from picture book reading.

They planned four bi-weekly hour-long sessions via Skype meetings to work on basic storytelling. After the skype sessions ended, they would meet four more times to work on the specific stories being used for the study. The storytelling training was to begin in the fall with hope that the research project would be able to start in the spring. They figured they were in great shape. Little did they know that all the plans for this study would change come February 2020.

The initial training went better than we could have ever hoped. Although Maria was a science major, she had grown up hearing lots of stories told by her family. They may not have been folklore, but they were historical and family lore. She fell in love with telling stories almost immediately. Before the December break, she began meeting with the other two volunteers, and we were working out exactly what they would tell and read to classes participating in the study.

In February, as they prepared to start the study, the world was struck with COVID-19 and the study could not proceed. Maria was terribly saddened that she didn't get to tell her stories for the study and promised to stay in touch. She said she would continue telling stories to the children in her family. It made her feel good in a way she found hard to describe.

Meanwhile Donna and Patrick put together a YouTube channel, *Stories Told by Heart*, on which they had professional librarian-storytellers record themselves telling stories. These were for younger children to watch while stuck at home. It was conceived as a project separate from the study but proved helpful to Donna's and Dr Demir-Lira's plans as circumstances changed. One benefit was giving Maria a chance to practice her newly acquired skills right away. Donna asked Maria if she would be willing to record her stories for the YouTube channel, even though she would be the only non-professional and non-librarian teller. Maria jumped right in. She recorded stories in English and Spanish. She is a confirmed believer in the power of storytelling. We could not have asked for a better outcome, although it was not the one we had planned.

The following is the outline of the four one-on-one training sessions Donna did with Maria. You'll recognize many of the same lessons pulled from the previous two case studies.

Week 1

The trainee was asked to bring two picture books she loved growing up. The first week's goal was to discuss the differences between reading aloud and telling stories. Dr Demir-Lira and Donna wanted to emphasize these differences, which were important for the study. And it was essential that the trainee see the differences for both the listener and the reader/teller when presenting.

1. We introduced ourselves, talked about the goals of this training and the research project.
2. We talked about some of the differences between shared reading and oral story:
   - Eye contact.
     - o For picture books children focus on the pictures.
     - o When telling children focus on the teller.
     - o Reader can learn to have eye contact with children by becoming very familiar with the material before reading to the listener.
     - o Teller will always be looking directly at the listener.
   - Flexibility of language.
     - o For picture books read aloud the reader, for the most part, reads the written words—which are independent of who's listening.
     - o When telling the teller can change wording to help the listeners' understanding and ability to visualize and focus on the story.
     - o Both the cadence and prosody can help the listener attend and understand the story.

- The ability to gesture.
  - o Hard to use your hands when holding a picture book so that the listener can see the pictures.
  - o The teller is not holding anything and can use natural (hopefully not exaggerated) hand gestures.
  - o Both can use facial gestures, but with picture book reading the listener infrequently looks at the reader's face.
3. Donna read *The Napping House* by Don and Audrey Wood.
  - There was discussion on what makes this a "good" picture book.
  - o Pictures match words in story.
  - o Pictures also extend the story.
  - o Pictures and words are age matched.
  - Donna read the book demonstrating how to maintain some eye contact while showing the pictures to the listeners.
  - o Trainee read one of the books she brought and was given feedback.
  - o Trainee read second book and received feedback.
4. Donna told the earliest collected version of *Snow White*, an ambiguous story with many possible interpretations.
  - We talked about how listening felt as opposed to how the teller felt when telling:
  - o Images.
  - o Characters.
  - o Story emotion.
  - o What the listener was left with.

The trainee was asked to tell both *Snow White* and one of the picture books for the next meeting. She was instructed to practice telling both stories aloud to herself during the week, and if comfortable to find someone to tell the stories to. They discussed different ways of learning a story and also the difference between memorizing (not recommended) as opposed to getting comfortable with the entire plot in your own language and prosody. They discussed appropriate age ranges for these particular stories (the *Snow White* story is not appropriate for young children or the faint of heart). She was told to contact Donna if she had any questions or if she wanted to practice with her.

Week 2

The goal for this week was to have the trainee TELL her stories and get comfortable with receiving feedback. When the session began, she was clearly nervous.

1. Trainee was asked to start the session by telling the *Snow White* story. The story is very short with much repetition, making it easy to tell.
2. After her telling, we discussed:
   - What she thought each of the three characters were thinking.
   - How she pictured them.
   - What the scenery looked like.
   - How far they traveled.
   - Were they cold or warm.
   - Which character she identified with.

She was asked to tell the story again identifying with a different character this time. The trainee began to relax and loved this imagination game. She did a great job of getting into what she was now purposefully "seeing" while she was telling the story. After this telling she said she felt energized and wanted to try telling that story again next week from a different perspective.

1. Donna gave the trainee a few minutes to now think about *Corduroy*, the story she was telling from the picture book. She decided to take the perspective of the young girl. She did a great job.
   - The trainee was totally relaxed now. Donna and the trainee talked about some small changes she could make that would greatly improve her telling by:
     o Not dropping her voice at the end of a sentence.
     o Trying to slow down when telling.
     o Maintaining eye contact throughout the telling.
   - The trainee told *Corduroy* again incorporating the feedback. We discussed:
     o How Corduroy was similar to a folktale with a classic story arc.
     o Why that is important.
2. Donna told *Epaminondas* (a story that was to be used in the study). They discussed:
   - How Epaminondas was similar to a folktale with a classic story arc.
   - Why that is important.

3. The trainee was told to prepare a 'family story' to tell for next session and given the following suggestions:
   - Think about it, using her imagination to visual the story and to try telling from different character's points of view.
   - Put it into a classic folktale style.
   - Tell it to herself and then practice it aloud with a group.

Dr Demir-Lira gave the trainee a copy of *Epaminondas*. She was asked to read it over a number of times before the next session.

Week 3
By week three, the trainee was no longer nervous but instead excited to tell. The goal for this week was to teach the trainee how she could learn a story by following the classic story arc from any tale. Also, they aimed to have the trainee become comfortable with *Epaminondas*.

1. Trainee talked about the family story she had chosen:
   - She told it in a lovely, enthusiastic manner.
   - We discussed how her story compared to a classic story arc.
   - We discussed some changes she could make in delivery.
     o Punching certain repeated phrases.
     o Pausing for emphasis.
     o Tightening the ending.
   - She asked to tell the story again.
2. We talked about *Epaminondas*, about what is a fool's story and why this story and stories like it, appeal to young children:
   - They get the problem before Epaminondas does.
   - There is a lot of repetition which they can join in on.
   - Even though he is young and silly, his mother loves him.
   - We discussed the folkloric structure of Epaminondas.
   - The trainee then "told" all the parts of the story she remembered.
3. Donna told *The Mitten*, another story that was going to be used in the study.

Dr Demir-Lira gave a copy of *The Mitten* to the trainee. For the following week the trainee was to learn *Epaminondas* as she had the previous stories and be prepared to tell it to Donna and Dr Demir-Lira.

Week 4

The goal for this week was to get the trainee comfortable when telling *Epaminondas* before an audience. This would be the fifth story the trainee had learned and told aloud. She was completely comfortable telling a story to a small group of people. It was delightful to watch. She was able to make the story "hers" and to play a bit with language and expression. After this session, the trainee was going to work with two undergraduates and prepare them to work on our study. They would be reading three picture books and telling three stories to the classes participating in our study.

1. The trainee was asked to tell *Epaminondas* to Donna and Dr Demir-Lira as soon as we began. This was to get rid of any nervousness about telling.
   • She was given feedback.
   • She was excited and enthusiastic, so we asked if she would tell Epaminondas to the whole Psychology Lab we were working in. She jumped right in and did a beautiful job.
   • We talked about how it felt to tell a story to a large group versus a small group and the following points were made:
     o Easier and less scary.
     o Easy to maintain eye contact.
     o Enthusiasm grew as the listeners showed their interest.
     o Generally felt wonderful for the teller.

Donna and Ece gave her a cupcake and congratulated her on a job well done. From here on in she would be able to learn any story she wanted to, or that we needed for the study. Now she would work with the other undergraduates that were going to present stories for our study. Or so we thought.

As we write, with schools likely to be closed indefinitely due to social distancing, the study's next phase was in doubt. Once Maria and the other undergraduate storytellers were trained, the plan was for them to work with classes of children. Dr Demir-Lira intended to gather data identifying and measuring the outcomes from listening to oral stories and shared picture book reading. Again, they were lucky that Donna developed *Stories Told by Heart*.

Recording the stories for our YouTube channel was a different type of telling from any kind we have talked about. There was no audience, no feedback, no eye contact, yet all the tellers, Maria included, found it exhilarating. Donna and Patrick also heard directly from children and their parents that the children were mesmerized by the stories, talked about them, imitated the tellers, questioned what happened, and wanted to hear more. This level of response wasn't anticipated. From long experience, both Patrick and Donna know being in the room with listeners is more effective than telling remotely, as discussed in Chaps. 1 and 5, but clearly remote telling can have an impact. With this in mind, the hope is to restructure Donna's and Dr Demir-Lira's study by having the undergraduate storytellers work remotely.

This is an unusual case study, although much like *KiR* and the ISB Summer Institute. It shows us that anyone can learn to tell stories. It's an empowering, pleasurable, and an intellectual exercise for both the listener and the teller. Part of its uniqueness is that it demonstrates an element of training different from the other case studies and our usual methods for teaching storytelling. It shows us that the *teller can gain a great deal by telling, and that the audience can be remote*. For this reason, we hope this account is helpful and of interest to anyone, no matter what their background, who wants to tell stories but hesitates in giving it a go.

Information on how to find stories used in this case study:

1. *The Napping House*. Wood, A. and Wood, D. 2010. Boston, MA: Harcourt Mifflin, Harcourt Publishing Company
2. *Snow White*. Grimm, J. W. 2014. Little Snow White. In *The Original Folk and Fairy Tales of the Brothers Grimm. The Complete First Edition*, trans. Jack Zipes, 170–177, 493–495. Princeton and Oxford: Princeton University Press
3. *Epaminondas*.
   - Bryant, S. C. 1905. Epaminondas and his Auntie. In *Stories to Tell to Children: Fifty-One Stories with Some Suggestions for Telling*. Boston and New York: Houghton Mifflin Company
   - Maestro, P. and Cabassa, M. 2010. *Epaminondas*. Madrid: Carretera
   - Merriam, E. and Schart Hymen, T. 1968. *Epaminondas*. New York and London: Follet Publishing Co.
   - de Valeri, M. and de Sesé, E. 1982. *Epaminondas*. Barcelona: La Galera, S.A. Editorial
4. *The Mitten*. Brett, J. 2009. *The Mitten, a Ukrainian Folk Tale*. New York: G. P. Putnam's Sons

5. *Corduroy.* Freeman, D. 1968. *Corduroy.* New York and London: Viking Books
6. Stories told by heart: the YouTube channel referred to in the case study: https://www.youtube.com/channel/UCwM6xM5iO7lrPD4SNlfbO0g.

INDEX

© The Author(s), under exclusive license to Springer Nature
Switzerland AG 2021
D. Schatt, P. Ryan, *Story Listening and Experience in Early
Childhood*, https://doi.org/10.1007/978-3-030-65358-3

183